Yasmeen Lari
Architecture for the Future

Yasmeen Lari
Architecture for the Future

Edited by
Angelika Fitz, Elke Krasny,
Marvi Mazhar, and
Architekturzentrum Wien

Architekturzentrum Wien, Vienna
The MIT Press,
Cambridge, Massachusetts,
and London, England

Introduction

Yasmeen Lari
Projects, Contexts, Concerns

10
Yasmeen Lari
Architecture for
the Future
Angelika Fitz and
Elke Krasny

26
Karachi Modernism:
Postcolonial Living
Angelika Fitz

36
Housing Equality:
Innovating Modernism
and Tradition
Elke Krasny

48
Icons for a
Karachi Boulevard
Angelika Fitz

58
Material Ecologies:
Building the Local
Elke Krasny
With additional research
by Marvi Mazhar

72
Heritage as Future:
Decolonizing Legacies
Elke Krasny

88
Building Policies, Laws,
and Institutions
Angelika Fitz

96
The Architect as
Humanitarian Worker
Elke Krasny
With additional research
by Marvi Mazhar

104
A Zero-Carbon Revolution
in Architecture
Angelika Fitz

120
Essentials for Life
Angelika Fitz

Yasmeen Lari
Interview

140
"Every decision
has a global impact."
Yasmeen Lari
in Conversation
with Angelika Fitz
and Elke Krasny
Karachi, 2022

Essays

154
Pakistan Under Construction
Chris Moffat

166
The Blossoming World of Yasmeen Lari
Helen Thomas

173
Recognition for Built Heritage: A Continuing Struggle
Anila Naeem

183
Karachi: Neoliberal Infrastructural Decisions and Development Crisis
Marvi Mazhar

193
The Gendered Impacts of Climate Change in Karachi
Abira Ashfaq

201
The Right to Housing
Interview with Raquel Rolnik by Elke Krasny

206
Care by Design: Women, Change, and the Climate Crisis
Anne Karpf

213
A Building Becomes More Beautiful by Its Usage
Runa Khan

220
The Stove Solution: Yasmeen Lari and the Reclamation of Feminist Knowledge
Rafia Zakaria

226
Teaching Zero-Carbon Design Methodologies
Cassandra Cozza

234
Building, Wounding, and the Future: On Planetary Care
Elke Krasny

246
Acknowledgments

249
About the Authors

253
About the Editors

255
About Yasmeen Lari

265
Bibliography

277
Index

285
Imprint

Yasmeen Lari
Architecture for the Future

Introduction

Introduction
Yasmeen Lari
Architecture for the Future

Angelika Fitz and Elke Krasny

In 2022, when torrential monsoon rains and increasing glacier melt in the Himalayas led to catastrophic floods in Pakistan that submerged one-third of the country, affected thirty-three million people, and destroyed hundreds of thousands of buildings, including homes, schools, health clinics, and other essential infrastructures, CNN reported that the architect Yasmeen Lari was "working around the clock to equip people in hard-hit Sindh Province with the skills and materials to construct prefabricated bamboo shelters."[1] How did a more than eighty-year-old woman architect come to be a climate activist counteracting the devastation of extreme weather events, inventing models to build outside of the international aid complex, and providing people with the skills to rebuild their homes and their lives? This volume takes its inspiration from Yasmeen Lari's relentless commitment to 'architecture for the future' and provides her body of work as a whole. It offers an in-depth introduction to Lari's entire career, which spans more than fifty years, and uses her work as an exemplar to study how architecture's relation to the future has changed tremendously since Lari trained as an architect and started practicing in the 1960s. Through her work one can learn that the responsibility architecture has to the future is now not only viewed very differently than it was fifty years ago, but can also be practiced in humble, future-making ways.

[1] Stephy Chung, "These bamboo shelters are empowering communities displaced by Pakistan's floods," CNN Style, September 30, 2022, https://edition.cnn.com/style/article/pakistan-floods-bamboo-shelters-climate-intl-hnk/index.html.

Decarbonize, Decolonize

This book is composed of three parts: our nine chapters on Lari's oeuvre titled *Projects, Concerns, Contexts,* a 2022 conversation with Yasmeen Lari, and eleven newly commissioned essays, which serve the critical purpose to provide further contextualization on issues addressed by the architect's work. Before we give a more detailed introduction to the three sections of the book, we will use the space of this introduction to explain our motivations and the reasons why we think that Yasmeen Lari's body of work matters to learning, or, perhaps better, relearning how architecture is responsible to the future. In 2015, we, Angelika Fitz and Elke Krasny, began to investigate how architecture can be understood and practiced as a form of materialized and spatial care, with care most broadly understood as all those material and immaterial supports that are essential to life-making. 'We,' in this introduction, refers to the two authors who speak and write from their research and thinking which develops through conversations and dialogue with each other and with many others. Acknowledging that care always starts within the given material, environmental, and infrastructural realities, and from the condition of interdependency, and being consciously aware of the harmful and violent effects of structural and infrastructural carelessness, we began to research the work of architects who do not avoid the conflicts around care and aim to practice architecture as the provision of care. It is in the context of our research on architecture as care that we first encountered Yasmeen Lari's work, in particular, we learned about her zero-carbon shelters, which, since their beginnings in the year 2005 when the disastrous Kashmir earthquake occurred, have become "the world's largest zero-carbon shelter programme."[2] While originally focusing on architecture as the spatial production of care in its cultural, environmental, material, social, and technological dimensions, we have, through many hours of research conversations with Yasmeen Lari and through the engagement with her body of work in Pakistan, come to think about architecture as the production of time and how caring architecture acts in support of future-making. Consequently, this led us to think about how architecture can be examined through its relation to the future, how architecture produces future effects, and how architecture, in ethical terms, can be viewed as responsibility to the future. Future is not understood abstractly as a faraway or distant time. Future is understood to begin in the present moment, in the here and now. Every second, every hour, every day in the lives of animals, humans, plants, as well as air, soil, rock, and water, are part of their future. Architecture, as one dimension of the built environment, is part of how each second, each hour, each day can or cannot be a livable future. We also understand that precisely because of

2 Jennifer Hahn, "Using 'ancient wisdoms and techniques' can lead to carbon-neutral buildings says Yasmeen Lari," *dezeen*, July 1, 2021, https://www.dezeen.com/2021/07/01/carbon-neutral-architecture-yasmeen-lari-interview/.

Man-made ruination resulting from the economic regimes of colonialist capitalism, Man, that is a specific understanding of Enlightenment-based human domination over nature and bodies as resources for capitalist extraction, and the impact of Man on the planet have to be seen at the scale of geological time, and thus also of geological futures.[3] While Man turned into a global climate predator putting the habitability of the planet at risk, the lives of the majority of human beings who are not the cause of this massive destruction and loss of future are being made more vulnerable because of the effects of planetary climate ruination. Amidst the enormity of climate destruction in Pakistan, which ranks among the top ten climate-impacted countries, Lari practices decarbonization and decolonization. Stating that the "International Colonial Charity model," which is the traditional response to crisis, views "affected people as supplicants," Lari argues for a "paradigm shift in the structure of the culture of giving."[4] According to her, homes and essential infrastructures can build dignity. The idea of dignity is crucial to an approach that sees the support given by architecture as fundamental and, at the same time, does not reduce those who lack this support the most as powerlessly dependent upon foreign aid or without agency. Lari's approach exemplifies that a different future in the here and now begins with architecture, with buildings not a spectacular end but a means to provide what is essential to everyday life and survival. So far, we have shared central reasons why Yasmeen Lari's work needs to be known and studied as part of architecture for the future, as her approach shows how architects can meaningfully contribute to building and rebuilding livelihoods in the midst of the ongoing climate catastrophe. Today, Yasmeen Lari's ways of practicing future-making architecture include what we see as direct-action architecture as a locally specific response to the climate catastrophe. Lari's architectural response goes beyond relief architecture conventionally understood as emergency shelters, very often taking the form of camps and containers, and results in building lasting homes with those whose homes in their villages have been damaged or destroyed. This includes a deep commitment to building up and passing on the knowledge needed to build zero-carbon shelters made with local materials and rooted in so-called traditional technologies. Passing on zero-carbon knowledge in architecture includes training and skill sharing with people affected by environmental harm, as they learn how to build their own homes and how to make their own building materials. It also includes teaching how to practice differently within architecture schools and together with universities. We share Yasmeen Lari's understanding commitment to knowledge as a social and ethical obligation and see our work as a contribution in support of sharing and expanding ways of knowing architecture differently.

[3] We follow here feminist anthropologist Anna Tsing, who capitalizes Man when she speaks of a specific idea of so-called universal modern Man, who, seeing Himself as supreme and different from nature, as well as all racialized and sexualized others, established the ideology of domination, exploitation, and extraction. See Anna Tsing, "Earth Stalked by Man," *The Cambridge Journal of Anthropology* 34, no. 1 (2016), 2–16.

[4] Lea Zeitoun, "'Lari Octa Green': Sustainable Bamboo Design for Flood Relief," designboom, October 26, 2022, https://www.designboom.com/architecture/lari-octa-green-emergency-bamboo-shelters-flood-relief-heritage-foundation-of-pakistan-10-26-2022/.

As curators, researchers, and theorists who focus on social and ecological dimensions of architecture, on an expanded understanding of architecture's histories and cultural meanings, as well as on "multidimensional and intersectional," transnational feminist epistemologies, we are most acutely aware of the fact that knowledge is never neutral, that knowledge is power, and that care is a form of knowledge historically silenced and marginalized, but also entangled with and used or abused in the name of power.[5] Knowledge is 'produced' and 'reproduced.' Knowledge is dynamic and can be changed. In the past, dimensions of caste, class, ethnicity, gender, race, religion, and sexuality, as well as geopolitical contexts and uneven geographies of power, have largely defined which architects and what kind of architecture, mostly singular architectural objects, were entered into the knowledge of architecture held to be canonical. 'Specialized' and 'canonical' knowledge of architecture is 'produced' and 'reproduced' through institutions of teaching, publishing, and exhibiting. Architecture and its modern histories, which were shaped by institutions such as architecture schools and art history departments at universities, books and journals produced by publishing houses, and museums of applied arts and architecture, were originally dominated by patriarchal coloniality. Patriarchal coloniality is a political and material process of cultural, social, and environmental domination. Challenging how architecture is being made, how architectural knowledge is defined, and what counts as architecture globally remains most difficult. In the period of the 1960s, when women entered into professions previously and at the time still dominated by men, and more importantly, by patriarchal ideas, they had to navigate the norms and complexities of the Man-made world. When an architect decides to bring a different way of knowing architecture into the making of architecture, to define their practice differently, or to challenge widely held assumptions and norms, then struggles ensue and persistence becomes paramount. Yasmeen Lari was the first woman to open an architectural office in Pakistan, where she started her practice in Karachi in 1964. This firm carried the name Lari Associates, Architects and Urban Designers. In 1978, Lari was part of the preparatory seminar for the first Aga Khan Award. In 1980, Lari was elected president of the Institute of Architects, Pakistan, and worked insistently on establishing the professions of architect and urban planner by law. This new law was introduced in 1983, when the Pakistan Council of Architects and Town Planners (PCATP) was formed. In 1980, Lari, together with her late husband Suhail Zaheer Lari, founded the Heritage Foundation of Pakistan, which was the first civic society institution concerned with architecture as built heritage and to this date provides the organizational framework through which her work is delivered. In 1984, Lari organized the first

[5] Françoise Vergès, *Decolonial Feminism*, trans. Ashley J. Bohrer (London: Pluto Press, 2021), 20.

Conference of Architects and Town Planners of Islamic Countries. While all these different 'firsts' warrant a monograph and a detailed examination of her work, we are actually wary of such narratives that place the emphasis on being the first, as this reinforces a notion of history as race and competition. Here, we are interested in developing a critical perspective on architecture in relation to the future by using Yasmeen Lari's body of work as a paradigmatic example and in using the format of the monograph to provide contextualization of specific concerns and themes in her work through the voices of different scholars and writers.

Imaginaries of the Future

We started this introduction by explaining how Lari's architecture today materializes what is urgently needed for the immediate and the long-term future. Her approach, at once analytic, systemic, material, locally specific, and conscious of the needs of the poorest and most vulnerable, with a particular focus on the oft-overlooked everyday spatial needs of women and children, sets a precedent from which many others can learn. At the same time, this volume does not focus only on her work today, but looks at her oeuvre, which spans more than half a century, as a body of work through which we can understand two essential dimensions of architecture's relation to the future: firstly, modern architecture, including in the context of nation-building in postcolonial societies in the second half of the twentieth century, which gave shape to the belief of building a different future; secondly, individual architects can change how they relate to future-making with their way of practicing architecture without disavowing or silencing the knowledge they draw from their own previous work. We came to understand this through our research process on Yasmeen Lari's work in dialogue with the architect. The curatorial research was spread out over a period of two years. Because of pandemic travel restrictions, we had regular research dialogues with Yasmeen Lari over Zoom in 2020 and 2021, and, finally, in 2022 we traveled to Pakistan to have time in her archive and to see her built work. Marvi Mazhar, a former member of staff in Yasmeen Lari's office and now an architect and activist herself, joined the curatorial team, and particularly the research in Karachi was supported by her.

The first part of the book, *Projects, Concepts, Concerns,* uses a narrative framework for Yasmeen Lari's body of work which provides information and contextualization of her projects in relation to relevant concepts and major concerns addressed by her work. Composed as analytical and visual essays based on photographs and plans researched in Yasmeen Lari's archive, as well as new photography, our nine chapters have a chronological and thematic structure. The first chapter, "Karachi Modernism: Postcolonial Living," focuses on Lari's own home in Karachi, recognized as an international icon of Brutalism and completed in 1973. This chapter also introduces her designs of other modernistic homes for clients from the urban upper and middle classes. The second chapter, "Housing Equality: Innovating Modernism and Tradition," locates Lari's work in the context of the slogan *roti* (bread), *kapda* (cloth), and *makaan* (shelter) for everyone, which, at the time, was promoted by the Pakistan People's Party founded by Zulfikar Ali Bhutto. Lari was given the opportunity to design social housing as part of the People's Housing Programme, established by the Bhutto Administration in 1973. What is of particular interest to the dimension of the future, envisioned as modern by way of innovation, is that Lari saw modernism and tradition on par for innovating. She used the spatial qualities of traditional morphologies in historical cities in Pakistan and translated them into her designs for modernist housing. Early on, Lari paid particular attention to finding spatial solutions for the specific needs of women in the mostly Muslim culture of her home country. The third chapter, "Icons for a Karachi Boulevard," brings together three of the most prominent, large-scale buildings, the FTC – Finance and Trade Centre, the headquarters of Pakistan State Oil, and the Amro Bank, which Lari realized in the 1980s and 1990s along Karachi's most prominent transport axis. This shows what was expected from architecture by national and international corporate clients who desired to articulate their reach of power into the future through representational and large-scale buildings. At the same time, Lari's big buildings give something back to the urban society. Communicative platforms and green atriums ensuring cross ventilation create generous spaces for the users, whom Lari considers to be her actual clients. To this date, these buildings have remained Karachi landmarks speaking of this notion of a past understanding of a powerful future. The fourth chapter, "Material Ecologies: Building the Local," examines how Lari has always experimented with materials and had, already at the time of her modernist beginnings, a high sensitivity and curiosity for building materials beyond steel, concrete, or glass. Aligned with the work of others, such as the Egyptian architect Hassan Fathi, Lari began to explore mud as a building material in the early 1970s. Later on, in her humanitarian work, lime and bamboo became the two other 'Lari materials.' We would like to highlight here that materials matter to the production of the Man-made climate. Today's most commonly used building materials in architecture and the construction industry are main causes of Man-made climate destruction. Materials, therefore, will be central for building 'architecture for the future' differently. Given the scale of housing and infrastructure that is needed globally, it speaks for instigating local prefabrication and low-tech seriality made from zero-carbon materials. The fifth chapter, titled "Heritage as Future: Decolonizing Legacies," looks at how Yasmeen Lari began to see the built legacies of her home country with her eyes sharpened only after returning from her studies in Great Britain. A Western architectural education had not equipped her with knowledge of the building traditions in Pakistan. Together with her husband Suhail Zaheer Lari, a passionate photographer, she set out on her own project of decolonial learning and began an extensive study and documentation of Pakistan's built heritage, including so-called vernacular buildings and urban structures. Multidimensional heritage as living knowledge, not heritage for heritage's sake, has remained a red thread in Lari's work since the 1960s. She has worked on two UNESCO World Heritage Sites in Pakistan, the citadel of Lahore Fort and the necropolis of Makli. Furthermore, she activates the knowledge stored in local buildings and local building traditions as innovations in her humanitarian work. The sixth chapter, "Building Policies, Laws, and Institutions," looks at a field of architectural work very often not considered architecture by architects themselves nor by scholars and theorists. This field of work includes policymaking, lawmaking, and institution-building. Very often, it is precisely this field of policy, law, and institutionalization that makes and remakes patriarchal power structures. All the more, it is of interest that Lari, early on, invested her energy in these fields. She was active as a policymaker to legally define the profession of architects and urban planners in her country. Among other initiatives, she set up civil society organizations, most prominently the Heritage Foundation of Pakistan. The seventh chapter, "The Architect as Humanitarian Worker," focuses on Lari's work in the context of emergency architecture needed because of earthquakes, floods, or situations of war. Highly critical of the paternalistic and colonial mindset of much of the international aid industry that not only practices forms of giving as top-down handouts and thus erodes local agency, Lari also became acutely aware that the emergency shelter industry relies on materials that are perpetuating climate ruination. She openly shares that she learned how to become a humanitarian architect by doing, by being in the field, which she began after she had retired from architecture as business as usual. She brought to this activist humanitarian work an ethical commitment to being attentive to the needs of those even more marginalized within vulnerable groups, such as women or children. Seeing the disastrous loss and damage, Lari learned in the field that a different architecture is needed and began to develop zero-carbon structures using the materials of mud, bamboo, and lime. The eighth chapter, "A Zero-Carbon Revolution in Architecture," introduces the guiding principles of Lari's work, which she has defined as low cost, zero carbon, and zero waste.

Closely examining her way of working and how she shares architectural knowledge as useful knowledge so people can build shelters and other infrastructures, but also build up local economies around the production of building materials and construction, one comes to understand that Lari turns to technologies identified in local building traditions and uses them to design structures that are as earthquake- and flood-resistant as possible and can be self-built. To implement this, Lari established a zero-carbon training center in Makli and uses digital channels to provide instructions on how to self-build. This resulted in people being enabled to self-build tens of thousands of zero-carbon shelters. The ninth and last chapter, "Essentials for Life," centers on the essential infrastructures that architecture can provide for the lives and livelihoods of those who are most vulnerable. Shelter, clean water, safe toilets, healthy cooking facilities, and community spaces, particularly also spaces where women can spend time together outside of their homes, are the essentials Lari has identified as central to architecture for the future. The Pakistan Chulah, a smokeless stove, 70,000 of which have been built by villagers, has received international recognition through the World Habitat Award. Finding cost-effective, ecological, and social solutions attests to pragmatism, optimism, and the hope that architecture can at once be responsible for providing what is essential and be responsible to the future.

Lari's body of work is often narrated through a timeline constructed as 'before' and 'after.' The architect herself has actively contributed to this perception of her work, with 'before' referring to her modernist and large-scale work for clients and 'after' standing for her self-initiated work as a humanitarian activist. Yet, after we listened to Yasmeen Lari in many hours of conversations and after we examined her work attentively and closely, we find that her projects placed in relation to concepts and concerns allow for a more complicated and more nuanced understanding. While it is certainly obvious that Yasmeen Lari at a certain moment in her career decided to design large-scale architecture for powerful clients, there are ethical and social commitments and a readiness to learn with heritage and traditional building technologies, as well as with materials beyond the hegemonic modern palette of concrete, steel, and glass, that characterize her entire body of work. Rather than a clear 'before' and 'after,' which is a continuation of the modernist ideology of rupture and immediate transformation, we see the development of her body of work as a response to how the imaginaries of the future are historically changing and how one can begin to develop more meaningful answers. Among her ethical and social commitments is the focus on the needs of those whose needs have historically been silenced. In her way of working, this began with focusing on the spatial everyday needs of women and children already in her early housing projects and with giving value to physical structures, recognizing them as a relevant architectural heritage to be maintained and to be used meaningfully by the public. Later, she joined the ecological needs of what is called nature or the environment, which had been largely silenced and even annihilated by modernist and hyper-modernist projects in architecture, to these other needs. Understanding the needs of humans, buildings, and the environment as interdependent is central to how to approach 'architecture for the future' today. The nine chapters on her work are followed by a conversation with Yasmeen Lari, entitled "Every decision has a global impact." which lasted several hours and was conducted by Angelika Fitz and Elke Krasny. The conversation took place in her office in Karachi and was also recorded as a video. In the conversation, Lari shares how she became the architect she is today, what opportunities of learning and growing her architectural work has presented her, and her tireless curiosity and energy to learn new things and to learn how to think differently. She arrives at stating that "all of us have to rethink our roles and the way we live basically."

Multiconflictual Contexts

Eleven essays focus on specific thematics and concerns that are deeply connected with Yasmeen Lari's work. Some of the essays focus directly on her work, while others provide more general contextualization. Taken together, the essays demonstrate that architecture needs to be meaningfully studied beyond a framework of singular objects within a narrowly defined discipline of architectural history. The contributions in this volume examine questions of nation/building, biography, heritage, neoliberal urbanization in Karachi, the gendered impacts of climate ruination, the right to housing, care by design, ways of providing protection and dignity by way of architecture for the most climate-impacted, local and feminist solutions for the essential infrastructure of stoves, teaching zero-carbon methodologies in architecture schools, and building as wounding in relation to the needs for planetary care. This range of subjects addressed and concerns analyzed is evidence that buildings, much like knowledge or conditions of living, are embedded in and entangled with larger constellations of local and global political, cultural, social, and environmental contexts. A building never has one story only; it is part of many different conditions, some of which more easily enter into its stories, while others have historically remained more absent or silent. Here, we seek to provide approaches that operate at different scales and allow for a more profound understanding of the complexities, contradictions, entanglements, and agencies that architecture is part of. The nation-state, the urban megalopolis, rural livelihoods, climate disruption, care, historically marginalized

knowledge, as well as the teachings of architecture schools are all contexts through which architecture operates. They come with their locally and historically specific material and political conditions, as well as with their social norms and cultural expectations that impact largely on how architecture finds solutions within these norms and expectations. Rather than focusing on one theme only, we have decided to concentrate on the multidimensional and multiconflictual contexts through which the production of architecture can be understood. In "Pakistan Under Construction," the political and intellectual historian of South Asia, Chris Moffat, focuses on the function of modern architecture in Post-Partition Pakistan. The architect and writer Helen Thomas, who is one of the editors of *Women Writing Architecture,* gives a succinct overview of how Lari's career unfolded, how she mobilizes others, those with influential positions just as much as those historically denied agency and power, and how her work ranges from the global to the intimate, as Thomas puts it. The essay "Recognition for Built Heritage: A Continuing Struggle" by the architect and researcher Anila Naeem provides an introduction to the complex understanding of what counts and matters as built heritage in the context of the Islamic Republic of Pakistan, bringing together issues of state ideology, political correctness, and material maintenance. The contribution by the architect, activist, and researcher Marvi Mazhar, "Karachi: Neoliberal Infrastructural Decisions and Development Crisis," describes how the megalopolis of Karachi, with a population of twenty million characterized by the copresence of many different ethnicities, religions, sects, as well as the huge importance of the so-called informal economy, is impacted both by the inheritance of colonial planning legislations, as well as by contemporary planning paradigms such as smart cities and public-private partnerships that, rather than preventing speculation and privatization, bolster it. The human rights activist and legal educator Abira Ashfaq shares in her essay, "The Gendered Impacts of Climate Change in Karachi," insights from her research on how rural women in the Malir District of Karachi, who have escaped conditions of bonded labor and exploitation and who now are faced with their unpaid and paid farm work, are being silenced and devalued in the urban context, while, at the same time, these women are at the forefront of organizing the resistance against the encroachment of privatization and so-called elite housing threatening to destroy their livelihoods.
The architect and urban planner Raquel Rolnik, a former UN Special Rapporteur on the Right to Housing and author of the book *Urban Warfare: Housing Under the Empire of Finance*, explains in an interview with Elke Krasny the effects of the financialization of housing and the responsibility that international aid and international cooperation following the logic of modernization have for ongoing massive

dispossession. Elucidating on the difference between the production of housing and the building of homes, Rolnik diagnoses that certain typologies of housing present a continuation of the colonial model of the plantation. Comparing industrialized housing and agrobusiness, Rolnik insists that public policies are central to who gets what, as she puts it, and therefore to human rights globally. The sociologist Anne Karpf, the author of the book *How Women Can Save the Planet,* looks at "Care by Design: Women, Change, and the Climate Crisis" in her essay. Karpf highlights how the low status of care work globally has been literally built into the built environment and has never been made central to what architecture organizes around. Highlighting that today women and girls are fourteen times more likely to die in extreme weather events such as floods or droughts, Karpf shares Lari's call for "a new activism among architects" and reads Lari's architectural focus on women's tasks as carers through a feminist lens. In her essay, "A Building Becomes More Beautiful by Its Usage," Runa Khan, the social entrepreneur and founder of the Friendship NGO, uses examples from her own work which commissions new architecture and infrastructures such as the Friendship Centre in Gaibandha, the hospital boats or the Friendship Hospital Shyamnagar. In her view, the built environment has to provide for protection, healing, spiritual peace, learning, and dignity, and becomes beautiful through being used. This offers a holistic ethics that links the value and meaning of architecture to the beauty of the mind, body, and spirit, as she puts it. The attorney and author Rafia Zakaria, who has written the book *Against White Feminism,* looks in her contribution to this volume at "The Stove Solution: Yasmeen Lari and the Reclamation of Feminist Knowledge." She traces a failed history of distributing clean cooking stoves in South India and Pakistan, which resulted from top-down developmental policies that sought to solve the problem of wood-burning stoves, at once an environmental problem, a health hazard, and an impediment to women working for wages outside of the home. She underlines how Yasmeen Lari's successful stove solution pushes back against the top-down regime of universal solutions and viewing those in need of new design solutions as incapable of developing locally specific, socially and ecologically meaningful and workable solutions. The architect, researcher, and educator Cassandra Cozza writes about her experience of "Teaching Zero-Carbon Design Methodologies" at the Politecnico di Milano. Her essay explains how the students made digital reproductions of Lari prototypes and then built physical maquettes at the scale of 1:5 and 1:2 in order to learn how to build with bamboo. Cozza locates her work in a wider network of educators active at universities in Pakistan and Bangladesh, who have begun to implement teaching strategies derived from Lari's Zero-Carbon Architecture. The essay by the cultural theorist Elke Krasny bears the title "Building, Wounding, and the Future: On Planetary Care." Placing the powerful imaginaries of the future held by word building against the realities of planetary wounding caused by the globalized building industry, the essay argues for reimagining building as future care.

Saving People and the Planet

Yasmeen Lari: Architecture for the Future locates architecture in the midst of things, as architecture can never be separated from bodily, ecological, social, political, material, and even spiritual concerns. For the making of architecture, the future has taken on many different meanings. Architecture was given the task to fulfil the representational needs of those in power. One can see this in historical imperial palaces holding amassed treasures or in contemporary spectacular museum or opera buildings to be consumed as icons. Such architecture was rooted in the idea of defining and dominating the future. Architecture was also widely seen as a universal problem-solver for the need of mass housing. At the same time, architecture was expected to design highly individualized homes expressing particular styles for people's future lives. As different and even contradictory as these functions of architecture in relation to the production of the future are—and only a few examples are pointed out here—these functions all converge in asserting the belief that architecture will shape the future and, most importantly, will last together with the future. In a certain way, this relation between architecture and the future can be summed up like this: the future was an architectural fact, and architecture was a future fact. Today, as the future of the planet has been put at risk and continues to be made vulnerable by ruthless extraction and pollution that aggravates climate ruination and causes climate-related loss and damage, architecture has to be understood as responsible for this situation and responsible to this situation: Architecture, and the construction sector, cause about half of the greenhouse emissions worldwide, but at the same time more and different architecture is urgently needed to provide homes and essential infrastructures to the unhoused, as increasing numbers are displaced and face the loss of their homes and livelihoods because of climate destruction. It is precisely in this most devastating historical moment, which is the global present today, that a different architecture for the future is most urgently needed. Such an architecture for the future understands both how human agency and livelihoods are supported by architecture attentive to environmental needs.

While we strongly believe that critical analysis remains a most useful tool when approaching architecture, its design and building, and its histories and effects, we also feel that critique alone has run its course and that the intellectual labor of analyzing and studying architecture today necessarily needs to contribute to 'architecture for the future' by means of reparation and care. Critical diagnosis needs to be linked to "critical care."[6] Becoming involved with the realities in critical analysis is never distanced nor neutral. As the coming together and intersecting of ethical, environmental, and social concerns in architecture and how these concerns are addressed by architects are coming to the fore today, Yasmeen Lari's work offers inspiration for a politics of hope and an ethics of dignity. We want to close this introduction by giving the word to Yasmeen Lari herself: "We need to do away with the prevalent colonial mindset and the desire to create imposing megastructures. […] Moving forward, we must all stand for a humanistic, inclusive architecture that is driven by environmental considerations, that treads lightly on the planet and responds to the needs of the majority – the vulnerable masses who have not been considered worthy of attention by architects."[7]

[6] See Angelika Fitz and Elke Krasny, *Critical Care. Architecture and Urbanism for a Broken Planet* (Cambridge, MA: The MIT Press, 2019).

[7] Yasmeen Lari, "We need to do away with the prevalent colonial mindset and the desire to create imposing megastructures," *dezeen*, November 5, 2021, https://www.dezeen.com/2021/11/05/yasmeen-lari-manifesto-dezeen-15/.

All quotations, unless otherwise noted:
Yasmeen Lari interviewed by Angelika Fitz
and Elke Krasny, February 15, 2022, Karachi
Yasmeen Lari interviewed by Angelika Fitz
and Elke Krasny, September 6, 2019, Vienna
Image credits: All photographs, plans, and drawings,
unless otherwise noted © Archive Yasmeen Lari

Yasmeen Lari
Projects,
Contexts,
Concerns

Karachi Modernism
Postcolonial Living

Angelika Fitz

Karachi was a booming, cosmopolitan center in the 1960s, even if it had to cede the rank of capital to the newly planned city of Islamabad, designed by the Greek architect Constantinos Doxiadis. Arising in 1947 from the Partition of India, an event marked by immense violence, death, and expulsion, the young Pakistani state wanted to look ahead to a new future. One of the double-faced aspects of modernism is that it is part of both colonial exploitation and the shaping of independence. As architectural history shows, the internationalization of modernism is by no means a one-way street from Europe to other regions. Rather, specific manifestations of multidimensional modernism emerge locally, in mutual exchange.

In 1964, after studying architecture at Oxford in Great Britain, Yasmeen Lari set up shop in Karachi, becoming the first woman in Pakistan to open her own architecture office, and began her career, like many other architects, with single-family houses. As with her first house, which was for her brother, her private homes were commissioned primarily by clients from the urban upper and middle classes. Modernistic in their open floor plans, they established a new, postcolonial feeling of living in Pakistan with flowing spatial structures often arranged in split levels. This also takes account of the permeability between inside and outside along generous glass fronts. At the same time, intimate courtyards refer to local traditions, and vertical, shaded window slits for natural ventilation correspond to the locally specific climatic requirements.

PREVIOUS PAGE Yasmeen Lari's own home in Karachi is internationally recognized as an icon of Brutalism, completion 1973.

Lari House, Karachi, 1973

In 1973, Yasmeen Lari completed her own house, which is regarded as an internationally acclaimed icon of Brutalism and was included in the *Phaidon Atlas of 20th Century Architecture* as one of the 750 most important buildings. The materials of concrete and brick dominate in their roughness; the tectonic forces are staged in a dramatic cantilever. Wind-catchers integrated into the design were intended as a locally inspired climate adaptation. Since then, the house in central Karachi has been her office and home.

The Lari House sits on the top edge of a steep sloping lot, adding drama to the six-meter overhang of the veranda. Made of reinforced concrete, the load-bearing structure is prominently visible throughout the building. The building site for the office extension can be seen at the left of the picture.

Split levels and a gallery structure the open space. Exposed concrete and traditional furnishing elements combine to create a homey and hospitable spatial experience.

Photograph: Angelika Fitz, 2022

For many years, the central living space served as a salon, a meeting place for intellectuals and artists in Karachi. The traditional 'floor living' offered ample room for the get-togethers to which the Lari couple had been inviting guests regularly since the mid-1960s.

After returning from England, where both had studied at Oxford, Yasmeen and her husband Suhail Zaheer Lari began to explore Pakistan, its cultural heritage, and everyday life in depth.

Lari had always deliberately kept her office small to be able to choose the assignments she would take on. In 2000, she left her architecture practice, Lari Associates, at first to devote herself to writing, later experimenting with new approaches in humanitarian architecture, which has been a major focus since 2005. Today, the employees of her Heritage Foundation of Pakistan, which is the head organization for cultural heritage projects as well as for her zero-carbon architecture, work in the office spaces realized as an extension of her house.

Photograph: Angelika Fitz, 2022

You must remember, when I went to England for studies, Pakistan had been independent for not even ten years, and we had gone through 150 years of colonial rule, where we had been told that our culture was really nothing, and that everything in the West was something to be emulated.

Yasmeen Lari, 2022

Naseeruddin Khan House, Karachi, 1969

Providing 279 square meters of living space, the house for an entrepreneur and his family is rather small compared to other villas of the era. The open floor plan makes it spacious; split levels and various references to the garden convey a relaxed atmosphere.

On the entrance side and towards the inner courtyard, ribbons of narrow windows ensure natural ventilation and shading, while the house opens generously to the garden side.

Photographs: M.N. Khan (left), published in *MIMAR: Architecture in Development*, no. 2, ed. Hasan-Uddin Khan (Singapore: Concept Media, 1981), 48, and Angelika Fitz, 2022 (right)

Section (left top), elevation (left bottom), and floor plan (right) of the Naseeruddin Khan House

Published in *MIMAR: Architecture in Development*, no. 2, ed. Hasan-Uddin Khan (Singapore: Concept Media, 1981), 48.

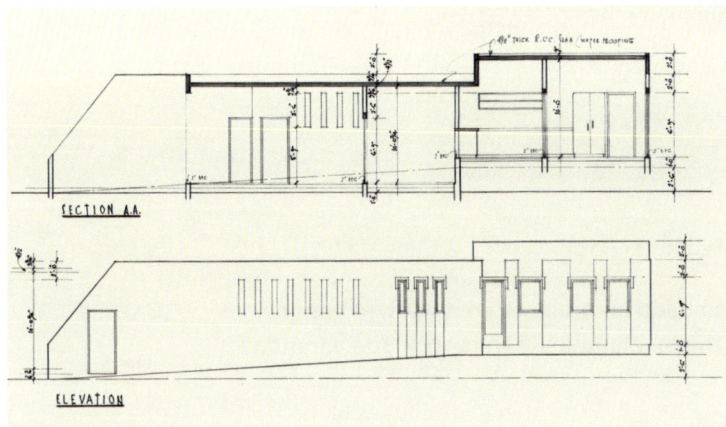

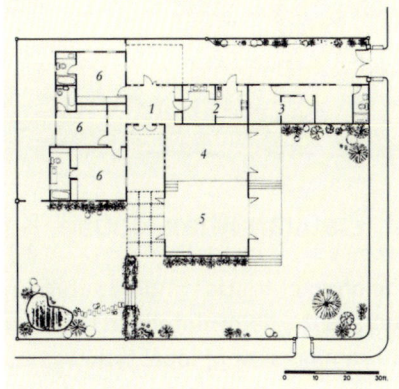

It just turned out that I was the first woman architect in Pakistan.
Yasmeen Lari, 2022

M. Ziaullah Khan House, Karachi, 1968

The characteristic window slits are also used on projects with a lower budget, such as the semi-detached house for the M. Ziaullah Khan family. The verandas are reminiscent of local typologies.

Photograph: Angelika Fitz, 2022

Family and Education

Yasmeen Lari received her early education in Lahore at Queen Mary's School and Adabistan-e-Soofia School, where she also studied Persian and Arabic at her father's wish, and at the Kinnaird College for Women. In 1956, at the age of fifteen, Yasmeen was sent with her siblings to England, where she first attended art school to improve her drawing skills and then studied architecture at the Oxford School of Architecture, now Oxford Brookes University. As she points out, her architectural training was influenced by the spirit of European modernism: "Le Corbusier was our god." In the meantime, the Western heroes of modernism were already busy designing entire cities in Pakistan, especially Doxiadis Associates. After her return in 1963, Yasmeen Lari—along with her husband Suhail Zaheer Lari, who had studied political science, philosophy, and economics at Oxford—traveled to historical places in Pakistan in order to see with her own eyes the cultural heritage, which, as Lari emphasizes, she had previously known only from the Victoria & Albert Museum in London.

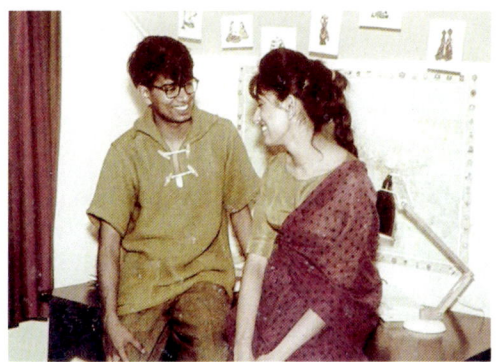

In 1961, while still studying in England, Yasmeen and Suhail Zaheer Lari wed—in an arranged marriage. The picture shows the two in their attic apartment in Oxford. Suhail had already maintained a lively intellectual network during his studies. He went on to become an entrepreneur but also worked both as a photographer accompanying the Pakistani cultural scene and the architectural work of his wife in Karachi for many decades and a passionate historian. He passed away from Covid-19 in 2020.

Yasmeen Lari's father Zafarul Ahsan (pictured in back) attained the rank of officer in the Indian Civil Service (ICS), which was mainly reserved for white Englishmen back then. After the Partition in 1947, he played an important role in the development of the young Pakistani state as Deputy Commissioner of Lahore and also oversaw modernist urban planning projects. Lari describes her mother, who worked to alleviate the post-Partition humanitarian catastrophe, as a deeply spiritual person. Suhail Zaheer Lari also came from an influential family. Before migrating to Pakistan, they lived near the family of the future Indian Prime Minister Jawaharlal Nehru. This led, among other things, to Nehru accepting Suhail's invitation to lecture in Oxford during a stay in London in the early 1960s.

The first of Yasmeen and Suhail Zaheer Lari's three children was born while they were still studying. The photo shows mother and daughter in Oxford in 1963.

Yasmeen Lari describes coming back to Pakistan as a 'shock' for a budding architect. One wanted to relegate her to being either the engineer or the beautifier of the façade. Representative architectural tasks often went to international architects. The Austrian-American architect Richard Neutra, seen here with Lari and prominent architects and artists in the mid-1960s, designed the US Embassy in Karachi in the late 1950s.

Housing Equality: Innovating Modernism and Tradition

Elke Krasny

Housing is essential to human life and survival. Creating access to adequate housing for all, in particular to those who are impoverished, displaced, or have no land, is one of the biggest social and economic challenges for ensuring equality worldwide. In the words of architectural historian Chris Moffat, the problem of home was the founding problem of Pakistan.[1] In the 1970s, the Pakistan People's Party founded by Zulfikar Ali Bhutto promoted the slogan *roti* (bread), *kapda* (cloth), and *makaan* (shelter) for everyone. A People's Housing Programme was established, and in 1973 the Bhutto Administration initiated a scheme to build the first 6,000 dwellings for low-income or middle-class families. Yet, the 787 units of Angoori Bagh designed by Yasmeen Lari were the only ones to actually be built. Lari describes this work as "life transforming." In her later humanitarian work, she was able to draw on this experience and to develop further approaches introduced here, including innovating tradition and focusing on the lived experience and needs of women.

Honoring the spatial qualities of traditional and organic morphologies characteristic of historic cities in Pakistan and translating them into modernist housing, Lari is convinced that this design strategy can afford women and children access to communally shared, semi-private, and private open spaces placed in such a way that they are protected from prying eyes. This is particularly relevant in the context of Pakistan's Muslim culture, where the home is still largely the center of women's lives. Even before planning Angoori Bagh, Lari had already successfully insisted on realizing such generous and protected spaces for women and children in her terrace design for the Naval Housing. Not realized according to her design, however, was her plan for the 1970s Lines Area Redevelopment Program, a large-scale, self-building project aligned with the notions of the freedom to build as promoted by architect John Turner, whose work Lari appreciated.

PREVIOUS PAGE **Angoori Bagh Housing, Lahore, 1975**
Photograph: Kazi Khaleed Ashraf, 1987. Image provided by the Aga Khan Documentation Center, MIT Libraries (AKDC@MIT)

The Story Behind the Large-Scale Housing Commission

How did a young architect like Yasmeen Lari, who had just opened her architecture office a few years earlier, end up designing such a large social housing project? Lari sees the seeds of Angoori Bagh in her 1969 Naval Housing, which she had realized for navy officers in Karachi. She happened to attend an elite social event, where she heard one of the men, who turned out to be Syed Mohammad Ahsan, Commander in Chief of the Pakistan Navy, speak about multistory housing as the best solution for new homes in the Naval Residential Area. Outspokenly refuting this idea, she was taken up on her challenge, invited to present an alternative design, and awarded the commission. This then led to Lari being summoned to a meeting with President Bhutto at the President House Murree in 1972. Given that her family's fortunes had been lost due to the government's nationalization of industry, Lari feared she would be asked to close down her modest architectural practice. Yet to her surprise, as she recalls, the president and his wife made her "feel treasured" and expressed their pride at her being Pakistan's first woman architect. Consequently, the engineer and humanist Mubashir Hassan, who was the Minister of Finance in the Bhutto Administration, invited her to present a design for Angoori Bagh with social housing as the flagship project of the Pakistan People's Party. She received a further invitation to develop a scheme for the Lines Area Redevelopment Program in Karachi in 1980.

Angoori Bagh Social Housing, Lahore, 1975

The land for Angoori Bagh (*angoori* means grape and *bagh* garden in Urdu) is located across from the famous seventeenth-century Shalimar Gardens in Lahore, which were originally built by Emperor Shah Jahan. It had been forcibly acquired by the Bhutto Government from old landowning families in Punjab. Angoori Bagh started with a large public presentation to marginalized communities, which was held in the Shalimar Gardens, previously used exclusively by the elite. Several thousand men and women attended this meeting. Focusing on the importance of the home as a site of cultural practices and subsistence production, Lari, in answering questions raised by women at the meeting, explained that the open-to-sky terraces allowed for watching one's children, keeping chickens, and growing vegetables. Yet, as Lari emphasizes today, none of the marginalized women attending the public design presentation actually moved into these 787 new dwelling units, which, in the end, were all distributed to middle-class families.

The 787 dwelling units are arranged in three-story blocks. They are grouped in clusters of fourteen with a special emphasis on open spaces for creating communal responsibility and caretaking.

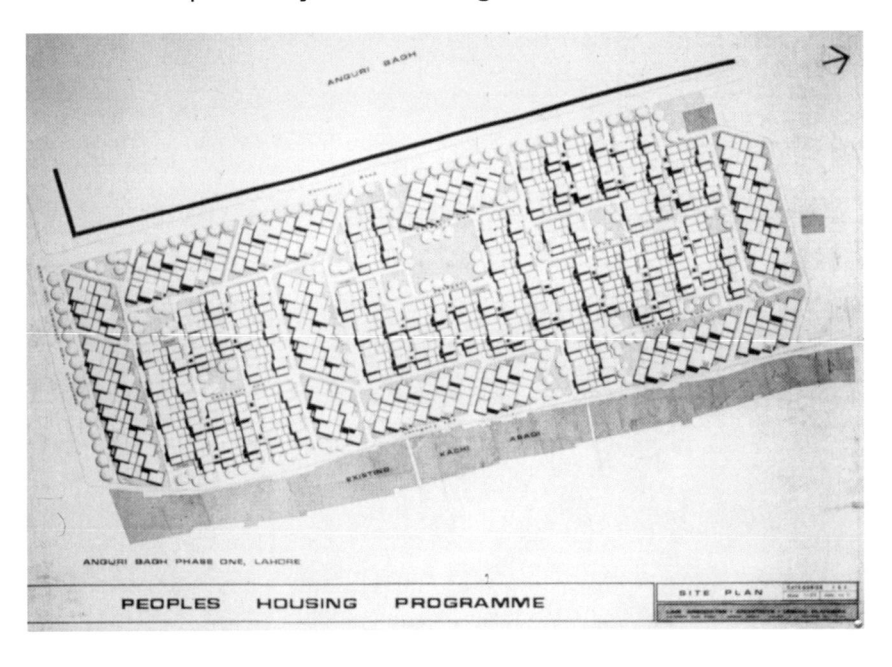

I had been very impressed by the traditional towns when I walked through them because I had not seen anything like them ever, and I think in a sense that unconsciously or subconsciously I was trying to replicate something like that, because I thought that allowed women to do a lot of things, and children had a much nicer place to be in.

Yasmeen Lari, 2022

Ensuring that the ancient wall of Angoori Bagh was maintained, activating building traditions of the walled cities in Multan and Lahore, and responding to everyday cultural practices and local needs, Lari connected these dimensions to the modern architectural principles she had studied in the UK. Tradition relevant to architecture is not only understood in terms of building here but as social and cultural traditions practiced at home and by communities in everyday life.

Responsive to the challenging climate, the limited budget, and using 100% local labor, with 70% of the workers previously unskilled and learning during construction, Lari's design relied on low-cost materials, in particular, locally manufactured clay bricks and simple bricklaying technology. The window frames are made of local timber, the floors are reinforced concrete slabs, and the walls are covered with a simple plaster wash. Only the steel was imported but rolled locally.

There were two different categories in the 787 dwelling units. While the first category had one room, a covered veranda, and an enclosed courtyard, the second category had two rooms. The kitchen was designed as an enclosure on the veranda. The sanitary unit and bath opened onto the courtyard.

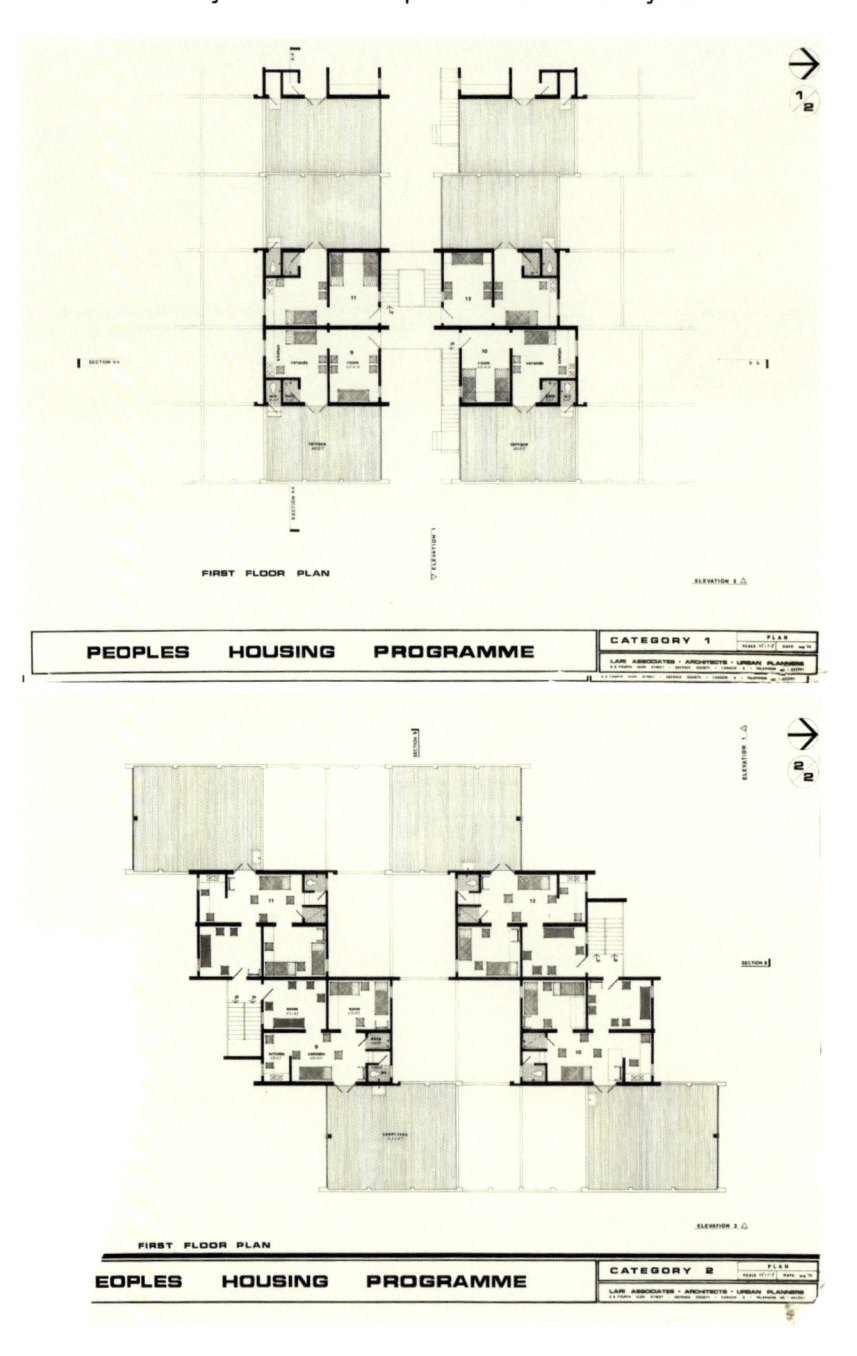

ELEVATION 1
CATEGORY 1

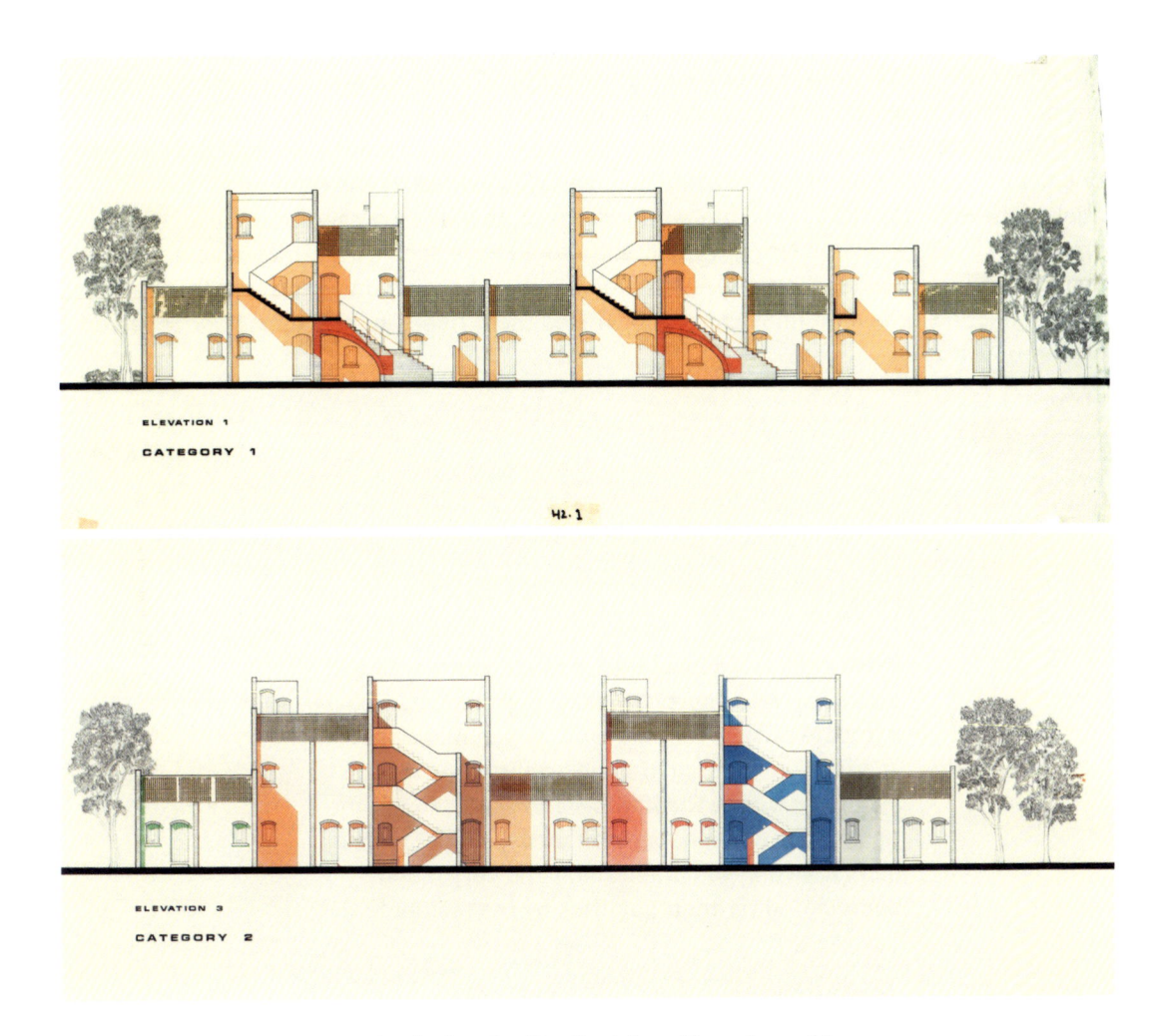

ELEVATION 3
CATEGORY 2

In her submission for the first Aga Khan Award in 1980, Lari states the following: "This particular approach is more applicable to the housing problems of the poor in developing countries than the western-type apartment block. I find the five-story walkup or the multistory apartment block totally unsuitable for the urban poor because of the confined space and the way it separates people from the ground and from one another." Paved pedestrian walkways enable access to the units, and staircases with overhanging bridges link the upper units with the terraces, which are key to the project and provided at all levels.

Naval Housing, Karachi, 1969–70

Only a few years after starting her own architectural office in Karachi, Yasmeen Lari was provided with the opportunity to design a collective housing project for the well-to-do middle class, the Naval Residential Estate. This allowed her to realize her specific spatial visions for collective, non-high-rise housing. Lari was invited by the Commander in Chief of the Pakistan Navy, Syed Mohammad Ahsan, to make a presentation to all the top officers of the Pakistan Navy, who initially would have seen a high-rise development as the modern way to go for the government-funded navy housing. Insisting that this renders families cooped up in matchboxes, Lari convinced the officers in attendance and received the commission.

Lari's design creates large, shared courtyards and a semi-private courtyard as an entrance, as well as a private terrace for each unit, which made for lively everyday communal life and, at the same time, ensured privacy. The photograph was taken at the time of completion. Up until today, all 276 housing units are very well maintained and very much appreciated for their qualities by the residents.

SECTION B B

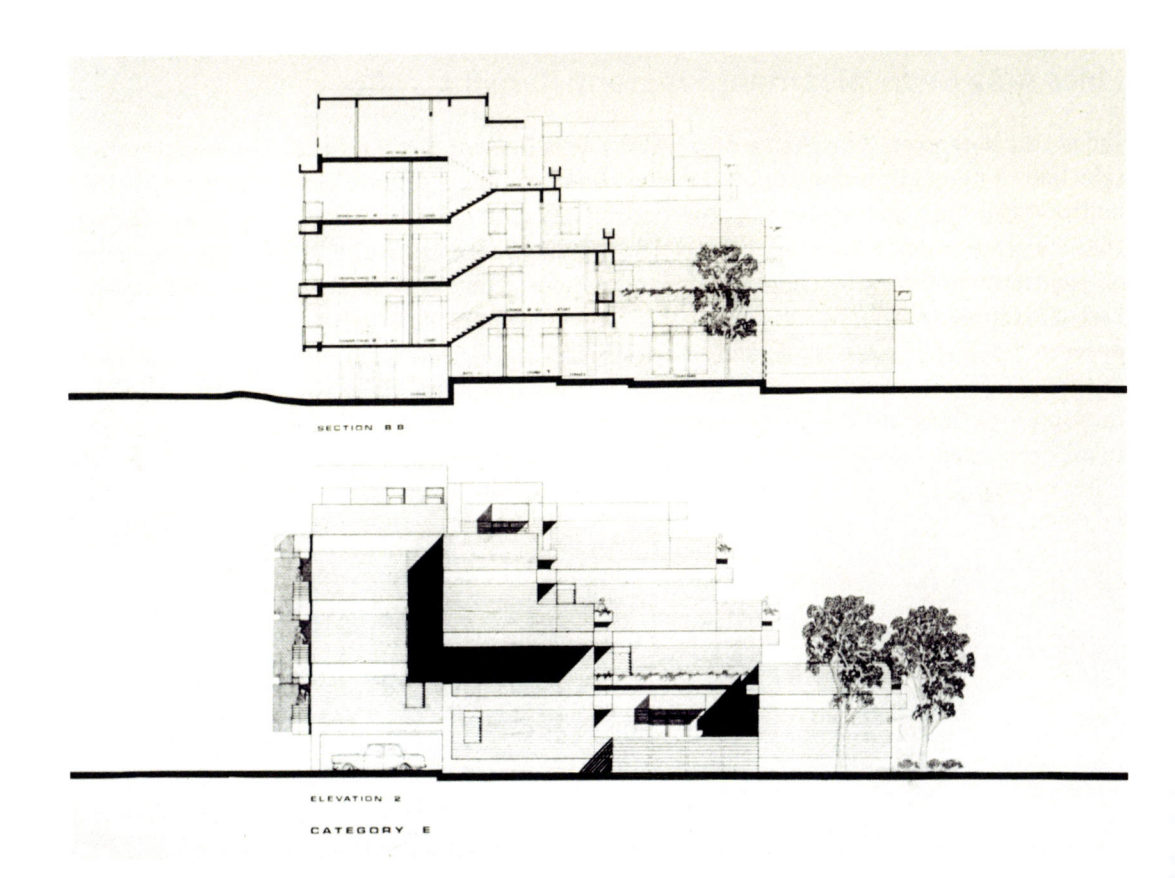

ELEVATION 2
CATEGORY E

Similar to her single-family homes, Lari designed split-level apartments, each with a spacious terrace. Trees separate blocks of six to eight units which, together, form courtyards.

I think the seeds of Angoori Bagh can be seen in the Naval Housing in Karachi. I was able to have these open-to-sky terraces, stacking back.
Yasmeen Lari, 2022

Lines Area Redevelopment Program, Karachi, 1980

When Lari worked on the scheme of the Lines Area Redevelopment for 13,000 people, more than half of Karachi's urban population lived under slum conditions. Having worked in close collaboration with the residents, Lari proposed her scheme to the authorities, suggesting that the state create the basic physical and social infrastructure and that people should be allowed to build their small homes, fifty square meters each, incrementally. According to Lari, it is important that nobody builds it for them. And that nobody should be resettled in order to preserve the economic and social structures. Her approach is completely different from the rationally planned Korangi township outside of Karachi. The Greek architect and town planner Constantinos Doxiadis had been brought to Pakistan by the Ford Foundation to plan this resettlement project for the Mohajirs, Muslim migrants from India.

Yasmeen Lari presents her plans for the Development Authority's Lines Area Redevelopment Program.
In order to enable self-determined social housing, parts of the 268-hectare, extremely valuable inner-city area were to be sold to private developers for commercial purposes. However, the goals of the cross-financing were not met.

FIRST FLOOR

SECOND FLOOR

GROUND FLOOR

Reproduced from Yasmeen Lari, "The Lines Area Resettlement Project Karachi," in *Designing in Islamic Cultures 2: Urban Housing*, ed. by Margaret Bentley Sevcenko (Cambridge, MA: Aga Khan Program for Islamic Architecture, 1982), 62.

The Lines Area, where British soldiers lived in colonial times, had gradually been taken over by informal settlements. Working in close contact with local residents, Lari's plan foresees self-help building and very simple construction methods. Emphasizing the importance of building privacy into the home, regardless of whether women were observing purdah (female seclusion as practiced in some Muslim communities including gendered spatial segregation and the requirement of women to cover their bodies), her plan includes enclosed courtyard spaces. Even though the density does not match the five-story walk-ups, it comes very close.

1 See Chris Moffat, "Lahore After the Modern: Architecture, equality and community in Yasmeen Lari's Anguri Bagh," *Global Intellectual History* (June 2022), DOI: 10.1080/23801883.2022.2062419.

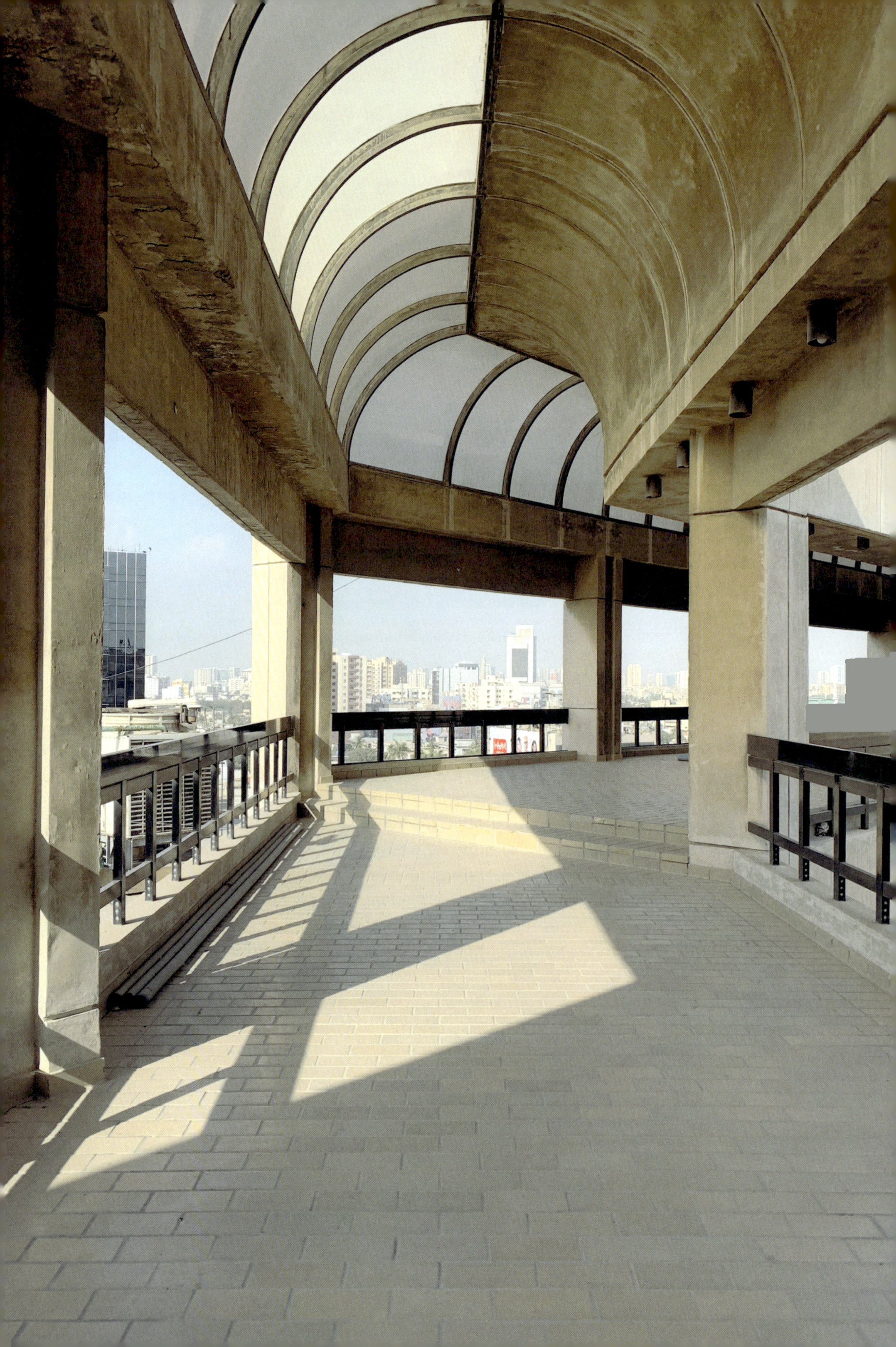

Icons for a Karachi Boulevard

Angelika Fitz

One of the most striking buildings on the drive from Karachi International Airport towards the city center is the FTC – Finance and Trade Centre: a megastructure of three skyscrapers connected by skywalks. This is one of several large-scale buildings that Yasmeen Lari realized in the 1980s and 1990s on a prominent transport axis. In Pakistan, infrastructures of this kind that are important for urban development were often developed in close cooperation between business, the public sector, and the military. As Lari explains, a scarcity of resources played no part in the planning. Glass, steel, and concrete—which were not (yet) available locally—were imported, and new industries, such as the local granite industry, sprung up as a result of the construction sites.

Looking back, Lari speaks of her time as a star architect, from which she retired in 2000. Decades later, in the face of water shortages in Karachi, the rapidly growing metropolis over twenty million people, she vehemently opposes new residential and office towers which, driven by a longing for a Dubai perceived as perfect (also known as 'Dubaiization'), are now being built en masse.

In contrast to the floor-space-maximized skyscrapers of twenty-first-century finance capitalism, Lari's large buildings give something back to the urban society. Recesses allow generous open spaces that expand the public realm. Elevated platforms and green atriums create communicative oases for employees and visitors. The varied structuring of the building and the integration of natural ventilation refer to the local context. Part of the ongoing erosion of public space in Karachi is the fact that the civic dimension of these buildings is threatened by increasing militarization and violence.

PREVIOUS PAGE **Skywalk FTC – Finance and Trade Centre, Karachi, 1982–89**
Photograph: Marvi Mazhar, 2022

FTC – Finance and Trade Centre, Karachi, 1982–89

In the 1980s, the question of what constitutes a specific Islamic architecture became increasingly prominent in the architectural discourse. Yasmeen Lari rejects stylistic interpretations and sees one strength of historic Islamic architecture in interiority as a concept. The large volume of the FTC is divided into three high sections and one low one, connected by a spine of open-air corridors, green atriums, and an extremely spacious entrance platform. More than ten large, state-related enterprises were involved in the development of the financial and commercial center. Many companies have been on site for over thirty years and the building continues to offer a most pleasant working environment to this day.

The FTC in the urban context of when it was created in the 1980s.

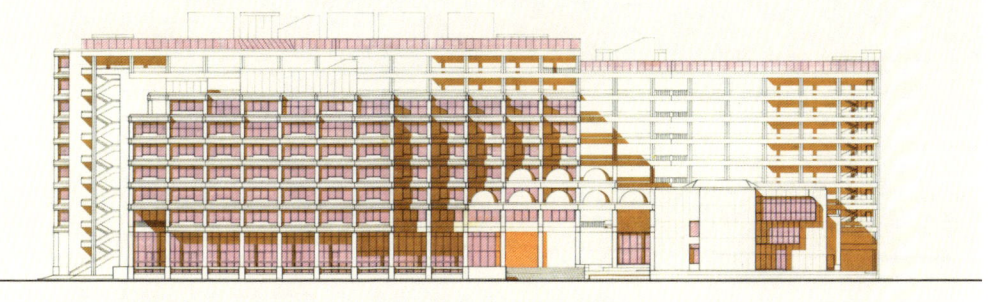

View from Shahrah-e-Faisal Boulevard

In 1980, Yasmeen Lari presented the plans for the FTC to investors and clients, including the military, who owned the land. In the background is the Vienna-born, Montréal-based architect Eva Vecsei, with whom Lari collaborated on the concept development.

For the concept of the FTC, Pakistan's largest building when it was completed, Lari looked for a partner who had experience with large-scale projects. The Hungarian-Canadian architect Eva Vecsei, born as Eva Hollo in Vienna in 1930, planned the Complex La Cité in Montréal in the 1970s, which was Canada's largest mixed-use, high-rise project at the time. The two met through the mediation of Canadian architect and landscape architect John Schreiber, with whom they both worked on an urban planning project in Karachi in the mid-1970s.

The central entrance platform serves as the distribution level and communicative meeting place. Opening the view of the city on two sides, the entrance arcades offer a pleasant and naturally ventilated place to escape from the hustle and bustle.

Photograph: Marvi Mazhar, 2022

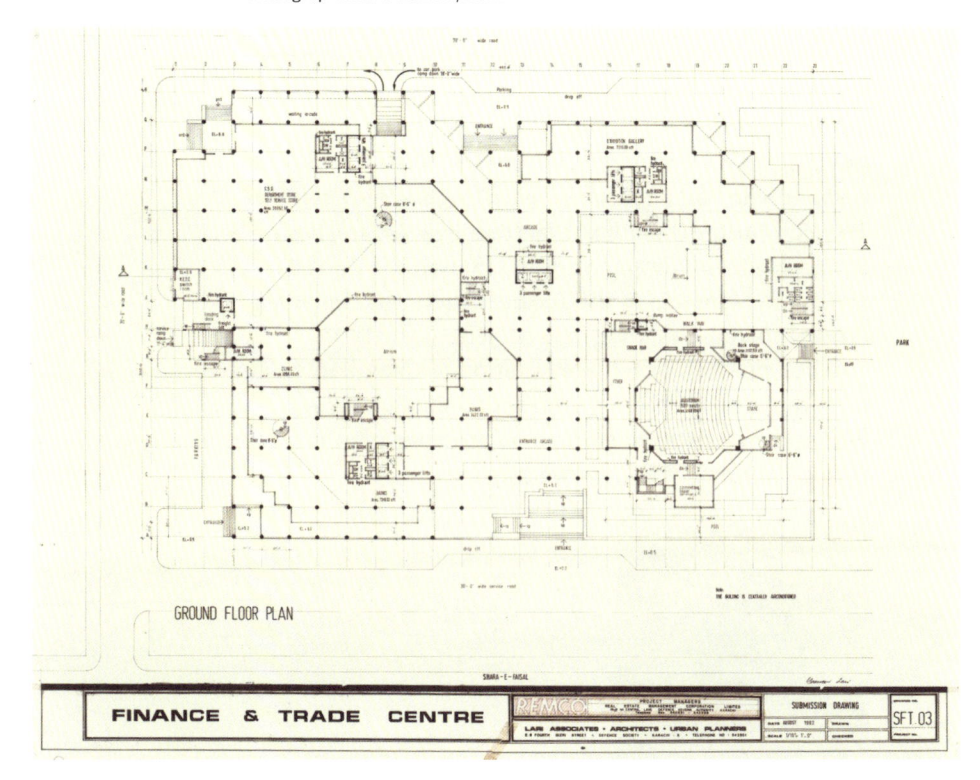

GROUND FLOOR PLAN

FINANCE & TRADE CENTRE

Islam suggests interiority as a concept. [...] The grandeur and beauty of a building is revealed only when you enter its portals.

Yasmeen Lari, 1981[1]

The skywalks encourage informal appropriation, from taking a break to repairing office furniture. The large courtyards ventilate and cool the building complex.

Photographs: Marvi Mazhar (left) and Elke Krasny (right), 2022

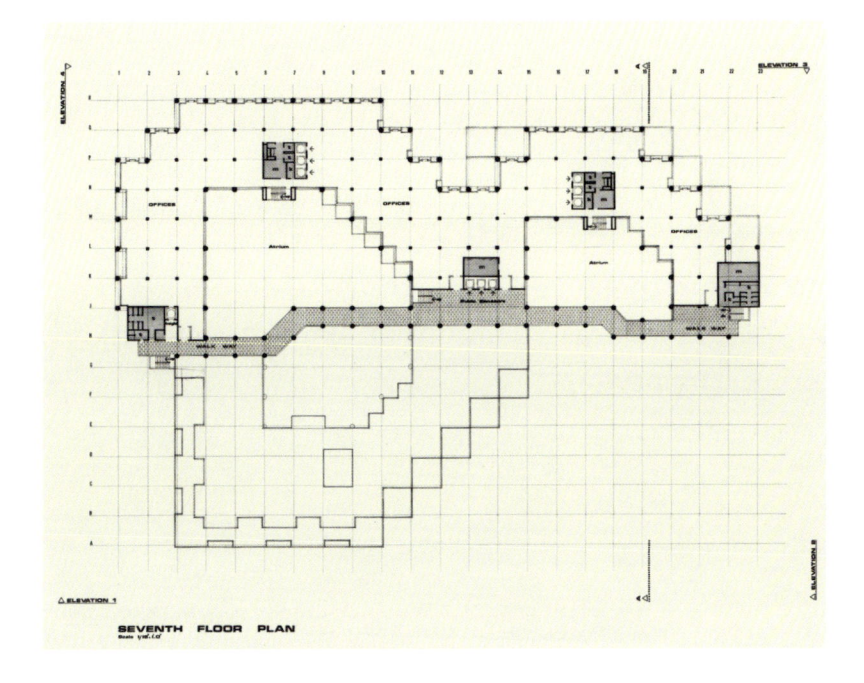

The experimental wind towers were later converted for building services. In the background, Karachi's rapidly growing skyline.

Photograph: Elke Krasny, 2022

I mean all of these public buildings are amazing because you want to do it as an architect, because you enjoy doing it. You are trained for it.

Yasmeen Lari, 2022

1 Yasmeen Lari, *MIMAR: Architecture in Development*, no. 2, ed. Hasan-Uddin Khan (Singapore: Concept Media, 1981), 45.

PSO House, Karachi, 1984–91

The PSO, the headquarters of Pakistan State Oil, is the first steel and glass structure of its size in Pakistan and bears witness to a growth-driven, resource-intensive vision of the future. Futuristic-looking panoramic elevators glide through the five-story entrance hall; solar control glass blocks out heat and noise; fountains, terraces, and front gardens offer relaxation areas in the hectic urban space.

The mirror glass façade reaches ten floors upwards, where the logo of the state oil company sits enthroned.

Photographs: Angelika Fitz (left) and Marvi Mazhar (right), 2022

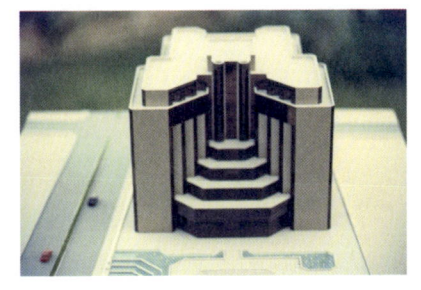

Model of the PSO, 1980s

Icons for a Karachi Boulevard

View of the steel construction and the panorama elevators in the entrance hall.

Photograph: Marvi Mazhar, 2022

Stepped structures react to the scale of the surroundings, recesses create public platforms. In recent years, safety barriers have severely limited accessibility.

Photographs: Angelika Fitz (left) and Marvi Mazhar (right), 2022

What is Pakistani architecture? Often there is the mistaken notion that if a building is 'Islamized,' as I call it, then it becomes Pakistani. But I don't believe in that, I feel that is a very false premise. I think what you need to do is, actually, maybe incorporate the spirit of something, rather than the actual expression of it.

Yasmeen Lari, 2022

ABN Amro Bank, Karachi, 1997

The branch for a European bank was Yasmeen Lari's final building with her office, Lari Associates. When the European clients wanted more Islamic elements in the façade design, Lari threatened to cancel the contract. She was not to be had for what she calls "instant Islamic" architecture. Instead, its postmodern stance draws on its most prominent urban neighbor, the neo-Gothic Frere Hall.

Frere Hall was erected in the mid-nineteenth century according to plans by the British general and architect Henry St. Clair Wilkins. The British colonial rulers originally intended it to be the city hall. Today it houses a library and gallery, surrounded by a popular public park.

Looking back: Lari's bank building in 2022, photographed through a window of Frere Hall opposite. In the 1990s, Yasmeen Lari wanted to design "a good neighbor" for the listed colonial heritage building. The tallest skyscrapers in Karachi are currently going up in the immediate vicinity.

Photograph: Angelika Fitz, 2022

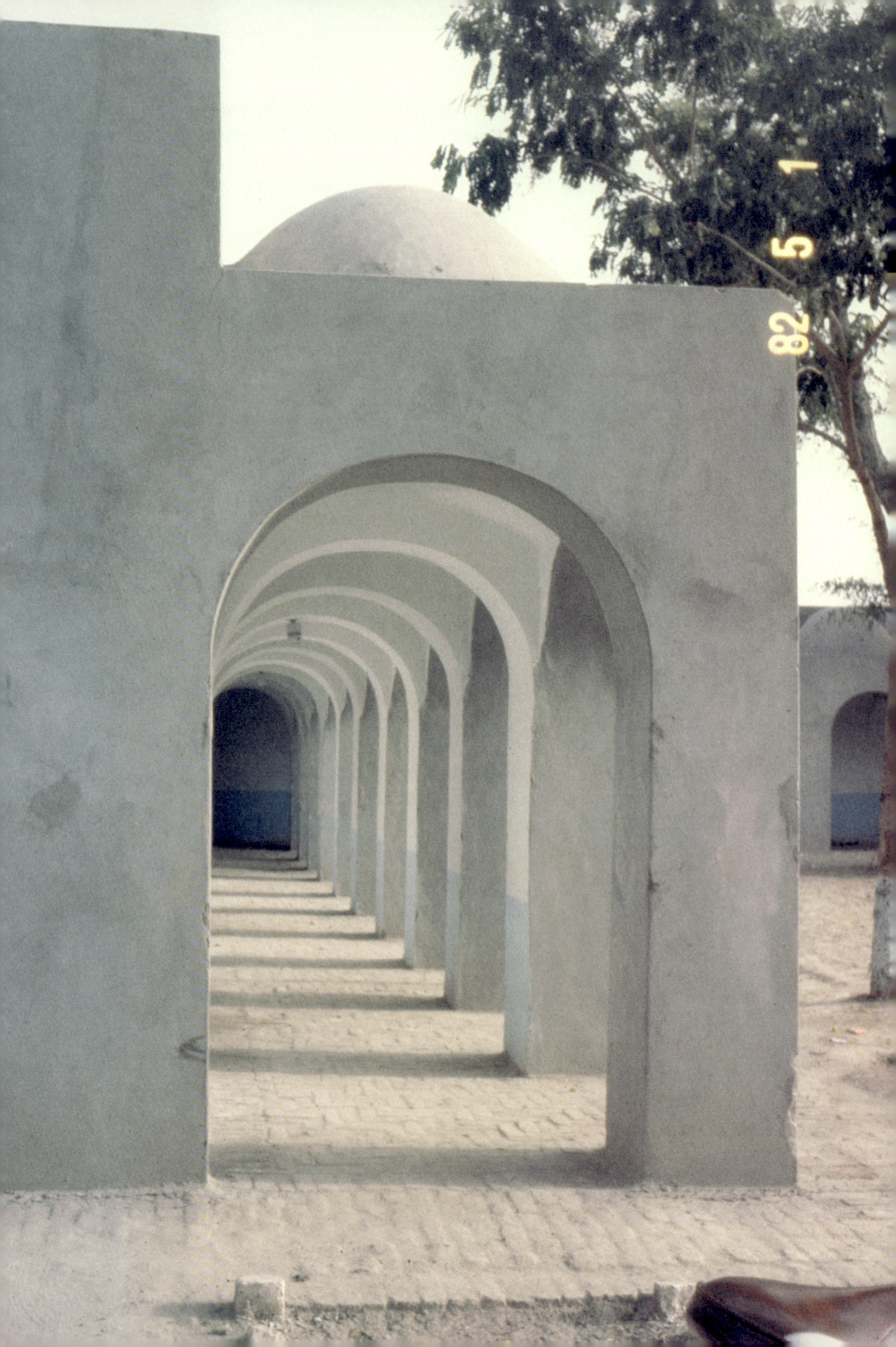
82 5 1

Material Ecologies
Building the Local

Elke Krasny
With additional research by Marvi Mazhar

Some architectural styles, and entire periods in architecture are known by their materiality. Steel, reinforced concrete, and glass are called to mind as the materials of modernism. From early on in her search for her own material language in architecture, Yasmeen Lari saw materials as having ethical and political implications beyond style or image. Materials and the resource economies and crafts connected to them matter to decolonization, to imagining a future beyond the Western industrialized material paradigm, and are a response to local climatic needs.

In 1972, when Lari was called to present herself to President Zulfikar Ali Bhutto and afforded the opportunity to have a conversation with him and his wife Shirin Amir Begum on Pakistan's future architecture, she not only spoke of housing, but also introduced the importance of materiality. The young architect promoted mud as a building material for the future. Invested in celebrating her own country's material heritage and fond of the work of the Egyptian architect Hassan Fathi, who used traditional mud architecture, Lari rallied for earth buildings. There was the political will to give a large number of commissions to her, including one to design an entire mud village. Yet, Lari's family had been expropriated by the Bhutto Administration and objected. This is why her first design for a village made out of earth bricks remained unrealized. But she stayed with mud. The President made it possible for her to have a first prototype of a two-room mud building constructed. It was a challenge to persuade the masons to work without shuttering molds. Having proven that mud can work, she received the commission to design the army barracks for sixty soldiers in Bahawalpur in 1981.

Later on, mud, lime, bamboo, and wind became central to her material ecological thinking. Yasmeen Lari is one of the very early proponents of what is understood today as material ecologies with, in her case, a focus on building locally and privileging the needs of women and children. Material ecologies as a design perspective is defined here as the relationships between building materials, economies of resources and labor, the knowledge of craft and construction technologies, environmental, climatic and atmospheric conditions, as well as the needs of humans and other living beings and inanimate objects.

PREVIOUS PAGE Army Mud Barracks, Bahawalpur, 1981

Working with Mud

In 1981, the Pakistani Army commissioned Yasmeen Lari to design barracks for sixty soldiers in Bahawalpur. Having successfully experimented with a mud prototype, she seized the opportunity to realize a large building of over five hundred square meters in mud.

This traditional building material in South Asia is commonly associated with rural life. Therefore, building accommodations for soldiers out of mud, and thus also creating an image for Pakistan's modern army, was met with serious doubt and public criticism at the time. Lari remembers that the barracks were not well received in the press, with one editorial in a locally important newspaper cautioning the government to not be led by a young architect into "muddy futures." According to her, there was talk at the Army Headquarters that the mud barracks resulted from the insistence of a "mad architect" and a "mad general" (Rahimuddin Khan, general of the Pakistani Army). All the building materials for the barracks were locally made and Lari encouraged the masons to trust their own construction knowledge when working with the drawings they were given.

When you are doing something, every time it is a learning process. And that is why, if you replicate something and keep on replicating, that doesn't help. It doesn't let you grow. I think it is very important that every time you do something, it is something new, something in which you are growing. You have to grow with every project.

Yasmeen Lari, 2022

The vault and dome building, which is organized around a generous L-shaped courtyard, was completed in only four months. At the time, Lari envisioned that soldiers would easily learn how to build such barracks themselves, so that neither labor nor materials would have to be imported.

Domes and walls consist of locally manufactured earth bricks. There are foundations of brick with a damp-proof course of bitumen. Cement concrete was poured in place and used for the floors.

Photographs: © Yasmeen Lari / Source: Aga Khan Trust for Culture

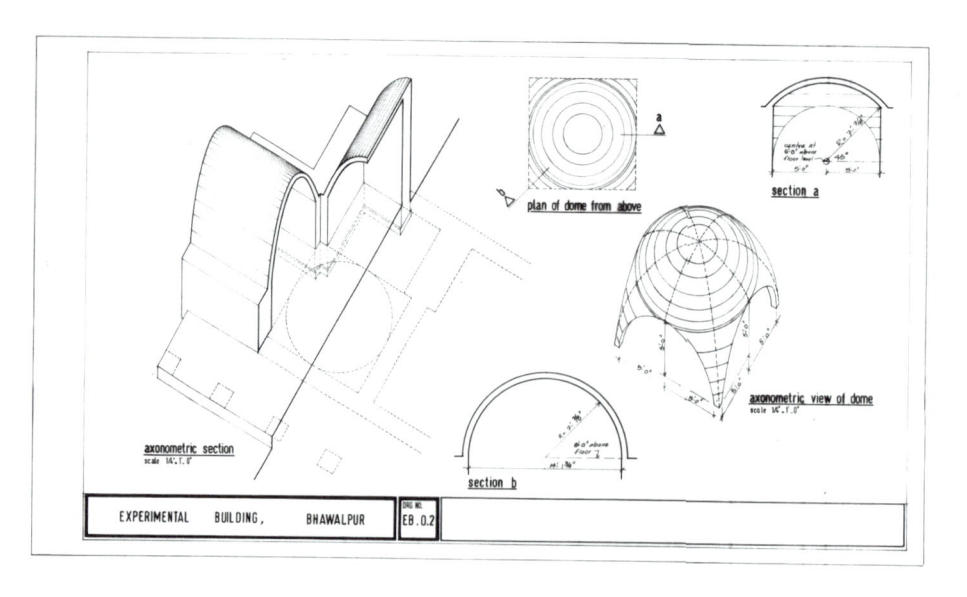

Referring to this as an experimental building in the plan makes it clear that Yasmeen Lari was well aware of the fact that her design for the army barracks was considered nonstandard and thus an experiment. Proof was needed that it could actually be done.

Decades later, when Lari was a full-time humanitarian worker and promoted zero-carbon ecologies, mud was central to the rebuilding efforts in rural areas undertaken together with villagers whose homes had been completely destroyed after the 2005 earthquake, as well as after the 2010 flood. This image was taken in 2012 and shows a woman learning how to build with mud in Kareema Village, close to Makli.

Lari's approach to material ecologies revolves around providing training for unskilled people. This also keeps traditional building skills alive. The large number of bricks shown here were produced by youths who participated in construction training funded by the United Nations Development Programme in 2016. They were fabricated to be used for the community center of Zindani in the Dera Ismail Khan District in Khyber Pakhtunkhwa.

Working with Lime

Traditional materials and building technologies are particularly relevant to heritage work. Maintenance and restoration require a profound understanding of the materials architecture is made out of, how to work with them, and how to respond to contemporary pressures on historic buildings, including the catastrophic impact of climate change. For Yasmeen Lari, her work in heritage and her humanitarian and zero-carbon activism are deeply interconnected. In particular, her own growing expertise in the use of mud and lime is connected to her work in heritage as well as her strong focus on local building traditions in the villages.

In 2012, the Heritage Foundation of Pakistan, founded by Yasmeen Lari and her husband Suhail Zaheer Lari, was entrusted with the maintenance and caretaking tasks at the Makli Necropolis by the Directorate of Archeology in Sindh Province. This enormous heritage site with thousands of funerary monuments from five centuries, from the 1400s to the 1800s, had been neglected. A lack of adequate funding for its management, as well as encroachment, waste, and siltation, caused severe problems. Furthermore, the necropolis, a World Heritage Site since 1981, was very badly affected by the 2010 flood in Sindh Province. The Heritage Foundation carried out material tests on site in order to work on the repair and conservation of decaying and crumbling structures. Lari turned to the use of lime to avoid the use of cement in restoration.

Photograph: Rahul Aijaz, writer/filmmaker, 2012

Earlier approaches to restoration included the use of cement, which had even been advised by the English archeologist John Marshall, who acted as the Director General of the Archeological Survey of India at the beginning of the twentieth century. Lari completely objects to the use of cement in restoration, particularly because of the harmful side effects of its rigidity. In all of her heritage work, the use of cement is forbidden.

Lime is a chalky, sticky material which was historically used as the principal binder for plasters or mortars. The Heritage Foundation team worked on site to test the method of wet slaked lime. Because of its properties, lime helps buildings withstand weathering. After the rocks called fat lime have been mixed with water to produce slaked lime cream, the lime can be stored safely in plastic containers for years.

On the occasion of one of the regular UNESCO visits to the Makli Necropolis, Yasmeen Lari explains how they produce the wet slaked lime needed for their restoration efforts.

Working with Bamboo

Unlike mud or lime, bamboo is not a traditional building material in Pakistan, where timber was usually used in combination with mud. In 2009, when Lari was working in the Shaikh Shahzad Camp to produce relief architecture for women and children who had been driven from their homes after a battle between the army and the Taliban, she saw that bamboo was the only easily available local material. Lari understood the potential of bamboo as a fast-growing ecological resource and very good building material in regions without established and sustainable timber production. Lari began to conduct tests and worked with structural engineers to use bamboo for building disaster relief shelters.
At the beginning of the 2020s, Yasmeen Lari extended the skill sharing around bamboo beyond training for self-building to include students. She collaborated with universities in Pakistan, Bangladesh, the UK, Italy, and Austria to integrate the practical experience of building with bamboo into design studios.

In 2010, Mariyam Nizam and Marvi Mazhar, who were members of Yasmeen Lari's staff at the time, conducted a workshop on self-building in the village of Darya Khan Sheikh in Khairpur for people who had been affected by the flood.

This is one of the shelters built in the village of Moak Sharif in 2011. The materials used are sun-dried mudbricks and bamboo.

This house was built in the village of Moak Sharif in 2011. It has a bamboo framework and lime mud was used for reinforcement. The load-bearing capacity of the roof was tested by members of the community. This photograph has become an iconic image of Yasmeen Lari's zero-carbon shelter program.

Yasmeen Lari perfected a system of local prefabrication and handmade seriality. These braced panels were made by people who were trained to build their own shelters after the 2005 earthquake in the foothills of the Himalayas in Dir in Khyber Pakhtunkhwa had destroyed their homes.

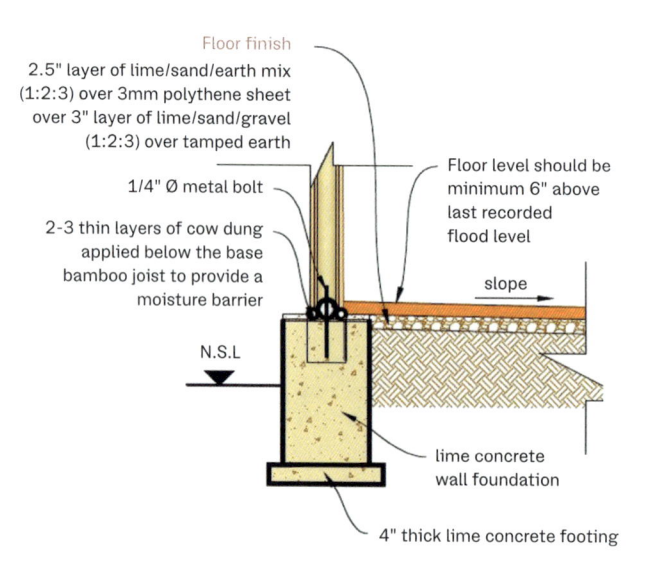

Floor finish
2.5" layer of lime/sand/earth mix (1:2:3) over 3mm polythene sheet over 3" layer of lime/sand/gravel (1:2:3) over tamped earth

1/4" Ø metal bolt

2-3 thin layers of cow dung applied below the base bamboo joist to provide a moisture barrier

N.S.L

Floor level should be minimum 6" above last recorded flood level

slope

lime concrete wall foundation

4" thick lime concrete footing

These technical plans for floors, walls, and roofs contain detailed instructions for construction. Shelters like these were mostly built in Moak Sharif and other nearby villages after the 2010 flood.

Roof detail

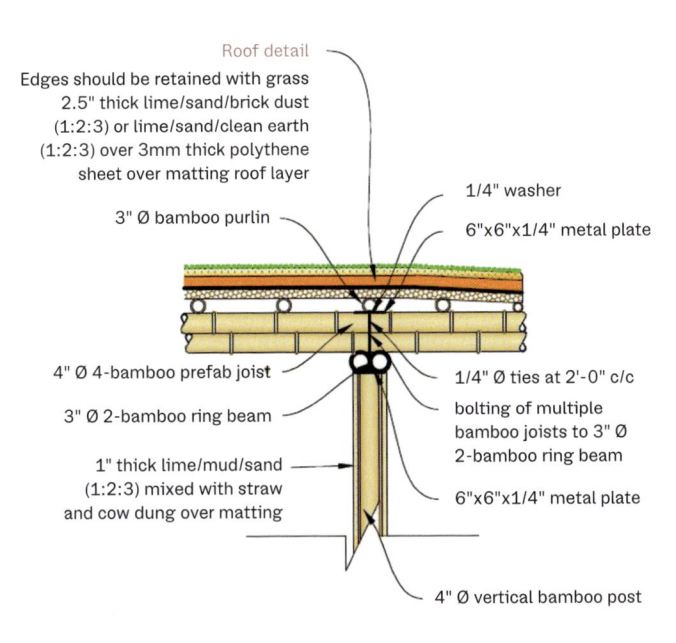

Edges should be retained with grass
2.5" thick lime/sand/brick dust
(1:2:3) or lime/sand/clean earth
(1:2:3) over 3mm thick polythene
sheet over matting roof layer

1/4" washer

6"x6"x1/4" metal plate

3" Ø bamboo purlin

4" Ø 4-bamboo prefab joist

3" Ø 2-bamboo ring beam

1" thick lime/mud/sand
(1:2:3) mixed with straw
and cow dung over matting

1/4" Ø ties at 2'-0" c/c

bolting of multiple
bamboo joists to 3" Ø
2-bamboo ring beam

6"x6"x1/4" metal plate

4" Ø vertical bamboo post

Working with Wind

Wind may be one of the most overlooked building materials. The technical-sounding term ventilation conceals rather than communicates the fact that naturally occurring winds and breezes perform the work of cooling. Historically, most local building traditions developed their distinct ways of interacting with the wind and of integrating the wind into their vernacular technologies. When Yasmeen Lari, together with her husband Suhail Zaheer Lari, set out to study the knowledge of traditional building and urban design in her country, she was particularly fascinated by the wind-cooling systems in Thatta.

The traditional wind-catchers of Thatta, also known as wind towers, became a life-long source of inspiration for Yasmeen Lari and made her consider wind as a building material in its own right, but also encouraged her to think more about the impact of the climate and the wind on buildings. Her use of wind-catchers as cooling and ventilation technology can be found throughout her urban modernist and post-modernist buildings and in her rural humanitarian zero-carbon architecture.

For the design of the FTC – Finance and Trade Centre on Karachi's Shahrah-e-Faisal Boulevard, Yasmeen Lari had wind studies conducted. To provide natural ventilation, Lari turned to the self-cooling interiority typical of local architecture and implemented this in covered arcades and courtyards. This is responsive to the needs of a subtropical climate with very hot summers when temperatures rise to over forty-six degrees Celsius. The design originally also foresaw the traditional technology of wind towers as a contemporary system for cooling and ventilation, but they were later filled with building services.

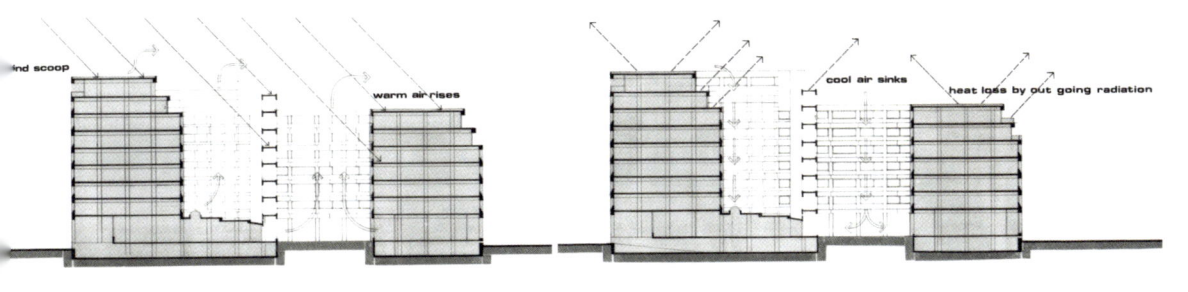

Air movement (day) Air movement (night)

Seeking to understand the best building techniques for both humanitarian rebuilding efforts and climate-responsive construction, Lari first introduced wind-catchers for the shelters. These were discontinued, because their maintenance proved to be challenging. As materials are of central importance for ecological and social justice in architecture, Lari is invested in ongoing experimentation to understand how traditional technologies can best be improved and innovated.

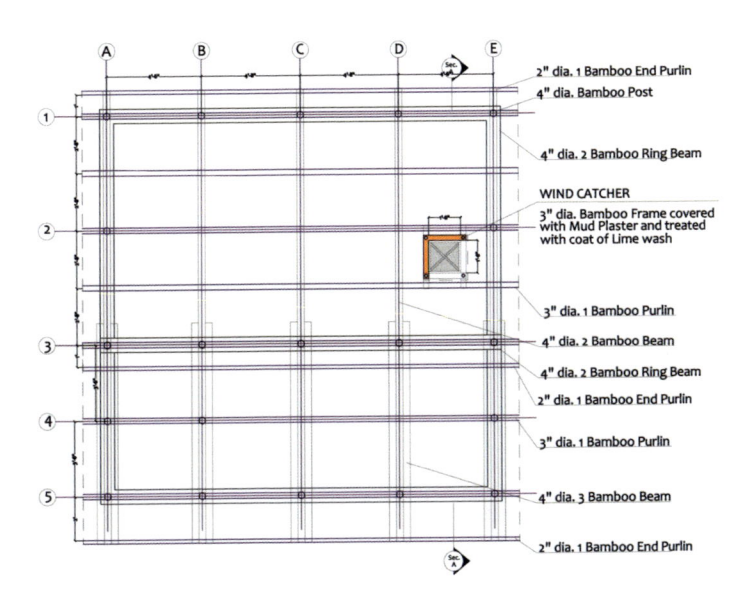

2" dia. 1 Bamboo End Purlin
4" dia. Bamboo Post
4" dia. 2 Bamboo Ring Beam

WIND CATCHER
3" dia. Bamboo Frame covered with Mud Plaster and treated with coat of Lime wash

3" dia. 1 Bamboo Purlin
4" dia. 2 Bamboo Beam
4" dia. 2 Bamboo Ring Beam
2" dia. 1 Bamboo End Purlin
3" dia. 1 Bamboo Purlin
4" dia. 3 Bamboo Beam
2" dia. 1 Bamboo End Purlin

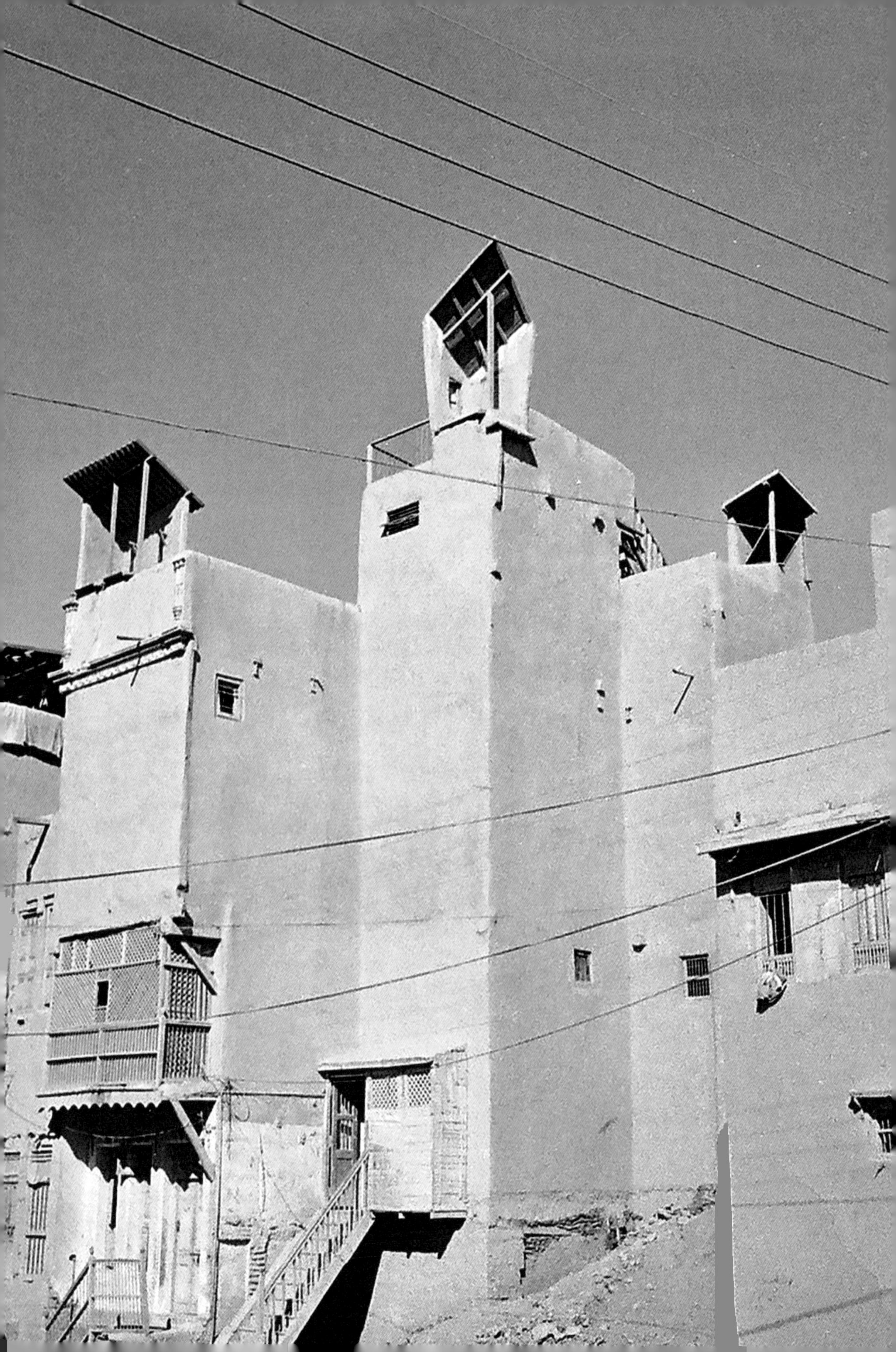

Heritage as Future
Decolonizing Legacies

Elke Krasny

Upon returning to Pakistan after her studies in England, Yasmeen Lari began to more fully understand the impact of over a century of British colonial rule on her own perspective on cultural values in architecture. What Kenyan novelist and theorist Ngũgĩ wa Thiong'o observed in his book *Decolonising the Mind* on linguistic decolonization and its importance to national culture also matters to the material decolonization of architecture and infrastructure. Together with her husband Suhail Zaheer Lari, the architect set out to research her country's architectural legacies, including the vastly overlooked vernacular traditions and mundane urban structures. Insisting that their cultural value should be rightly recognized was a first step towards redefining what counts as heritage in Pakistan.

The wholehearted commitment to creating futures through architecture was extended into heritage work, which, in Lari's case, not only meant conservation, but also the active translation of vernacular materials and highly sophisticated, low-tech technologies into her own ecological architecture practice. Together with her husband and like-minded friends, she set up the Heritage Foundation of Pakistan in 1980, through which she continued to deliver her later humanitarian and zero-carbon work in architecture.

By expanding her heritage, conservation, and restoration expertise through exchange with international practitioners and scholars and cultivating her ties with UNESCO, Lari's sustained heritage activism ultimately led her to become the architect who has worked on two UNESCO World Heritage Sites in Pakistan: the citadel of Lahore Fort and the necropolis of Makli. Her interest is not in heritage as an object but in heritage as living knowledge meaningful to people's livelihoods. Making traditional craft techniques used in restoration and repair available to village women means investing in building local, ecologically sound, and gender-responsive economies. Bringing together research, documentation, self-initiated publications and public education, advocacy and public policy advising, as well as large-scale civic activism, Lari became the key figure in redefining, reclaiming, and ultimately restoring and saving architectural heritage in Pakistan.

PREVIOUS PAGE Traditional wind-catcher houses in Thatta, photographed by Suhail Zaheer Lari in the 1970s.

Wind-Catchers in Thatta

Already in 1964, the ingenuity of the wind-catchers attracted attention. Bernard Rudofsky included Hyderabad's wind-catchers, which he called air-conditioners, in his book *Architecture without Architects.* While appreciative of spatial and technological dimensions of vernacular buildings, the coinage architecture without architects may have added to upholding the separation between local building traditions and the international architectural canon. Yasmeen Lari counteracts such a colonialist separation and emphasizes the value of local architecture as architecture. The houses in Thatta used timber lath and mud plaster construction. A wind-catcher for each room is installed on the roof to provide cross-ventilation and passive cooling.

With the Heritage Foundation, Lari published a book on Thatta in 1989.

A passionate photographer, Suhail Zaheer Lari documented the vernacular architecture of Thatta in Sindh Province, approximately ninety kilometers from Karachi.

Lari was interested in studying the traditional technologies that helped make homes more comfortable in sweltering heat and high humidity. She emphasizes that in traditional Muslim culture the space for women was the home, with women separated from public life outside. Therefore, these traditional technologies had an important dimension of providing comfort to women and children, who spend most of their time in their houses.

Traditional towns and villages had very narrow streets so that the shade could protect pedestrians and the streets acted as a cooling device.

The Mohenjo-daro archeological site (left), Thatta Heritage Mapping (right)

Together with the German archeologist Michael Jansen, who conducted a German-funded project at the archeological site Mohenjo-daro at the Indus River between 1978 and 1987, Lari did an in-depth documentation of the vernacular architecture in Thatta in 1979. Lari remembers that through her collaboration with Jansen she learned all the relevant methods for archeological documentation, which she later used for the documentation of urban heritage in Karachi and in Makli. Characteristic of Lari's way of working are her openness to always learning more and willingness to adapt methods to the needs of specific contexts. Today, most of the traditional structures and wind-catchers in Thatta have disappeared because of development.

Karachi Documentation, since the 1980s

During the late 1980s, Yasmeen Lari, with the Heritage Foundation, began to map the urban heritage of Karachi as systematically as possible. At the time, as Lari recalls, Pakistan was really a left-out place and there was hardly anything published on Karachi's urban heritage or architecture. Because of more than one hundred years of colonial rule, no historical maps seemed to have been made available to the public. Drinking countless cups of tea with registrars and sub-registrars of the city of Karachi in their offices and persuading them to open up old and dusty cupboards, Lari was able to track down maps from 1870, which she then published in her book on Karachi.

Working with paintings, a large number of rare, historic photographs, and the different maps she had been able to gather, Yasmeen Lari, together with her son Mihail Lari, who took new photographs of Karachi's urban heritage, published a comprehensive book on Karachi's urbanization and its architecture: *The Dual City: Karachi during the Raj* (1996).

National Advisor for Lahore Fort, 2003–05

In 2003, after Lari had already closed her architecture office, she was persuaded by the then Director of the Islamabad UNESCO office Ingeborg Breines, a humanist who focuses on women and peace-building, to come out of retirement and act as a National Advisor at the site of Lahore Fort. In 1981, Lahore Fort was inscribed as a UNESCO World Heritage Site in acknowledgment of its Mughal monuments. Traveling regularly between Karachi and Lahore, Lari completed a survey between 2003 and 2005. Together with the field archeologist and international consultant Ayesha Pamela Rogers, she also co-authored the proposition for the master plan.

Lahore Fort is the citadel in the city of Lahore. The first historical references to the citadel date back to the eleventh century. Under Mughal rule, Lahore Fort was completely rebuilt in the seventeenth century.

Since 1981, Lahore Fort has been inscribed in the UNESCO World Heritage list.

As UNESCO's National Advisor, Lari was instrumental in saving the endangered Sheesh Mahal ceiling in the Shah Burj of the Lahore Fort, which she visits here with an international team.

As part of public heritage education and to strengthen the material understanding of the structures and its relations to heritage, Yasmeen Lari arranged for students to be able to participate in the cleaning of Lahore Fort.

Sethi House, Damage Assessment and Protection Measures, 2011

The Sethi House is located in the old city of Peshawar and is named after the Sethis, a Hindu trader family from Punjab. Lari adheres to a 'first aid' imperative in heritage work. This includes documentation and damage assessment together with providing initial protection measures for the continued existence of buildings. Lari first visited the neighborhood in the 1980s and, due to family connections, was granted access to the famous Sethi House. She recalls that achieving its stabilization and conservation was very challenging. Ingeborg Breines from the UNESCO office in Islamabad collaborated with Lari on a report, which made it possible for Lari to introduce the idea of a Heritage Center. This aligns with her understanding of making heritage publicly accessible, which is even more important in this case, as it was the very first time that the Sindh Province government bought a private house to make it open to the public.

Originally, this house had been the *zanakhana* (female quarters) of the central Sethi House. This photo is included in the documentation of the building's restoration, which was published by the Heritage Foundation in 2015.

Poor plumbing and rainwater seepage had caused the decay of the wooden rafters. The replacement of joists and rafters had to be carried out with extreme care. Master artisans from Lahore worked on the conservation in 2011.

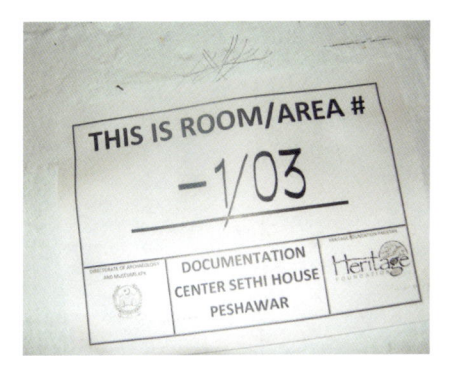

Almost fourteen tons of earth had to be removed from the site. Lari supervised the work on-site, and meticulous daily documentation of the work was carried out, a practice Lari had established during her earlier work at Lahore Fort.

The Makli Necropolis, Damage Assessment and Conservation, since 2011

The vast Makli Necropolis, with graves and tombs from the fourteenth to the eighteenth centuries, is spread over an area of ten kilometers and located close to Thatta. Makli demonstrates the coming together of different multiethnic and religious architectural expressions for honoring the dead, including pre-Mughal and Mughal funerary architecture. This resonates with Yasmeen Lari's heritage ethics of viewing architectural legacies as multidimensional and of equal importance regardless of their time of origin. Suhail Zaheer Lari took a particular interest in Makli and made proposals for its conservation. In 1981, the site was inscribed into the UNESCO World Heritage List. In 2011, with financial support from the Prins Claus Fund, the Heritage Foundation made a damage assessment of the historic monuments and their varying states of decay, which became the basis for measures taken over the next decades.

According to Rabela Junejo, who completed a dissertation on Makli in 2020, there are 125,000 burial ensembles.

Photograph: © Daily Times, 2020

Yasmeen Lari worked on the documentation of the highly ornamented stone structure of the tomb dedicated to Jam Nizamuddin II, the Sultan of Sindh between 1461 and 1508. In its 36th session in 2012, the World Heritage Committee noted this work and recommended further investigation and monitoring.

The Heritage Foundation carried out work at Makli focuses on the repair, repointing, and grouting of brickwork and masonry rather than on stone replacement. Such minimum interventions were recommended by UNESCO.

One of the frequent UNESCO visits to Makli. In 2012, this World Heritage Site came under the custody of the newly founded Directorate of Archeology in Sindh Province, which "outsourced" the maintenance and conservation work to Lari's Heritage Foundation, with whom they drew up a Memorandum of Understanding for joint caretaking. Since then, UNESCO delegations have been visiting regularly to monitor the progress of the conservation efforts and check whether their recommendations, such as the implementation of visitor services or the protection of the site boundaries, are being carried out.

Yasmeen Lari and Vibeke Jensen on a visit in Makli. In November 2014, Vibeke Jensen was appointed Director of the UNESCO Office in Islamabad and UNESCO Representative in Pakistan.

The problem, of course, has always been that since most of us have been trained in the West, our focus always is the West. When I came back after my studies, I felt as if I had no idea about my own roots. You know, now we talk about the one percent because of Thomas Piketty, but the fact is Pakistan has always been like that. So, being part of the one percent, you never even looked at other things, which was a great tragedy.

Yasmeen Lari, 2022

Workshop with experts from Bangladesh, Iran, Jordan, Nepal, Oman, and Pakistan in Makli in 2017. At the top in the center is Naheem Shah, who works as the Heritage Foundation's project manager. This workshop was part of the World Heritage, Sustainable Development and Community Involvement project established under the UNESCO/Republic of Korea Funds-in-Trust in 2014. Makli was specifically chosen as the pilot for this project.
In order to improve the quality of glazed tiles needed for the conservation work in Makli, a Glaze Tile Atelier was established and tile specialists from Italy were brought in. With the project's express aim to connect conservation work to income-generating craft practices, it is thanks to Lari's insistence that the training in ceramic production was made available to women from nearby villages, who had no other source of income. Now the ceramic production of the newly trained craftswomen is linked to conservation efforts at the World Heritage Site, which makes heritage, as Lari points out, meaningful to their lives.
Photograph: © UNESCO / ActuA, 2017, CC BY-SA 3.0 IGO

Karavan, since 2000

With public space under enormous pressure in Karachi, Yasmeen Lari felt it was more important than ever for urban streets in Karachi to offer space for people to move freely and peacefully, and she saw heritage as a vehicle to make a claim to civic presence in public and to promote peace. This led to regular programming around heritage for the entirety of the year, culminating in a heritage festival called KaravanKarachi in September 2001.

Every Saturday there were preparatory meetings in her office with people pouring in and freely volunteering their ideas and their help. September witnessed four weeks of public celebration, guided tours, workshops, craft activities, and performances. Strongly believing in the communal power and creativity of citizens and in heritage to provide the reason for a culture of belonging and civic pride, Lari, together with many others, made this claim to public space and peaceful movement in a time of deadly violence.

Since then, KaravanKarachi has been transformed into KaravanPakistan and serves as an umbrella for organizing public heritage education and civic action, in particular, community outreach and youth action programs.

Beginning in March 2001, a temporary pedestrian zone was organized to honor specific historic buildings every Sunday. Volunteer tour guides provided historical explanations of the history of the buildings.

With the support of the British Council, 13,000 schools participated in the festival. Students were encouraged to celebrate all their contributions rather than be invited for a competition, as is often the case.

In the Rahguzar walking street, where Lari has been working for over a decade, Karavan events such as the cleaning of Denso Hall, a historic library building, take place. Fazal Mansion, at the corner of the street, is in dire need of restoration and under threat of being delisted. Lari appealed to citizens for their support in efforts to save the building. The Rahguzar site is linked to the craft-based heritage economy which Lari initiated. The terra-cotta pavers are produced by local craftswomen who have learned the skill through heritage training in the villages next to Makli.

Heritage as Future

YASMEEN LARI

Building Policies, Laws, and Institutions

Angelika Fitz

For Yasmeen Lari, architecture is more than buildings. Architecture shapes the future. As an architect, Lari works on changing the underlying conditions to realize the social and ecological potential of architecture. Lari is not satisfied with a symptom diagnosis. Once she identifies flaws or deficits, she seeks to change the systems around architecture or design new ones. Today she is considered a public figure in Pakistan, whose portrait can be seen as a mural next to those of human rights activists on the streets of Karachi.

Lari has (co)founded civil society organizations, the most prominent being the Heritage Foundation of Pakistan, with which she is still active today. She has created new public spaces, such as the Karachi Artists' Gallery, the first permanent exhibition space in Pakistan, which she founded in 1964 together with her husband Suhail Zaheer Lari. She has achieved the enshrinement of job descriptions for architects and town planners into law and the establishment of urban monument protection in Pakistan. She is very skeptical about the state and politics but, if necessary, she takes the path through state institutions and even served as a member of parliament for a short time.

Although Lari has built exclusively in Pakistan, her professional networks are international. She seeks exchange in three areas in particular: the question of housing, dealing with cultural heritage, and Islamic building traditions. In 1976, she was a speaker in the forum of the legendary first UN Habitat Conference on Human Settlements in Vancouver. She has been involved from the very beginning in two World Heritage Sites and in the architectural activities of the Aga Khan Trust for Culture.

PREVIOUS PAGE **Mural in the Defence Underpass, Karachi**

A series of murals of courageous women was originally commissioned by the civic platform I AM KARACHI for the walls of the Karachi Press Club as a response to the murder of the human rights activist Sabeen Mahmud. Similar murals later appeared in a busy underpass (pictured here) on the initiative of a provincial government administrator. Video still: Imran Gill, 2022

Heritage Foundation of Pakistan, since 1980

"Pakistan's Heritage is the best kept secret of the country," says the founding statement of the Heritage Foundation of Pakistan. The civil society foundation was founded in 1980 by Yasmeen and Suhail Zaheer Lari, with private resources from his insurance company and her architectural practice. According to Lari, it is important to preserve the built heritage in all its diversity, including buildings from the British colonial era as well as Mughal, Hindu, or Buddhist architecture. While the British Antiquities Act of 1901 focused on grand monuments, the Heritage Foundation draws attention to everyday historical structures and their qualities, such as human scale, climatic adaptation, and local craftsmanship traditions.

The Heritage Foundation's Karavan event series and the practical work to save built structures have involved a broad public for decades and taught Lari "that you do not have to attain high levels of education to be heritage savvy." She also used the foundation's institutional framework for international networking and her own further education in monument protection.

Angelika Fitz

After the 2005 earthquake, the Heritage Foundation, whose CEO to this day is Yasmeen Lari, also covered her humanitarian and zero-carbon projects. Pictured is the Heritage Foundation meeting table at the Lari House in Karachi.

Photograph: Angelika Fitz, 2022

Sindh Cultural Heritage (Preservation) Act, 1994

With this law, Lari succeeded, against great political resistance, in having around 600 buildings in the province of Sindh listed as historical monuments. The Heritage Foundation's list was compiled with special consideration for small-scale urban structures because "this is what shapes our built environment today and most of our cities."

I fought for a lot of things. And there were some really troublesome times. But I managed to get through. It's been very exciting at times.

Yasmeen Lari, 2018[1]

UNESCO

The United Nations Educational, Scientific and Cultural Organization is a specialized agency of the United Nations (UN) that manages the "world heritage of humanity," consisting of world cultural and natural heritage, in accordance with the World Heritage Convention of 1972. Yasmeen Lari became an important cooperation partner for the two Pakistani World Heritage Sites: the Lahore Fort and the Makli Necropolis. The picture shows her in 2004 with Ingeborg Breines, born in Norway in 1945, who first worked at the UNESCO headquarters as head of the "Women and a Culture of Peace Program" before becoming director of the UNESCO office in Islamabad.

Aga Khan Award for Architecture, Lahore, 1980

Since the early 1980s, the Aga Khan Trust for Culture has been the leading institution for the discourse and promotion of architecture that "successfully address the needs and aspirations of societies across the world, in which Muslims have a significant presence."[2] The prominent architecture prize of the same name and the establishment of a program for Islamic architecture at Harvard University and MIT proved decisive. In 1978, Yasmeen Lari attended the preparatory seminar for the first Aga Khan Award at the Aga Khan's residence in Aiglemont, France, where she met Hassan Fathy, an Egyptian architect she admired greatly. Born in Alexandria in 1900, Fathy was a pioneer of regional building and mud-brick construction. At Lari's initiative, the first Aga Khan Award was presented in 1980 at the Shalimar Gardens in Lahore.

Yasmeen Lari in 1980 hosting the gala dinner of the Institute of Architects, Pakistan (IAP) for the Aga Khan.

The picture shows Yasmeen Lari with the Aga Khan Group in Karachi, including Mona Serageldin, professor of architecture at Cairo University and Harvard University, and the Indian architect Charles Correa (left). Lari was a guest lecturer at MIT in the 1980s and repeatedly brought international experts to Pakistan, for instance, at the MIT-Harvard seminar "Housing Design in Islamic Cultures" in Karachi in 1982.

Institute of Architects, Pakistan (IAP)

After the Partition of India in 1947, there was a lack of architecture schools in Pakistan. Engineers prevailed in the corridors of power, while architects were reduced to façade cosmetics. When Lari was elected president of the Institute of Architects, Pakistan (IAP) in 1980, her main concern was to establish the professions of architect and urban planner by law. Many before her had failed in this endeavor, as the political and economic lobbies were too strong. Lari went to extremes, becoming a member of parliament for a short time—against her family's will—and defying full-page advertisements in daily newspapers mobilizing against her. In 1983, the law came into effect and the Pakistan Council of Architects and Town Planners (PCATP) was formed. Lari served as its chairperson until 1986.

In 1984, Yasmeen Lari organized the first Conference of Architects and Town Planners of Islamic Countries.

At the First Asian Congress of Architects in Manila in 1984, she gave a keynote address entitled "The Expanding Role of an Architect in the Asian Context."

The Architect as Public Figure

Not only with her Heritage Foundation but also beyond that, Yasmeen Lari remains a tireless voice of civil society to this day. In 2021, she took over the chair of Transparency International Pakistan. In the twenty-first century her work is recognized locally and internationally. In 2006, she was awarded the Pakistani Sitara-e-Imtiaz (Star of Excellence), in 2016, the Japanese Fukuoka Art and Culture Prize, and, in 2020, the Jane Drew Prize of the Royal Institute of British Architects (RIBA). In 2018, her Pakistan Chulah program received the UN Habitat Award and in 2021 she became the first woman to be conferred an honorary doctorate degree by the Politecnico di Milano, on a par with prominent international architects such as Alvar Aalto, Louis I. Kahn, Kenzo Tange, Álvaro Siza Vieira, or Steven Holl.

Yasmeen Lari in 2006 with the Sitara-e-Imtiaz (Star of Excellence), one of the highest civilian awards in Pakistan.

[1] "In conversation with…Yasmeen Lari." Interview by Alison Cleary and Susie Ashworth, Parlour, August 31, 2018, https://parlour.org.au/series/in-conversation/in-conversation-with-yasmeen-lari/.

[2] Mission Statement on the website of the Aga Khan Award for Architecture, accessed September 28, 2022, https://www.akdn.org/architecture.

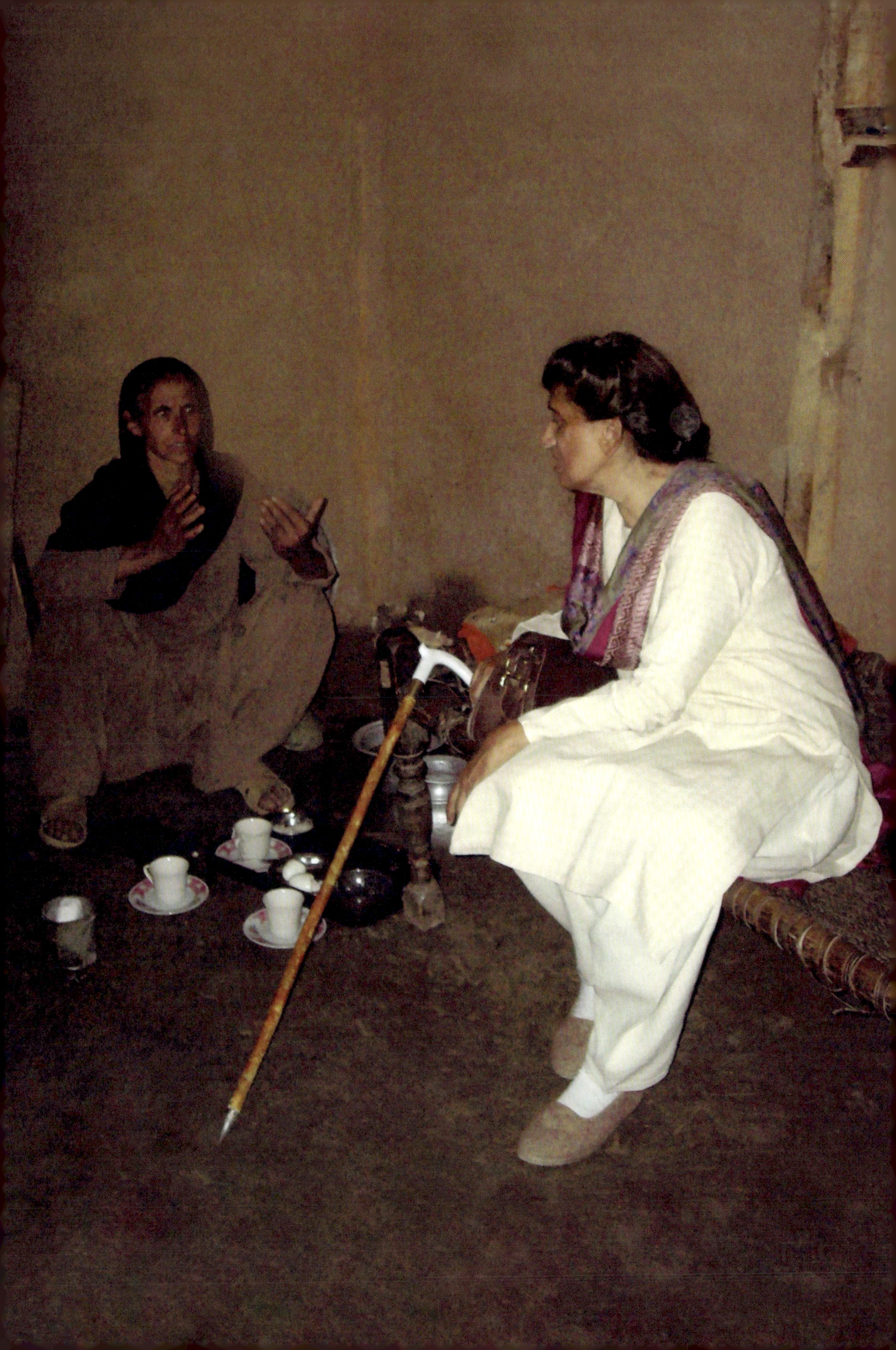

The Architect as Humanitarian Worker

Elke Krasny
With additional research by Marvi Mazhar

In 2000, at the age of 59, Yasmeen Lari very deliberately decided to retire from architecture. She no longer wanted to be Pakistan's woman star architect, who works for the rich. After the Amro Bank, the last commercial client she ever worked with, questioned her decisions and wanted her to design in a style that Lari considered as a Western view of instant Islamic architecture, she no longer wanted to serve the aims of capital. Yet, her retirement only lasted three years. By 2003 she had already begun dedicating her time to heritage and restoration, acting as the National Advisor for the Lahore Fort. In 2005, she went back to working full time, no longer as an architect following the commission-based model, but as an initiative-based humanitarian worker who donates her time and knowledge for free and only uses money to pay staff members, provide self-building training, and buy resources. That year a devastating earthquake measuring 7.6 on the Richter scale struck the territories of Afghanistan, India, and Pakistan. It left four million people homeless and took more than 80,000 lives. Not only did the earthquake mobilize the whole country like never before but it also triggered a huge international response. Volunteers and representatives of many different aid organizations traveled to Pakistan, and the international community pledged about $5.8 billion for recovery and rebuilding.

Seeing the impact of the loss of homes on human lives and very aware of local and global aid, Lari felt she needed to go to the earthquake area of Khyber Pakhtunkhwa to find out what she as an architect could usefully contribute. This marked her turn toward proactively practicing architecture as humanitarian work. Through her previous work for the army, Lari was included in several high-level meetings with army and government representatives and introduced to international organizations. Immediately understanding that the international aid industry was set on an industrialized system most often based on cement and steel, Lari ardently argued for using materials salvaged from the debris with lime as mortar. Lari's humanitarian architecture is at once ecological, social, and reliant on cheaply available, environmentally-friendly materials and self-help building techniques.

PREVIOUS PAGE **Yasmeen Lari visiting a private home in Mardan after the 2005 earthquake.**

Rebuilding Livelihoods after the 2005 Earthquake
Kodar and Jabbar, Siran Valley in Mansehra District

Mansehra was one of the most affected regions of the October 8, 2005 earthquake. With buildings collapsed, homes in ruins, and people desperately in need of shelter after the disaster, Lari and her local team, together with many international volunteers, focused their efforts on the remote villages in Siran Valley, helping families to rebuild homes. Rebuilding livelihoods starts with rebuilding homes, essential shelter for life and survival. By March 2006, 1,200 homes made of salvaged stone, reclaimed timber, and donated lime, steel mesh, and galvanized iron sheets had been constructed in devastated villages.

    Much like in the aftermath of war, post-earthquake recovery and housing reconstruction are linked to the globalized aid industry and the construction sector and therefore dominated by their interests. The paternalism of the post-crisis aid industry is often compared to aid programs in the globalized model of development, which is seen as a present-day, neocolonial continuation of colonialism. While Lari is highly critical of these dimensions of the aid sector and aware of the vested interests of the construction industry, she pragmatically and purposefully works together with international donor organizations, focusing on those that are making it possible to rebuild differently and to invest in training people in self-building and repair.

Massive destruction in Siran Valley, 2005

Massive destruction as a result of Earthquake 2005.

We worked in the North; we worked in the South. And what it has done for me is help me understand what is necessary to give people safe structures and allow them to build them themselves.

Yasmeen Lari, 2019

Unlike the international aid industry (in the background), Lari relies on a local workforce and low-carbon materials, such as stones salvaged from the debris, wood, and lime mortar, to rebuild the houses.

First women's assembly at the orchard in Kodar Bala.

Seeing that the local army and the international aid industry were both ignoring the needs of women, and aware of the violent effects of such uncaring neglect on women's everyday lives, Lari reached out to women and invited them to a meeting. 150 women from villages in Siran Valley responded to her invitation and gathered in an orchard in Kodar. Through this meeting Lari found out about their essential yet unaddressed needs. In particular, the issue of an urgent lack of toilets was raised, with women forced to relieve themselves only before morning prayers or not until after dark. This meeting was crucial for the decisions concerning what rebuilding would focus on next. Financial support came from Nokia.

Working solely with local materials and improved vernacular building techniques, Lari's team built 132 household latrines, 50 household kitchens, three primary schools, one community center and a heritage museum. Reforestation began with the planting of 35,000 saplings, and over eight kilometers of mountain bridle pathways were created.

Community meeting with architect Yasmeen Lari after the earthquake in Jabbar.

In 2005, volunteers conducted workshops on how to self-build vernacular houses, which are called KaravanGhar. Workshops were held in 75 remote villages in Siran Valley. The structural design was provided by Amin Tariq & Associates.

Construction of three primary schools in the villages of Jabbar and Kodar in 2006.

Relief Architecture in the Shaikh Shahzad Camp, Mardan, 2009

In 2009, after the Second Battle of Swat between the Pakistani Army and Tehrik-i-Taliban Pakistan militants when people were displaced and moved to tents in the hot plains of Mardan, somebody called Yasmeen Lari to tell her that she was needed at the camp. Working with women and children at the Shaikh Shahzad Camp and in cooperation with the camp authorities, she and her team constructed community kitchens. Seeing that only bamboo was available, Lari turned to this material for the first time, combining it with mud and lime. Bamboo allowed for speedy construction; within three days the community kitchen was ready. Learning by doing with this 'first aid' construction, Lari's experience was immediately transferred to building shelters out of bamboo.

In 2009, after the Second Battle of Swat between the Pakistani Army and Tehrik-i-Taliban Pakistan militants, displaced persons lived in tents in the Shaikh Shahzad Camp.

Having tried out bamboo for community kitchens in the Shaikh Shahzad Camp, Lari used this new-found knowledge of bamboo construction for shelters, first combining timber and bamboo in 2009. Lari conducted extensive studies on how to build without timber and realized her first bamboo-only shelters in 2010. Since then, Yasmeen Lari has referred to bamboo, mud, and lime as 'Lari materials.'

Building Shelters after the Awaran Earthquake in Balochistan Province, 2013

The Awaran Earthquake, which hit this thinly populated area of Balochistan Province in northwest Pakistan in 2013, registered 7.7 on the Richter scale. Many traditional mudbrick structures suffered severe damage. According to estimates of the local government, 21,000 homes were destroyed. Working on post-earthquake recovery and focusing on building shelters, Lari further improved the design of the bamboo shelters to increase their seismic resistance. Reinforcing the mud walls with bamboo in the corners, as well as in the internal and external faces of the wall, and anchoring and joining them together produces structures that can withstand even very severe earthquake jolts. The roofs are very lightweight, which helps save lives if they collapse.

The devastated, barren landscape of Awaran in Balochistan Province, 2013

Working on the seismic improvement of bamboo shelters.

Many of the traditional mudbrick structures were badly hit in the 2013 Awaran Earthquake. This photograph shows the artisans Bhoira, Dharmoo, and Fida. They are laying the base of a model unit in Moak Sharif village, which shows how mud is being reinforced and thus made more resistant to climatic pressures and extreme weather events. The land of Moak Sharif village is owned by the Rashidi family. Agricultural land in Pakistan is owned by a small number of powerful and politically influential families. The landowners are known as *wadera.*
In this system of feudalism the peasants are laborers, who are known as *haris.* They live at subsistence level and perform the actual agricultural labor. Ever since Paras Rashidi, a daughter-in-law of the land-owning Rashidi family, first reached out to Yasmeen Lari for help immediately after the 2010 flood, Lari has been very active in this rural area.

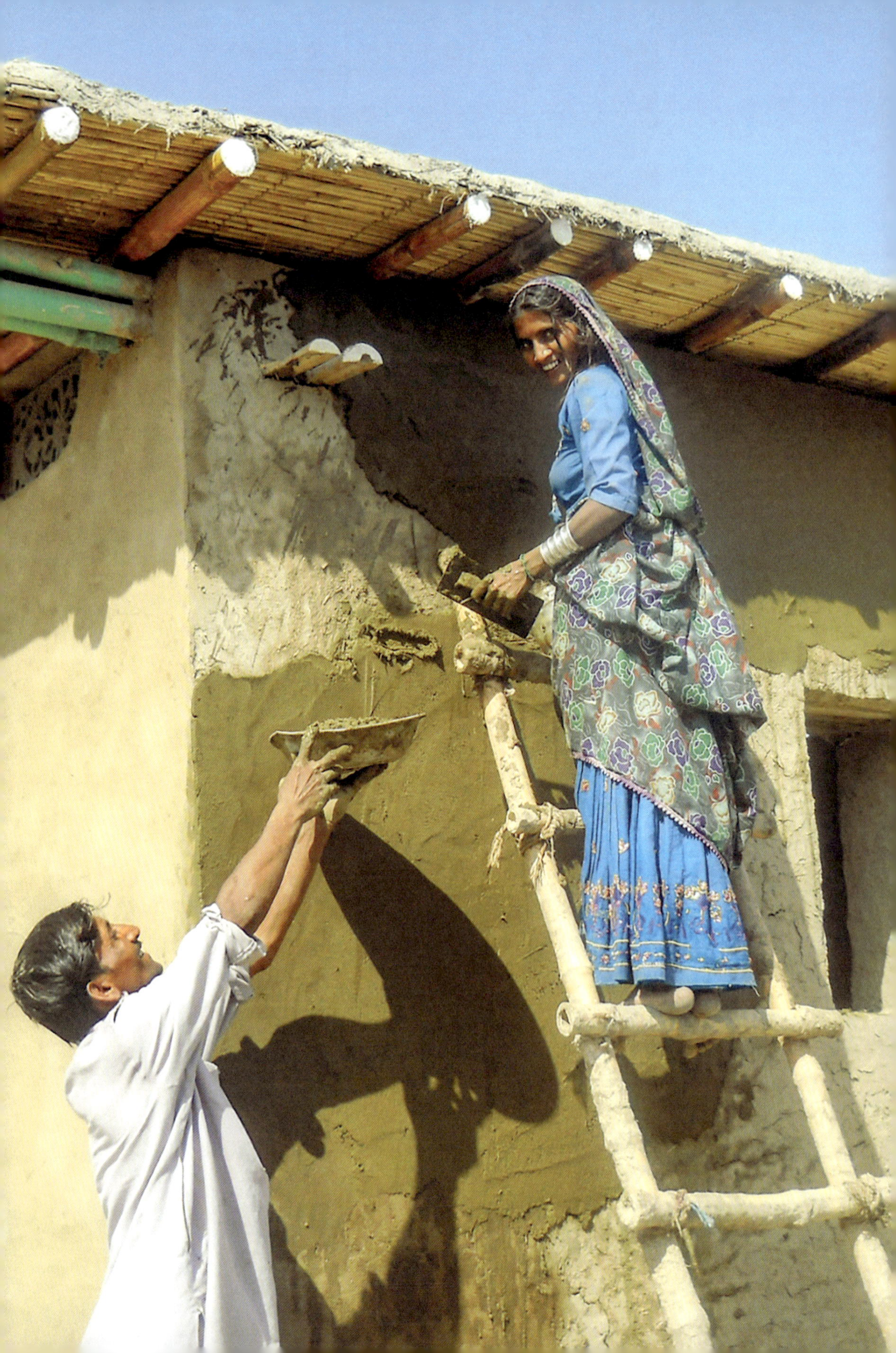

A Zero-Carbon Revolution in Architecture

Angelika Fitz

The construction sector is one of the world's largest CO_2 emitters and one of the main causes of the exploitation and devastation of our planet. The effects of Man-made climate change are dramatic all over the globe, but some regions are affected more than others, including Pakistan. In cities like Karachi, where temperatures topped nearly 50 degrees Celsius in the summer of 2022, the heat is unbearable and the annual monsoon rains are increasingly turning into extreme floods. At the time of writing, one-third of Pakistan is flooded. Today and in the future, construction must be disaster-resistant and at the same time make an active contribution to climate change mitigation.

For more than a decade, Yasmeen Lari has been further developing her system of humanitarian architecture along the guiding principles of low costs, zero carbon, and zero waste. In contrast to the global aid industry, which is stuck in an ecological and economic negative spiral with containers, cement, and concrete, Lari has been using only zero-carbon or low-carbon, low-cost, and locally available materials such as mud and bamboo since 2010. Methodologically, she takes up local building traditions and improves them structurally in terms of flood and earthquake resistance. Most of the money is invested in passing on knowledge so that the houses can be built by the people themselves. To promote this, Lari established her own training center in Makli and set up a digital channel for instruction via mobile phone. Tens of thousands of zero-carbon houses have been implemented so far and are withstanding extreme weather events.

It is debatable whether completely zero-carbon construction is actually possible, since Lari also needs lime treatment, means of transportation, and digital aids for example. Lari's approach is revolutionary in its simplicity, affordability, systematization, and transferability to many regions of our planet. Her zero-carbon architecture enables a life in security and dignity, especially for those most affected by poverty and climate change.

PREVIOUS PAGE Self-built, zero-carbon, and flood-resistant houses, Sindh Province, since 2010

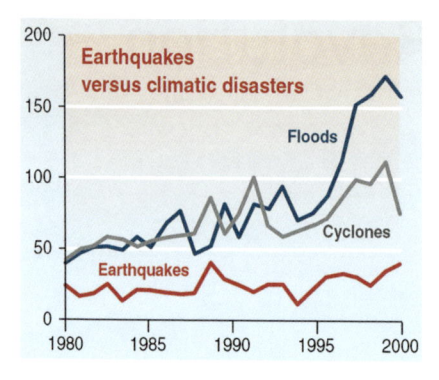

The rapid increase in extreme weather events such as floods and cyclones compared to earthquakes shows the influence of Man-made climate change.

This section is an excerpt of the original graphic from *In Dead Water—Climate Change, Pollution, Over-harvest, and Invasive Species in the World's Fishing Grounds*, cartographer: Hugo Ahlenius, UNEP/GRID-Arendal, 2008; source: https://www.grida.no/resources/7199

In the summer of 2022, Pakistan was again hit by enormous flooding. At the time of writing, one-third of the territory is under water, 33 million people are affected, more than 1,500 are reported dead. "Pakistan has been thrown into the front line of the human-induced climate crisis,"[1] the UN says on its website.

Photograph: Zahid Hussain / AP / picturedesk.com

Sindh Flood Rehabilitation, 2010

In 2010, when millions of people were made homeless in Pakistan by an extreme flood and more than one thousand died, Yasmeen Lari systematically developed her work in humanitarian architecture. She started a broad program in Sindh Province that empowers the population to build flood-resistant and climate-friendly housing. All materials are locally available either free of charge or very cheaply. The walls are made of mud stabilized with lime with bamboo used for the cross bracing. In perfecting the method, Lari draws on her decades of experience in renovating historic architectural monuments made of mud. On the flat roofs, which can serve as roof gardens, wood is replaced by bamboo, which grows rapidly. No tree is felled. The houses are self-constructed under the guidance of master trainers, many of whom are women who received training from Lari's Heritage Foundation. Women are particularly endangered by floods because they mainly work in the fields and at home.

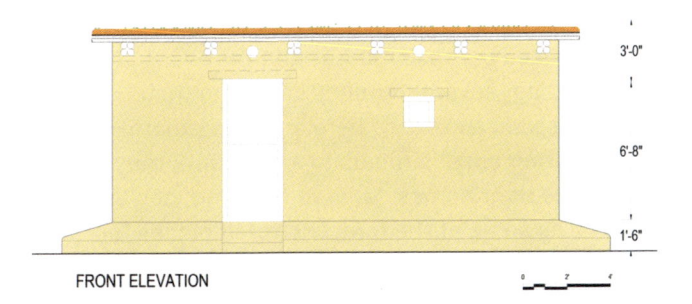

FRONT ELEVATION

In 2011, Sindh Province was hit by heavy monsoon rains. The zero-carbon dwellings, with their raised platforms made of mud and lime, withstood the floods. In cooperation with the International Organization for Migration (IOM), among others, over 40,000 houses were built by the residents.

Parallel to the flood-resistant mud houses, Yasmeen Lari designed communal buildings on stilts made of prefabricated bamboo modules. In the event of severe flooding, several families can store their household goods and seeds here and bring themselves and their small animals to safety until they can return to their homes. Most of the time, however, they serve as some of the rare, sheltered places for women to meet and gather, like here at the Green Women's Centre in Khairpur, Sindh Province.

Schools are also built on bamboo stilts as safe zero-carbon architecture. In the hot dry season, the covered space provides shade. This image shows the primary school in the village of Darya Khan Sheikh in Khairpur, Sindh Province.

A master trainer shares knowledge on how to further develop traditional building methods into disaster-resistant, zero-carbon architecture. Most of the financial resources provided to Lari's Heritage Foundation through international grants are invested into training. Lari speaks of "barefoot entrepreneurs" to describe this systematic development of local economies around zero-carbon architecture. The expansion of local skills means that people in endangered regions are no longer solely dependent on international or national aid but are better prepared for disasters.

Zero Carbon Cultural Centre, Makli, since 2016

Yasmeen Lari sees the Zero Carbon Cultural Centre as an incubator for CO_2-free architecture. She opened the facility with the Heritage Foundation in 2016 near the Makli Necropolis World Heritage Site. It functions as a training site, experimental field, production facility, and event venue. Master trainers, who then pass on their knowledge in the villages, gain experience here, and workshops for architecture students from local and international universities also take place. They live in zero-carbon accommodations, and a huge bamboo hall offers space for training courses, as well as for larger conferences. In between, it serves as an airy manufacturing plant for women from surrounding villages, who can earn their own income for the first time by producing ceramics.

The land for the Zero Carbon Cultural Centre is made available to the Heritage Foundation by a local large landowner. Colonial-era laws perpetuate a feudal system of landless rural workers in Sindh Province. Empowering them socially and economically is part of Lari's zero-carbon system.

The central hall of the Zero Carbon Cultural Centre consists of prefabricated bamboo modules. Erected without columns, the event, training, and production space is twenty-seven meters long, eighteen meters wide, and up to eleven meters high. Accommodation and experimental growing fields are grouped around it. The more than 16,000-square-meter-large area serves as a test site to further develop Lari's zero-carbon architecture. In addition to various house shapes, always derived from local typologies, experiments are also being carried out with cooking areas and eco-toilets. The picture shows a workshop in 2019 with the INTBAU Foundation set up by the former Prince of Wales. Lari is the Chapter Chair of INTBAU Pakistan.

My own dictum is: low costs, zero carbon, zero waste.
Yasmeen Lari, 2019

The dissemination of knowledge and skills on how to build in a zero-carbon, safe, and cost-effective manner with local resources constitutes the core of Lari's zero-carbon architecture. At the Zero Carbon Cultural Centre in Makli, both the theoretical basics and practical skills are taught.

Workshop for making and processing sun-dried mudbricks to build smokeless chulahs, an award-winning program for healthy and eco-friendly stoves.

Numerous built witnesses of shared learning, such as the prototypes of smokeless Pakistan Chulahs, can be found on the grounds of the Zero Carbon Cultural Centre in Makli.

Photograph: Angelika Fitz, 2022

Whether or not one can read or write: the training courses at the Zero Carbon Cultural Centre are open to everyone, as a list of participants shows.

In the villages around the Makli Necropolis there are large communities that depend on begging for their livelihood. At the Zero Carbon Cultural Centre, women from these communities learn various ceramic techniques and can use them to generate income.

Women from the neighboring villages meet in the shady and airy bamboo hall to make ceramic tiles together, which are also used in Lari's projects in Karachi.

Photograph: Elke Krasny, 2022

Zero Carbon Channel, since 2020

With the onset of the Covid-19 pandemic, physical meetings to share knowledge became difficult. Yasmeen Lari reacted immediately and has been operating a digital Zero Carbon Channel since 2020. Over twenty tutorials can be accessed via mobile phone. The digital step-by-step instructions are accompanied by a close-meshed monitoring system with checklists. This ensures that the resulting zero-carbon architecture is stable and safe. The Zero Carbon Channel serves the training and further education of craftspeople and provides information for the general public.

During the 2022 flood disaster, Lari expanded social media communications with step-by-step building instructions and Q&A sessions.

Video stills from Yasmeen Lari's Zero Carbon Channel on YouTube, https://www.youtube.com/c/YasmeenLarisZeroCarbonChannel

Rahguzar, Karachi, since 2019

With the Rahguzar project (*rahguzar* means passage or path in Urdu), Yasmeen Lari brings her zero-carbon architecture into the urban metropolis, specifically into the historic center of Karachi, where traffic, noise, bad air, extreme heat, and annual flooding, as well as a lack of security, are some of the burdens of everyday life. Her vision is a series of green, pedestrian-friendly streetscapes. After long negotiations with homeowners, business operators, and the city administration, she was recently able to implement a first part. Terra-cotta pavers, made by women at her Zero Carbon Cultural Centre in Makli and laid according to the sponge city principle, replace the asphalt. Fast-growing green spaces counteract urban heat islands. The new pedestrian zone begins at the historic Denso Hall, which was rescued from a state of disrepair by Lari's Heritage Foundation. Other adjacent historic buildings are being renovated or at least stabilized, since nothing is more sustainable than preventing demolition and new construction. Lari hopes to bring about a rethinking in public space with this private initiative.

The skepticism of the shopkeepers has meanwhile vanished, says Yasmeen Lari: "It is the first time they are able to breathe fresh air."

Video still: Imran Gill, 2022

Bamboo platforms invite people to linger. Platforms are elements of community, tranquility, and security that already appeared in Lari's large buildings and also play a major role in her village infrastructures.
Video still: Imran Gill, 2022

150,000 terra-cotta pavers replace concrete and asphalt. They were produced at the Zero Carbon Cultural Centre in Makli and on the underside bear the signature of the respective craftswoman—all women from so-called beggar communities who live in the villages around the Makli World Heritage Site. Decades of applied research in restoration work makes the glazed terra-cotta resilient, Yasmeen Lari explains. "Every household, every bathroom could use such tiles," she adds. The laying of the paving stones leaves enough space for seepage. This sponge city principle has already proven itself during the devastating floods of 2022. Rahguzar was one of the few streets in Karachi that wasn't flooded.
Photograph: Angelika Fitz, 2022

The greening follows the method of the Japanese botanist Akira Miyawaki. His concept of "potential natural vegetation," similar to how it would proliferate without human intervention, achieves high biodiversity through the combination of many different species. Optimally adapted to the local conditions, the plants grow quickly and become particularly dense in a "multistory" system.

Photograph: Elke Krasny, 2022

The Rahguzar Project begins at Denso Hall, built by the British in 1881 as a library. In 2019, Lari's Heritage Foundation cleaned the building with the help of volunteers and made it publicly usable again. Such 'first aid' for historic buildings will continue along the Rahguzar walking street. Extending the future of these structures is ecologically sustainable and preserves the memory of a multidimensional past.

On Sundays, when the shops are closed, Yasmeen Lari invites people to public events on Rahguzar. By doing so, she continues her KaravanKarachi series and insists once again that public space should not be abandoned to violence, but belongs to everyone, including women.

Photographs: Elke Krasny, 2022

Yasmeen Lari's declared goal is to anchor the teaching and learning of zero-carbon methods in architectural education worldwide. Pictured here is a workshop in February 2022 with architecture students from Pakistan and Bangladesh. In addition to lectures and discussions in public space, the young women are building a "Lari OctaGreen" out of bamboo—a system for zero-carbon shelters—in the middle of the Rahguzar walking street.

Photographs: Angelika Fitz (top), Elke Krasny (bottom), 2022

1 "Pakistan: More than 6.4 million in 'dire need' after unprecedented flood," UN News, September 2, 2022, https://news.un.org/en/story/2022/09/1126001.

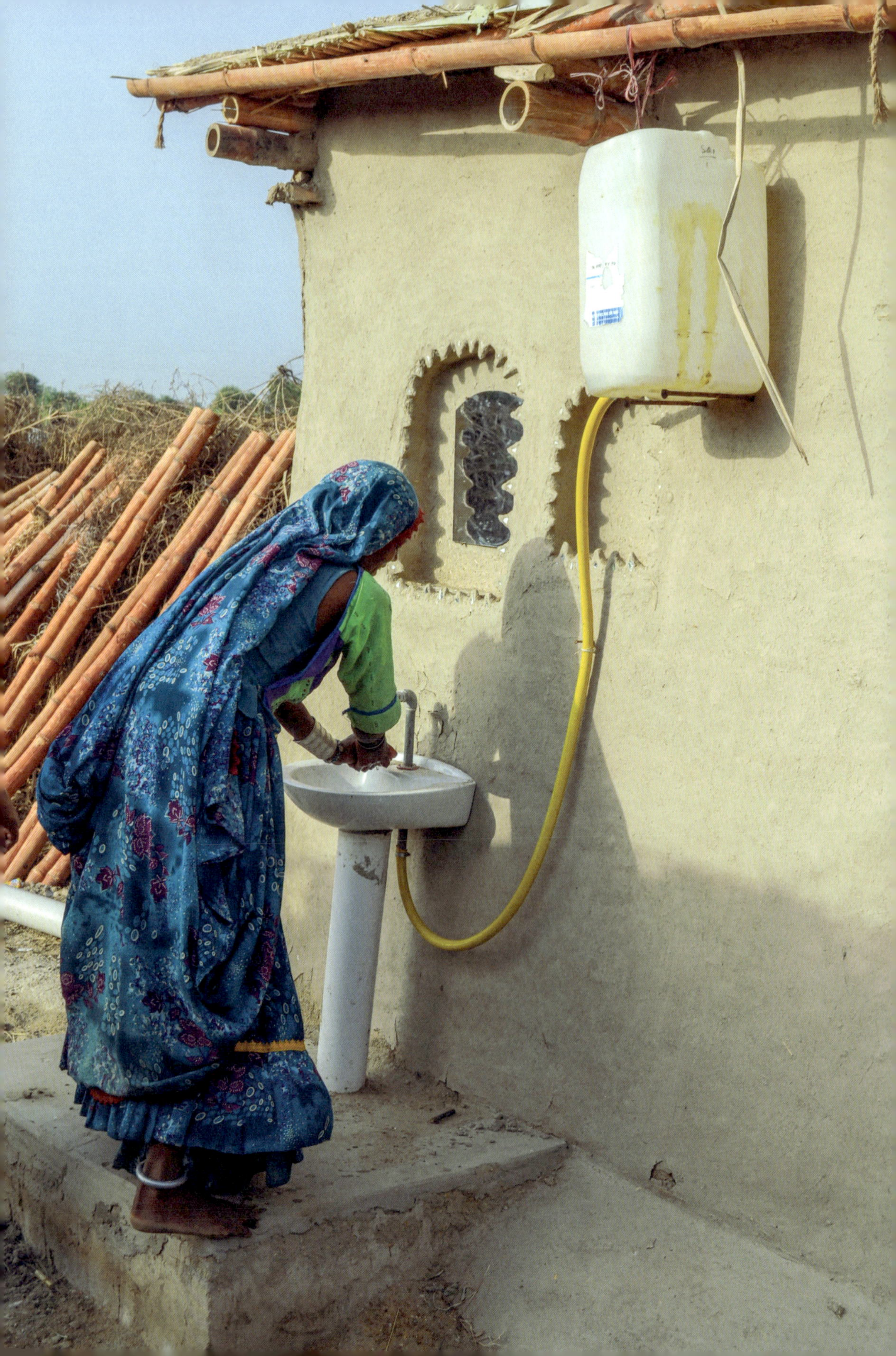

Essentials for Life

Angelika Fitz

Millions of people live without a safe roof over their heads, without access to clean water, or without sanitary infrastructure. Deprived of basic human rights, they are particularly vulnerable in the event of a disaster. Yasmeen Lari sees the discipline of architecture as the duty to develop viable and sustainable solutions for essential infrastructure. Not just a small minority but the majority of the world's population should benefit from architecture in the future. As always, her architectural thinking and actions go beyond the individual building. She designs and tests a systemic approach that aims to tread lightly on the planet.

It is about finding out which method is the most cost-effective, safest, and most ecological, and then implementing it en masse, says Lari. In her integrative approach, this applies not only to accommodation, but also to the supply of clean water, safe toilets, healthy cooking facilities, and community spaces. For these basic needs, she develops zero-carbon infrastructures that take care of the planet as well as work toward the survival of people, and especially toward improving the lives of women, who are responsible for many life-sustaining activities. A Pakistan Chulah (smokeless stove) uses half the fuel, can be built by families themselves, and provides a pleasant place to work and gather, which remains functional during floods, as do the water pumps raised on platforms. The safe toilets spare the women the dangerous nocturnal walk in the fields.

There are almost no building costs, since local materials such as mud, lime, and bamboo are used for construction. People can do it themselves, guided by those members of the community who have received training from the Heritage Foundation and who, by passing on this knowledge, generate an income that contributes to their livelihoods. A handmade seriality ensures efficiency and clearly regulated reporting systems for security. The poorest meet the needs of the poorest, that is how Lari describes this economy and adds that not only essential infrastructure is built, but also a life in dignity.

PREVIOUS PAGE **Safe houses and sanitary infrastructure are a human right and particularly important for women**

Shelter

According to Yasmeen Lari, the immense need for affordable and safe accommodation in countries like Pakistan cannot be met with conventional social housing programs. Concrete and cement homes are too expensive for millions of people, and they harm the environment in a region particularly hard hit by the catastrophic effects of climate change. Moreover, they are often not safe due to poor material quality and construction.

Working in earthquake and flood areas, Lari has continuously developed self-construction methods for extremely inexpensive zero-carbon houses. Tens of thousands of such structures were built within a few years. The house forms are derived from vernacular traditions in different regions of Pakistan, the materials also vary regionally from stone to mud and straw. Transverse bracing made of bamboo and lime mortar guarantee stability that withstands even strong earthquakes. The possibility of prefabrication takes the time factor into account. With the Lari OctaGreen (LOG), accommodations can be erected in a very short time with serially prefabricated bamboo modules.

The overhanging roof construction made of bamboo can be designed as a flat roof that can be walked on and greened with plants or as a pent or gable roof.

The areas surrounding major rivers such as the Indus, which crosses Pakistan from north to south, are scenes of catastrophic flooding but also a resource for clay processing. Unfired clay can be used in Lari's zero-carbon architecture in the form of sun-dried mudbricks and adobe construction. Lime mortar and bamboo provide stability. Where trees are scarce, the fast-growing bamboo is more environmentally friendly than wood. Fossil fuel is only needed for the preparation of lime, but the environmental balance is significantly better than with cement as Lari explains. All materials are available locally, mostly free of charge, and can be processed by the residents according to Lari's detailed instructions.

So, the most affordable, the most inexpensive, the safest thing that you can do, you need to do for everybody.

Yasmeen Lari, 2022

Shaking Table

At the NED University of Engineering & Technology in Karachi, under the supervision of Vice Rector Sarosh Hashmat Lodi, the earthquake resistance of the house construction made of mud, lime, and bamboo was tried and tested on the "shaking table"—simulating tremors many times greater than the 1995 earthquake in Kobe, Japan, where a magnitude greater than 7 was first measured on the JMA Seismic Intensity Scale.

Video still: Heritage Foundation of Pakistan, 2017

When you work for the poor, you are trying to save their lives, but you are also trying to save the planet.
Yasmeen Lari, 2019

With Lari's zero-carbon techniques, existing buildings in the village setting can also be replaced, repaired, and made disaster-resistant. Elevated platforms create safe communal spaces, like here in Sindh Province.

In contrast to concrete, mud is a material that women without an income of their own can produce and process. Mud is also used by them to decorate their houses, as part of a personal appropriation. In the picture is the house of Rani and Dharmi Bibi.

Lari OctaGreen (LOG)

The octagon-shaped LOG buildings can be erected in a few hours from prefabricated bamboo modules and offer immediate protection from rain, wind, and snow. By filling the bamboo panels with clay or small stones, the 'first aid' shelters become permanent houses that can be connected to form larger structures. They are plastered with a mixture of mud and lime. Derived from traditional forms in Sindh Province, the cone-shaped roof becomes disaster-resistant with structural improvements. The roof construction is sealed with mats of straw, mud-lime plaster, and then with a pozzolana-like mixture of lime and brick dust.

In the Heritage Foundation training program, craftsmen and unskilled workers learn how to manufacture modules for the Lari OctaGreens (LOG). They are prefabricated jointly at central locations in the villages, so the quality and safety of the construction are constantly checked before they are erected by the villagers. The cross braces are derived from traditional dhijjis in the northern provinces of Khyber Pakhtunkhwa and Kashmir—this construction method proved to be the most stable during the 2005 earthquake. The panels are covered with mats woven from palm straw.

During the devastating floods of summer 2022, bamboo modules for Lari OctaGreens (LOG) were being prefabricated at the Zero Carbon Cultural Centre in Makli to provide emergency relief to homeless villagers.

Drinking Water

Access to clean water is another basis of life. Groundwater is mostly available in Pakistan, says Yasmeen Lari, but rarely to villagers in close proximity. In the Heritage Foundation program, five families each share the cost of a well. To ensure that they remain functional during the increasingly fierce monsoon rains, the wells are built as elevated platforms. Again, the load is especially taken off women, who are responsible for the care of people and animals and often have to transport the water over long distances.

A well is used jointly by several families. The elevated platform protects against contamination, especially during floods.

The essential infrastructures built locally under the guidance of the Heritage Foundation are part of a predefined reporting system. The quality control lies in the hands of the individual households, who receive a checklist.

Cooking

There is no life without food. A good infrastructure for the daily preparation of meals is essential. Poorer families in Pakistan—and in many other countries—rely on open fires for cooking. This repeatedly leads to burns, especially suffered by children, and sometimes to threatening fires. The heavy smoke that develops when cooking damages the respiratory organs and the eyes, which restricts the living situation of the women affected. Last but not least, the high consumption of fossil fuels is bad for the environment.

Yasmeen Lari developed the smokeless Pakistan Chulah (Pakistani stove), which consumes only half the fuel. In contrast to international aid programs, no industrially manufactured metal stoves are used. The Pakistan Chulahs can be built by the families themselves from the local materials of mud and lime under the guidance of the "Chulah Adhis" (Stove Sisters), who received training from the Heritage Foundation.

In 2011, Lari started the first experiments in Moak Sharif. Systematic training was carried out in 2014 with the support of the ILO (International Labor Organization) and in 2015 by the IOM (International Organization for Migration). The process is now self-sustaining: the Chulah Adhis and their husbands show the families how they can build the innovative stoves themselves and get paid two hundred Pakistani rupees (approximately two US dollars) for doing so. Seventy thousand Pakistan Chulahs have been erected in this way so far. In 2018, the Pakistan Chulah received the UN Habitat Award.

For the Pakistan Chulah, a platform made of sun-dried mudbricks, plastered with a mud-lime mixture is erected. Far more hygienic than cooking on the ground, the elevated workstation is also protected from flooding. The position of the women responsible for cooking rises symbolically, too. Additional structures for storing cooking utensils are individually designed by the women.

The Pakistan Chulah enables two cooking zones to be operated with one fire chamber. Waste materials such as cow manure or sawdust and only a little wood are used for firing. The chimney reduces any direct exposure to pollution and can be used as an additional heating plate.

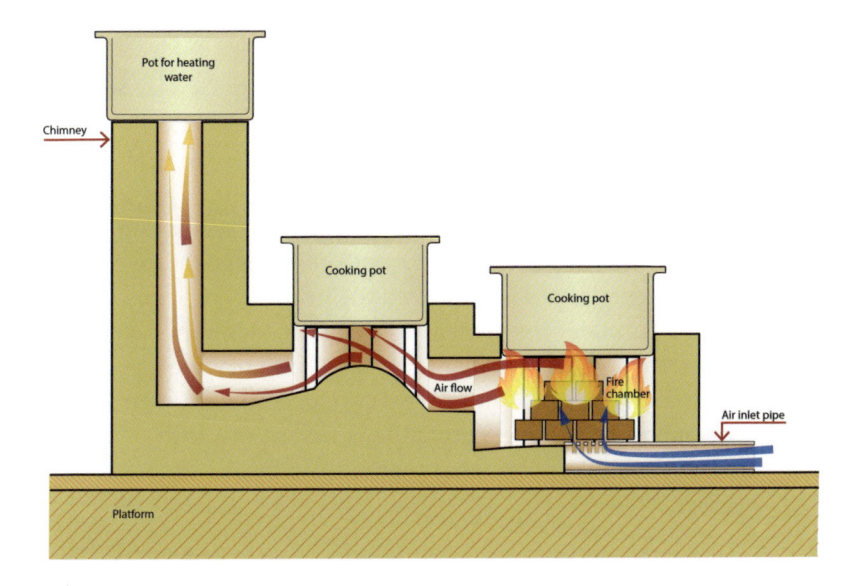

The platforms of the Pakistan Chulahs are not only secure working spaces, but also pleasant and communicative places for women and children.

The Story of a Chulah Adhi (Stove Sister)

Together with her husband Kanji, Champa has guided the self-construction of thousands of Pakistan Chulahs and thereby improved the living conditions of the families. They live in Mirpur Khas in Sindh Province and, as members of a local minority, were able to overcome their own precarious situation with the income they generated. In the meantime, they have already trained other teams.

Video stills: Heritage Foundation of Pakistan, 2018

Safe Toilets

Visibly moved, Yasmeen Lari describes why toilets are one of the most important infrastructures for a life in dignity, especially for women: "When I asked women, 'What do you do for toilets?' they said: 'Well, in the morning, before early morning prayer, the Fajr prayer, and after Maghrib, which is the sunset prayer, we go behind the bushes, that is where the toilet is.'"

The toilets developed by Yasmeen Lari once again follow the principles of utilizing extremely low-cost, local, and mostly zero-carbon materials and self-construction so that everyone has access to sanitary facilities. As with Lari's zero-carbon houses, the walls are built from sun-dried mudbricks or from prefabricated bamboo panels plastered with mud and lime. The floor is preferably hygienically sealed with a pozzolana made of lime and brick dust. A closable pit contains the bucket for the excrement used to make fertilizer. Next to it is space for a shower.

Hygienic sanitary rooms that ensure privacy enable women in particular to live in dignity and security.

Karavan Toilet

On her digital Zero Carbon Channel Yasmeen Lari shares instructions for building toilets. "Karavan Toilet" is the name she gives to the prefabricated bamboo version.

Video stills: Yasmeen Lari's Zero Carbon Channel on YouTube, 2021

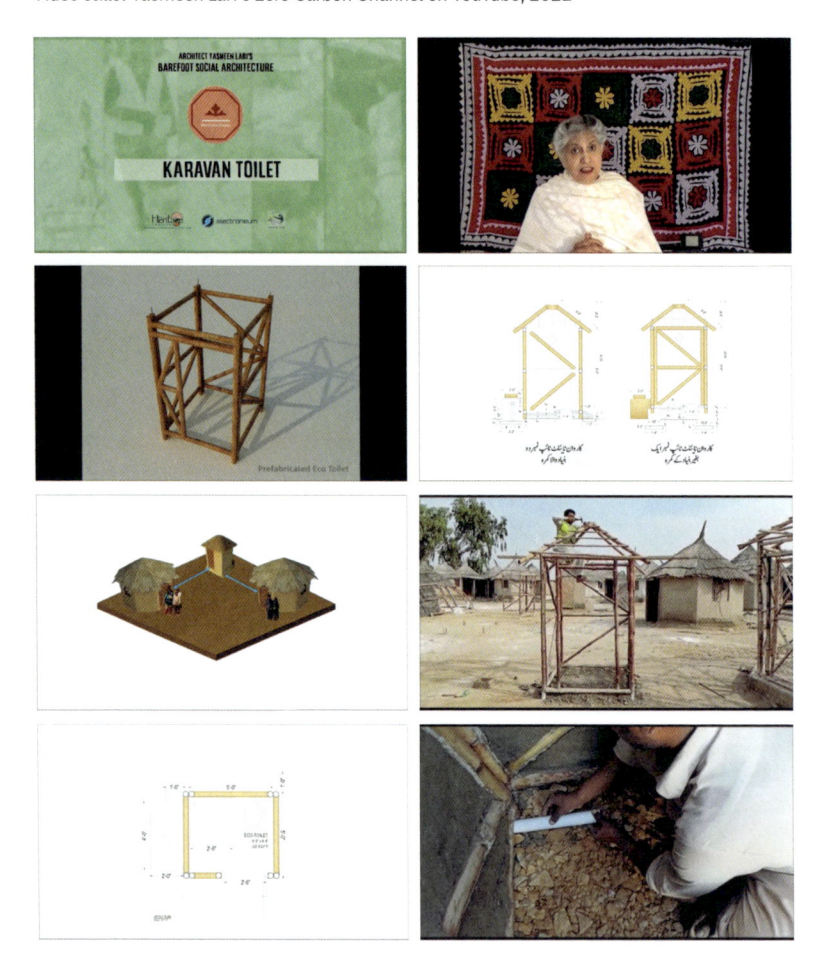

There is not a single woman I have spoken with who is not willing to do anything to improve her life.

Yasmeen Lari, 2022

Community

Yasmeen Lari's work is exemplary of how architecture can create vital infrastructure for millions of people without exploiting the planet and polluting it with emissions. Life and survival not only include physical integrity but also the basic human need for social exchange and cooperation. In addition to schools, Lari sees a great need for community spaces for women who are tied to a small area by their domestic work and only have access to social gatherings on rare occasions, such as weddings or funerals. Lari's Green Women's Centres provide shelter and opportunities for collective action. Lari says she has not met a single woman who was not willing to do whatever it takes to improve her life.

The Green Women's Centre in Darya Khan Sheikh, Sindh Province, is a meeting place and shared learning space for women. In the event of flooding, household goods and small animals can be brought to safety on the upper floor.

The construction site of the Green Women's Centre in Darya Khan Sheikh made of bamboo.

Women gather at the Green Women's Centre in Darya Khan Sheikh in 2011 for a meeting with Yasmeen Lari. For Lari, women are important partners on the way to a zero-carbon future.

Yasmeen Lari
Interview

Portrait of Yasmeen Lari. Photograph: © Archive Yasmeen Lari

"Every decision has a global impact."

Yasmeen Lari in Conversation
with Angelika Fitz and Elke Krasny
Karachi, 2022

^{AF} In 1964, you returned to Pakistan after graduating from the Oxford School of Architecture. What was it like for you when you came back to Pakistan from the UK?

^{YL} In 1964, I was finally able to see a lot of the old cities with my husband, who was a great photographer. Before, I had not had a taste of how things were in Pakistan. Because I had never been out of our, literally out of our home. You did not mingle with others, you only kept to yourself or your own close friends. I had no idea how much poverty there might have been, or what cultural traditions there were. You must remember, when I went to England for studies, Pakistan had been independent for not even ten years, and we had gone through 150 years of colonial rule, where we had been told that our culture was really nothing, and that everything in the West was something to be emulated.

So when I came back, we were going around traditional cities and old towns, and that was a wealth of understanding of what lives had been here. I think that has opened up quite a few thoughts and processes for me. First, I used to call it 'unlearning,' but now I call it 'relearning.' I think unlearning is a little bit harsh, because I think I learned a lot when I was being trained in the West. It is really like a relearning of your own self, as to what you are. And, looking at people, really understanding what made Pakistan.

EK Like many other architects, you started your career with private residences. In 1972, you were given the commission to design a large-scale social housing project, Angoori Bagh. Can you tell us how you approached the design of social housing?

YL I think the seeds of Angoori Bagh can be seen in the Naval Housing in Karachi. I was able to have these open-to-sky terraces, stacking back so there was never a kind of slab like this, you know (indicating a vertical line with her hand). Because if you look at our historic cities, there is never a straight line. The streets are meandering, the buildings follow that, and everything is kind of stacked on top of each other but set back. In a sense, I was trying to capture that even at that time, because I thought that allowed women to be able to do a lot of things and children had a much nicer place to be in. And then the social housing of Angoori Bagh, which was in Lahore, came along.

EK Did you design Angoori Bagh for internally displaced people?

YL Well, the story is that a populist government had taken over, the People's Party regime of Zulfikar Ali Bhutto. It was the first time that this group of people, who really were very poor, had any kind of attention paid to them to be able to provide them with housing. And that is how the Angoori Bagh housing came about. They took over this very old piece of land. It had been in a family, who had been loyal to the Mughals, from generation to generation. The Minister of Finance, Mubashir Hassan, who had been a friend actually earlier on, led a gathering in the famous Shalimar Gardens, which is the beautiful, seventeenth-century Mughal paradise garden. On its walkway, we had these hundreds of people congregating, to whom I presented the whole project. And because I had been having chats with them, I knew what the women wanted. The question for me was when the women said, "If we move into these flats or apartments, where will our chickens go?" Because chickens are where they get protein for their children. So, I was very happy to tell that every one of them had a terrace. They were again stacked back (illustrating stacking with her hand), and it had to be very carefully done because it couldn't be expensive. In the Naval Housing, I could play around. Here, I have a very simple system of load-bearing walls, of burnt brick, which is a very common and popular material in Lahore.

Learning from Old Towns

^{AF} The urban design of Angoori Bagh is small-scale and quite varied. This is very unusual for the time. What was your inspiration for this?

^{YL} Something I had learned from our old towns is that if you don't have a gridiron pattern and you have meandering streets, and semi-public, semi-open spaces, then you have much more chance of interaction with each other. And that is the feeling I wanted to convey in the new housing. Now that I am talking to you, I am thinking of my childhood when I saw the settlements that my father had been instrumental in creating. He was this high-level bureaucrat, under whose care something like five or six cities had been built. We had gone to one or two quite often. There were these large roads and there were no people walking around. When I went to the old town, I could see the contrast. I didn't quite get to do what the old towns achieve, but I think I was getting quite close. But I have to tell you that none of the peers, any architects, gave any importance to it. Nobody said that it was anything of value, because it was for the poor. For a long time, I also felt that what I had done was something that I enjoyed doing, but not necessarily something that would break the mold in architecture.

^{EK} But in the end, it did.

^{YL} (Smiling)... No, it taught me a lot, that is the important thing. When you are doing something, every time it is a learning process. And that is why if you keep on replicating, that doesn't let you grow. I think it is very important that every time you do something, it is something new. You have to grow with every project.

^{AF} There is one more housing project we would like you to talk about, the Lines Area Redevelopment.

^{YL} There is a huge area that was full of these slums and informal settlements, which is right in the middle of the city. And we had had this experience of a very famous planner called Doxiadis, who planned Islamabad. In the late 1950s, he was commissioned to work on the slums of Karachi, and he had moved a huge number of people into a new settlement called Korangi (Township), which again is a (grid)iron pattern. All of these people from the slums in the middle of the city were forcibly taken to the new settlement and everybody thought they were doing them a favor. Lo and behold, most of the people came back to the city, because that is where their jobs were. This is something that no political government understands even to this day. We are still willing

to trample human rights. We don't really care what is good for them, we only think about what they should have or do.

I had always in my mind that people should have a right to be able to build as they wish. A family is not a static unit, families are growing. A family knows best what they need. So, I designed these very little units, only about sixty square yards [about fifty-two square meters], on a very small lot, but you could build a two-story unit on that, and you could have two or three rooms and a toilet, plus a small courtyard. And then they could build incrementally. Nobody was building it for them. Because the tragedy of Angoori Bagh was that the people for whom it was designed never actually lived there. Because social housing by any kind of government is used as a political tool. They use it to give favors. They are not really interested in the welfare of the poor. And I think this is by and large true for many, many countries and many governments. And so, after that experience, I believed that the best thing would be for people to be given those lots. They had a right, they had been living there, and that is where their jobs were, where their livelihoods were. But unfortunately, again as corruption levels are high in countries like mine, only one sector could be done in that way.

Designing for Women and Children

^{EK} Early on you started to pay attention to women and children and to design spaces with their needs in mind. Can you please tell us more about this?

^{YL} Well, women in Pakistan traditionally need their own space. Because they are mostly not allowed to be outside their homes. Traditionally there are either courtyards, either the buildings are introverted, inward-looking, or there are terraces that are protected from prying eyes above. It is very important to continue that tradition, because if you don't, it is very difficult for them to survive. And that is why, for me, the old town and what I call the small, semi-public, semi-open spaces are very important. In Peshawar, there are these beautiful city houses. They are full of all kinds of craft, strong traditions from central Asia, beautiful wood carving, metal work, and stucco work—oh, it is out of this world! I had the privilege of restoring one of them, and we made a good study of that area. They have linkages at the upper level of closed walkways. That is for women to go from one side to the other, which is very interesting. It creates a beautiful urban character there.

EK Your heritage work was a very important source of inspiration for your humanitarian work and your zero-carbon architecture. Can you please tell us how your interest in heritage influenced your own architectural work even before your turn to relief housing and principles of ecological justice?

YL The problem has always been that, since most of us have been trained in the West, our focus always is the West. And very few of us have had the opportunity to study other things. And because I was lucky, I never had a very large office that I had to be able to provide work for. It never became a factory. Because this mostly is a vicious circle. I could decide and take a pause, and that is what helped me to do my heritage research and documentation, and everything that I do. Because there were really long, lean periods, I can tell you (laughing).

I don't think there is another Pakistani who has had the run of two major World Heritage Sites. I mean, I had the privilege of staying in the Lahore Fort, because Ingeborg (Ingeborg Breines, Director of the Islamabad UNESCO office) said "I want you there." And I was walking in the nights, on the same route as Nur Jahan, the empress, would have walked. I have just been very blessed, that is all I can say.

AF At the same time, when you were doing research in the heritage field, you had what you call your 'star architecture' phase. Maybe you can share with us how you got into these large projects, and how you conceptualized them?

YL So, there were these large commissions that came my way. The FTC – Finance and Trade Centre was about putting different organizations together. I had a very strong backing of the army at the time. The army department that owned the land was very interested in somehow maximizing whatever they could get out of it. Something like ten or twelve very large, state-run corporations decided to join hands, and that is how the whole Finance and Trade Centre came about. And then we invited Eva Vecsei, whom I had worked with before, from Canada, and she and a couple of her colleagues came, and we developed the concept together. Eva had this tremendous experience of building very large projects, and she taught me a hell of a lot, although her stay might not have been more than two or three weeks. How to do the massing, how to break up the large spaces, and so on. The good thing was that we were on the same wavelength and did not have just straight blocks. I think that was a very good learning experience.

We have this spine that connects three blocks. And then the breeze wafts into the whole building. And then we have the courtyards in the middle, inverted spaces again, back to tradition. I have never felt that

I needed to replicate the imagery of the past. There are lots of other aspects that you can build into the design, which would evoke the feeling of the tradition without just replicating something. There has been a debate all the time: What is Pakistani architecture? Often there is the mistaken notion that if a building is 'Islamized,' as I call it, then it becomes Pakistani. But I don't believe in that, I feel that is a very false premise. I think what you need to do is to incorporate the spirit of something, rather than the actual expression of it.

The Users as Clients

AF Your big buildings became landmarks in Karachi. How do you see this period today?

YL In the 1980s I felt that, you know, money was no object. I could use the best materials, wherever they could come from. I specified them, and if the granite was not available here, then hell I said, "No, I want granite," and then we got it. Incidentally, the FTC spawned a totally new granite industry in Pakistan. The PSO house granite is actually Pakistani. But, you know, at that time, there was a very strong criticism against me, and really, it made sense.

The fact is that a lot of time we are led by, in our minds basically, the need to please our client, and that if they want something, it is their right that we give it to them because they are paying for it. But for me, the design that I produce is not their property. Because they may have paid for it, but it is used by common people. I feel I have a responsibility to the people who are going to use the building and not to the person who pays. What is right for the users, that is important. How are you going to transform their lives with your conception? That is far more important than pleasing somebody's whim.

I think we need the profession to be strong. You know, the training as an architect equips you to deal with so many situations. You know how to collaborate with people, how to conceive, how to put things together. I would very much like for architects to give up this whole concept about pleasing the clients and go into the humanitarian field where you should please the common person, where you can really transform their lives.

EK In 2000, you decided to stop architecture as a business, but, as it turned out, you retired from one thing to do another thing.

YL (Laughing) I never thought I would do anything else when I retired. My husband ran this very lucrative insurance company, had to sell it, and retired. He had always wanted to be an author, and he became a historian. I felt that I was trying to do things, and, in a sense, within architecture, you are pleasing your clients. And I said, "Maybe the best thing is to give up and just retire and write books?" That was my intention actually. I had no thought of doing anything else in my life. And then in 2000, the KaravanKarachi phenomenon happened, because my guidebook on Karachi heritage came out *(Karachi: Illustrated City Guide)*, based on my big Karachi book *(The Dual City: Karachi during the Raj)*. Some people started to come to me and say, "We did not know that Karachi had so much wealth, so why don't we do something about the city?"

Now, at that time there were a lot of disturbances. The Afghan War had been affecting our lives for a long time. Nobody realizes the toll that Pakistan has had to pay for that. There were a lot of bomb blasts. And we decided to celebrate the city. First, we started organizing heritage street fests. Thousands of people would turn up. And I remember the British Council director laughing and asking, "Do you think that you can go and sit on the street and celebrate British colonial heritage?" Because at that time, nobody really wanted this heritage. Nobody thought it was of any importance. Lahore was a big cultural capital, where you had these amazing Mughal buildings. But in Karachi? So, every Sunday we would put a big stage in front of a historic building. And then a policemen said to me, "You know, the Karachi roads have always been blocked for VIP traffic to make way for very important people. For the first time, they are blocked for a common person."

I have always felt that streets are the place if you want to spread something. I mean, now, with social media, of course, it is different. One day there had been a killing, of two people, I think, very prominent mullahs (religious scholars). And the deputy commissioner, who had always been very supportive, called me and said, "Okay, madam, I think you should postpone this one." I remember telling him, "You know, thank you very much for warning us, but why don't you just double your security? We will not cancel anything." If they have an agenda, we also have our own agenda (which was to normalize the city).

Against the Aid Industry

EK And then you became a humanitarian worker?

YL Well, I don't know whether I can take credit for this, because a lot of times I am just led into situations. I think my bad habit is that, even if I don't know what is going on, I tend to just jump into it. An earthquake happened at that time, in 2005. We had never seen devastation of that kind. And here were all these people in the remote areas, and nobody knew how much destruction had actually taken place. It mobilized the whole country like never before. And I felt I had to go there. At that time, I had never done humanitarian work, I had never known what is needed; I had never designed for an earthquake area.

Somebody told me that the army was in charge, and, for some reason, I was invited to this conference that was being held with different INGOs and NGOs. I was also included in that particular group, which the president at the time, General Musharraf (Pervez Musharraf), was addressing. I go to attend this meeting, and there is talk of using galvanized iron structures. I get up, and first they don't listen to me. I kept on raising my hand, and when they said, "the last question," I raised my hand again (raising hand). So, he said, "Well, give her a chance." I went on a rant and said, "You know, you've got to go back to whatever had been done before, and not these kinds of industrialized systems. Whatever is there, we should use it." And they said, "Okay, okay, all right. You go and meet the general who is now in charge."

The next day I arrived at the doorstep of that general, who happened to be the big boss of the whole reconstruction there, General Nadim. He said, "So you are an architect. As an architect, what do you think you are going to do?" I said, "Well, you know, general, I think I would use lime to work with." He said, "Lime? Well, that is a very novel idea." I said, "Well, maybe novel to you, but the Mughals used it five hundred years ago. It is there, we can use it." Anyway, he said, "Okay, fine. We will tell you where to go."

Now the biggest issue was that I had no workforce. My office more or less hardly existed. I mean, Lari Associates were completely gone, and the Heritage Foundation was a very shoestring kind of thing. But we managed to do everything. I mean, my volunteers were just amazing. It was real hardship because cold weather had set in. And then we had a conflict with the army. Because first I was told that I could use the army camps, and then the army people had another order to only use galvanized iron steel for structures. We were saying recycled stone, recycled everything. Whatever you find there, you use. And we worked out a whole methodology, and their implementation partners would come, saying to the people, "If you repair your room, we will not give you a new one, we will not give you any help." This whole international system is totally skewed, I think, because nobody is looking at what the reality is. Funding is in short supply, and you keep on destroying whatever can be salvaged.

Saving People and the Planet

AF You have completely changed the system of humanitarian architecture, introducing both low-cost and zero-carbon principles.

YL You know, what happened really was that I saw a lot of destruction in the name of helping people who were affected by these disasters. By 2010 all of us had understood that climate change was there and that we all had to be careful as to what we did. Ever since I went to the Lahore Fort World Heritage Site, I have never used cement in anything. Pakistan is the fifth most vulnerable country as far as climate change is concerned. And our poverty levels are really high. Whatever resources we have, they should be maximized in the best possible manner. There is nothing that you can throw away or waste. There is nothing you can destroy and rebuild away, you know. The most affordable, the most inexpensive, the safest thing that you can do, you need to do for everybody. And it is not only Pakistan, it is, as you know, all of South Asia, the whole of Sub-Saharan Africa. They are saying today there are three billion people in the world who are shelterless. Probably there are more now. So, what is the future for these people?

EK Again, you address the needs of women and you work with women.

YL When the General Officer Commanding, who was in control of the whole emergency operation after the 2005 earthquake, heard that I was inviting women over, he said, "Madam, they never come out of their houses. You will just be wasting your time." So I said, "Okay, general, I will try and see what happens." I sent out the invitation, and you wouldn't believe that at least two hundred women turned up, walking, I don't know how many hours, to get there.

We did community kitchens and a lot of toilets for them. Because again, I mean the stories are just horrific. When I asked women, "What do you do for toilets?" They said, "Well, in the morning, before early morning prayer, the Fajr prayer, and after Maghrib, which is the sunset prayer, we go behind the bushes, that is where the toilet is." (Becomes emotional) This is how they live their lives. I couldn't believe it.

AF Since then, your zero-carbon architecture has gone beyond providing shelter to adding essential infrastructure.

YL So, I believe that especially with my bamboo LOG (Lari OctaGreen), which is a prefab structure, you can very easily build basic infrastructure. If you teach people, it is perfectly doable. The same panels are used for the shelter, and for the toilets. They are all safe the way we build them. One safe shelter for every family, that is their right, if you look at human rights and housing as a right. Then you have one toilet that may be shared, but at least women have access to it, so they have dignity. And then clean water, that is again a right, every convention says that. And then I add on clean cooking, the Pakistan Chulah, which is self-built, can provide clean cooking and also dignity for women. I want these four elements; I would like every family in the world to actually have them. But certainly every family in Pakistan.

The route I am taking is very simple. First of all, we are providing these video tutorials that people can watch on their cellphones and follow them. Secondly, we are also training artisans. We get funding from elsewhere or we pay to train artisans ourselves. I am not taking any large-scale funding from anybody. That means we get a trained workforce within each village who can then say how these things need to be done.

Taking Zero-Carbon Architecture to the City

AF Finally, you transferred zero-carbon architecture from the rural areas to the city.

YL The Rahguzar has been my dream for some time, and, again, I took my chance. There was this Chief Justice of Pakistan who had been talking about the state of Karachi and saying, "I want the glory of Karachi to be brought back." Because Karachi is a city that has now been labeled as an 'orphan city,' where it seems that nobody cares for it. So, the Chief Secretary, who is the head of the administration, decided to call a meeting of architects and planners. And I said, "If you want the glory back, then you have to restore all your historic buildings, because that is what the city is about." They said, "Okay, fine, let us have your proposal." I wanted this trail, which would be lined with historic buildings. In 1994, I was instrumental in getting this law to protect urban historic architecture with the Heritage Foundation. By that time we had made inventories of about six hundred historic structures.

One could walk along this trail, pedestrian, of course, with lots of plantings and greenery. You know, like every civilized country actually has. I decided to take this one segment, close to Denso Hall, which we had been restoring. But this street was, really again, urban blight of the worst order. We had got the women in Makli to make the tiles. There are 150,000 of these terra-cotta cobbles. The whole work is derived from what we have done at the Makli Necropolis in restoration. Because we learned the art of making terra-cotta, as well as glazed tile through that.

We have got these aquifer wells, so the rainwater goes into them. We have got sponge pavements with gaps in which the water is absorbed. Since it is zero-carbon, there is obviously no cement or steel here. And then we have got full Miyawaki-style forests. The whole climate has changed with cool air now. The shopkeepers say that it is the first time they are able to breathe here. They now have joined hands with us to start restoring heritage façades. What I really would like is to stabilize every structure, every historic structure. I am not interested in totally revamping something. But as long as I can make them safe, that has always been what I wanted. I would like very much to see how I can transform this entire area.

EK When you think about the future, what do you want to share with the readers?

YL You know, I think it is a very difficult one you are going to face. I don't see enough movement in trying to come to terms with the kind of challenges that exist today. I think not enough people are thinking or even aware of the damage that is being caused all the time. I mean, I talk about injustices, social injustice in the global South. But there are also ecological injustices in the West, where consumption levels are so high. All of us will have to rethink our roles and the way we live basically. Whether in the South, to take care of each other, and in the West, this kind of extravagant living and capitalist exploitation has to be reduced. But of course, every country has to decide on its own. But now we know that every decision any of us makes, even as an individual, has a global impact. And this is something that was probably not there before, but will be more and more in your lives I think.

The interview was recorded in Karachi on February 15, 2022, and edited by Angelika Fitz.

Essays

Pakistan Under Construction

Chris Moffat

I. Nation/Building

The call for Pakistan, an independent homeland for the Muslims of South Asia, was formally adopted as a political goal by the All-India Muslim League in 1940. Its creation only seven years later, with the partition of British India, has been presented by scholars and partisans variously as an astonishing act of political efficacy or as a case study in the calamities of historical contingency. Pakistan's abrupt appearance on the map, its borders drawn by a British official who had never before been to India, fueled the spiraling violence of 1947. A new era of postcolonial, independent states in South Asia was to be inaugurated by civil war: riots, looting, murder, and mass migration.[1]

One of the defining early architectural forms of Pakistan was, accordingly, the refugee camp—sprawling landscapes of tents, mud, fear, and anger, but also relief and expectation.[2] These spaces of migrants and strangers, arriving within the new borders of Pakistan from India and bringing with them their own histories, languages, and experiences of loss, illuminate some of the challenges that faced the new state. How to create a national community out of this hugely diverse populace, bound (for the most part[3]) by affiliations to Islam but otherwise riven by cleavages of sect, ethnicity, caste, and class? The

[1] Shruti Kapila, *Violent Fraternity: Indian Political Thought in the Global Age* (Princeton, NJ: Princeton University Press, 2021), 237–9.

[2] Anooradha Iyer Siddiqui and Vazira Fazila-Yacoobi Zamindar, "Partitions: Architectures of Statelessness," *e-flux*, March 2022, https://www.e-flux.com/architecture/positions/454156/partitions-architectures-of-statelessness/.

[3] Anushay Malik, "Narrating Christians in Pakistan through Times of War and Conflict," *South Asia* 43, no. 1 (2020): 6–83.

task was further complicated by the fact that Pakistan was composed of two 'wings,' separated by a thousand miles on either side of the new Indian state.

Because Pakistani nationalism could not rely on common histories or shared relationships fostered by language, blood, or soil, it has frequently coalesced around an aspirational, future-oriented vision of what an Islamic polity could or should be.[4] The country is often referred to as a purposeful, built structure. The common refrain, *'Pakistan masjid hai,'* imagines the nation-state as a mosque, a site for assembly, a sacred place.[5] Scaling this up from building to built environment, scholars have noted the desire within the movement for Pakistan to construct 'a new Medina,' modeled on the Prophet's capital city, from whose streets might emerge "an Islamic utopia that would be the harbinger for renewal and [the] rise of Islam in the modern world."[6] The historian Faisal Devji, with a nod to Hegel, evokes another built form in the conclusion to his book *Muslim Zion,* where he suggests that Pakistan is a *sepulchre,* a mausoleum. The country's founding in 1947, for Devji, can be seen as "the grave of Islam as an ecumenical religion,"[7] where a more expansive realm of political identifications and practices were sacrificed in order to set the foundations for a bounded, modern nation-state.

Assembling, founding, building, making: Pakistan remains a place under construction. This is not simply a story of bricks and mortar but of ideological contest, public debate, popular movements, and global forces. Architecture is not a passive backdrop to these processes but a product of and prompt for critical discussions around history, identity, and belonging. Architects—and especially those of Yasmeen Lari's

4 Faisal Devji, *Muslim Zion: Pakistan as a Political Idea* (London: Hurst, 2013).

5 Naveeda Khan, *Muslim Becoming: Aspiration and Skepticism in Pakistan* (Durham, NC: Duke University Press, 2012), 21–2.

6 Venkat Dhulipala, *Creating a New Medina* (Cambridge: Cambridge University Press, 2015), 4.

7 Devji, *Muslim Zion,* 248.

The unfinished Bab-e-Pakistan Monument, built on the site of a former refugee camp, Lahore, 2019

generation—have been enthusiastic participants in such discussions, engaged as much in educational and campaigning work as they are with the world of sketchbooks, site surveys, models, and materials. The following sections introduce the early history of Pakistan through scenes of construction. They trace the emergence of architecture as a profession in Pakistan, considering the purchase of these pasts for architecture in the present.

II. Lahore, 1947

In the market area of Shahalami, within Lahore's Walled City, the fires burned for many nights. Well-known as a commercial hub for Hindu and Sikh traders, it drew the wrath of Pakistan supporters in a moment of fear, suspicion, and anger. Their fury was propelled by rumors that Muslims were being targeted in places like nearby Amritsar, Lahore's historic sister city, now partitioned off across an international border. In Shahalami, houses were looted and places of worship vandalized. Buildings were torn apart and the bricks used as weapons. Petrol bombs were placed in drainage pipes. The centuries-old Shahalami Gate, one of twelve entry points in the city wall, crumbled to the ground.[8]

    Partition reordered the subcontinent, though in this part of Punjab— and in Bengal in the east—once-familiar geographies were shattered by the bloody drama of separation. In the years that followed, the revival of Shahalami as a market area was supervised by the Lahore Improvement Trust (LIT), an organization with its roots in the colonial period but which adapted itself to the work of post-Partition repair. Visiting Shahalami today, its distinction from other parts of the Walled City is obvious. In contrast to the warren of narrow streets and *galis* (alleyways) nearby, one finds a main boulevard lined with multi-story concrete, glass, and

[8] Pervaiz Vandal, "Architecture in the Post-Colonial Lahore," in *Portrait of Lahore*, ed. idem. (Lahore: THAAP, 2012), 204–7.

The Walled City of Lahore, 2019

steel buildings. Alongside the vehicle traffic channeled by the road, covered shopping arcades and brightly signposted storefronts draw pedestrians into the area, busy with commerce once more.

The LIT Chairman who oversaw this work, Zafarul Ahsan, was also responsible in his role as Lahore's Deputy Commissioner for planning several new neighborhoods in the city. Working alongside the town planner S. A. Rahim, areas like Gulberg, Samanabad, and Rifle Range on Multan Road were laid out with modern planning principles in mind and a desire to cater to a nascent automobile age. With these neighborhoods, the immediate, emergency work of reconstruction gave way to broader projects of urban expansion. They served as thresholds to a wider, postcolonial agenda of 'development.'[9]

Though Ahsan was immersed in the city's rhythms, his daughter Yasmeen, born in 1941, recalls her childhood in Lahore as one of isolation. Safely ensconced in a leafy, domestic compound, her exposure to the city was limited to the trip to school and the circulations of her family through Lahore's elite social network. It was only years later, after completing her education in England and returning to Pakistan with her married name, Lari, that Ahsan's daughter would come to know Lahore in all its variety. She relished the opportunity to explore places like the Walled City on foot, a young architect eager to learn lessons from the historic sections that had survived the passage of time, the wreckage of partition, and so too the bulldozers of postcolonial development. In doing so, she registered the need in Pakistan for an architecture that was cognizant of older, organic practices of building and dwelling in the region and which did not surrender completely to the enchantments of the future.[10]

III. Karachi, 1954

The Hyderabad-born architect Mehdi Ali Mirza convened a regular meeting of practicing and aspiring architects at the Café Al-Mehran. An employee of Karachi's Public Works Department (PWD), Mirza was alive to the challenges facing the architectural profession in the young country. Mirza himself was trained at the prestigious Sir J. J. College of Architecture in Bombay and, prior to partition, taught architecture at Delhi Polytechnic. Both of these specialist institutions were now partitioned off to India. There was, in fact, no provision for architectural education in Pakistan until Mirza's meetings set the foundations for a new Government School of Architecture (GSA). The GSA was supported by the PWD, desperately in need of local draftsmen, and in 1956 it moved to a purpose-built space on Shahrah-e-Kemal Ataturk.[11] The Café Al-Mehran meetings had another important outcome. They led, in 1957, to the creation of the Institute of Architects, Pakistan (IAP), an advocacy

---

9 Markus Daechsel, *Islamabad and the Politics of International Development in Pakistan* (Cambridge: Cambridge University Press, 2015).

10 Chris Moffat, "Lahore After the Modern: Architecture, Equality and Community in Yasmeen Lari's Anguri Bagh," *Global Intellectual History* (June 2022): 1–23, https://doi.org/10.1080/23801883.2022.2062419

11 The GSA would not grant a Bachelor of Architecture degree until 1972. In 1974, the institution was absorbed into the Dawood College of Engineering and Technology. See Neelum Naz, "Development of Architectural Education in Pakistan," *GBER 7*, no. 2 (2010): 8.

Karachi street scene, 2019

group for which Mirza served as the first president. Mirza was joined in the initiative by other senior architects whose careers spanned the partition event: Zahir-ud Deen Khwaja, Minoo Mistri, Tajuddin Bhamani, M. A. Ahed, and others.[12] The aim of the IAP was to articulate and defend the professional interests of architects, support the creation of new schools, establish a code of ethics for practitioners, and to connect with other professional bodies around the world.

Histories of postcolonial nation-states in the age of decolonization are very often histories of building. The desire to 'catch up' with the West—to break free from the 'waiting room of history'—manifested in large-scale development programs across Asian and African states: new buildings, new infrastructure, new neighborhoods, even entirely new cities. In some cases, these building projects were inaugurated to consolidate a young state's claims to self-sufficiency and autonomy. But very often, the complex demands of 'five-year plans' and other developmental leaps forward provided a new alibi for western intervention, in the form of 'technical assistance,' financial loans, and the supply of materials and equipment.

The latter was certainly the case in Pakistan's early decades, where a lingering British presence was superseded by growing alignment with the United States of America. American organizations—governmental, philanthropic, and private—invested heavily in the new state, their motives determined in no small part by the global dynamics of the Cold War. In the late 1950s, when the Pakistani government began to take seriously the problems caused by a lack of homegrown Pakistani architects, it drew on support from the Ford Foundation and the Fulbright Program, alongside the United Nations Expanded Programme

12 Zahir-ud Deen Khwaja, *Memoirs of an Architect* (Lahore: Self-Published, 1998), 56.

of Technical Assistance and the Commonwealth-administered Colombo Plan, to help establish new schools. In 1958, the Mayo School of Arts—founded in 1875 by the British artist and educator Lockwood Kipling—was 'upgraded' to become the National College of Arts (NCA). Its first principal was the Ohio-born sculptor and art historian Mark Sponenburgh. Though figures like Zahir-ud Deen Khwaja advised on its pioneering five-year Diploma in Architecture, the early years of this program drew on visiting Fulbright Professors from the Universities of Oregon, Oklahoma, and elsewhere. In Dhaka, the East Pakistan University of Engineering and Technology established its Faculty of Architecture and Planning in 1962 in a direct collaboration with Texas A&M University, funded by the United States Agency for International Development (USAID). Its founding dean was another Ohioan, the architect Richard Vrooman, alongside early faculty members Daniel Dunham and Jack Yardley.

In spite of these new institutions in Lahore, Karachi, and Dhaka, many of the major figures who constitute Pakistan's first 'postcolonial' generation of architects—defined, loosely, as those who were born around the time of partition and who grew up in and established practices in Pakistan—were trained abroad in the late 1950s and early 1960s: Kamil Khan Mumtaz and Habib Fida Ali at the Architectural Association in London; Muzharul Islam at the University of Oregon and Yale University; Arif Hasan at the Oxford School of Architecture; Anwar Said at the University of Liverpool; Pervaiz Vandal at the American University of Beirut; the list goes on. A notable exception is Nayyar Ali Dada, who joined the first batch of the NCA's architecture program in 1958. Yasmeen Lari trained at the Oxford School of Architecture, which is today part of Oxford Brookes University, from 1959 to 1963. After completing her diploma, Lari received her accreditation from the Royal Institute of British Architects and returned to Pakistan in 1964 to establish a private practice in Karachi. Benefiting from family connections, her early commissions included private residences in upper-income areas—notably Khan House (1969) in Karachi's Defence Officers' Housing Society—which were designed in the modern style and helped build her reputation. Her own home, Lari House (1973), composed of blocky concrete and cantilevered forms, demonstrates the influence of Brutalism on Lari's early practice.

The 1960s remained a period dominated by foreign architects in Pakistan, with public and private patrons attracted by the experience and prestige offered by figures like Edward Durrell Stone, Louis Kahn, Michel Écochard, and C. A. Doxiadis, all of whom designed major schemes and structures in this decade. It would be inadvisable, however, to stick too starkly to a 'foreign'/'local' divide when narrating Pakistan's architectural history. In the first place, even those Pakistani practitioners and educators who had no international experience or connections were drawn into a global consensus around modern architectural forms, technology, and planning prominent across the post-WWII world. Meanwhile, international architects like Stone, Kahn, Écochard, and Doxiadis were all deeply concerned, in their own ways, with how to 'adapt' modernist practices to the peculiarities of region, climate, and Pakistan's Islamic identity. In some cases, this sensitivity formed a central element of their design approach; in others, it was a product of pressure exerted by their patrons, as when designs for official buildings in the new capital of Islamabad were returned for not being appropriately 'Islamic.'[13] What is clear is that the rising generation of Pakistani architects, Lari included, would begin to foreground critical questions of place, purpose, and authenticity as they developed their practice in the young country. What could, or should, a Pakistani architecture look like? How might it balance divergent notions of history, geography, and community? What is the responsibility of the architect to the people, places, and political context around and in which they work?

[13] See Daechsel, *Islamabad and the Politics of International Development in Pakistan* and Farhan Karim, "Pakistan Papers: Louis Kahn's Designs of a Past and Future in Islamabad and Dhaka," *Comparative Studies of South Asia, Africa and the Middle East* 40, no. 3 (2020): 507–25.

IV. Dhaka, 1971

Under the Constitution of 1962, the old Mughal capital of the Bengal Subah, Dhaka, was made Pakistan's 'second capital,' after Islamabad. On the one hand, this was an attempt by the military regime of General Muhammad Ayub Khan to address growing demands for autonomy in East Pakistan; on the other, it provided another excuse for the President to demonstrate his power through the spectacle of construction and development. The monumental new parliament complex, designed by Louis Kahn, was to be centered in a neighborhood called 'Ayub Nagar.' But in 1968, a long period of dissatisfaction with martial rule erupted into mass uprisings led by peasants, students, and workers across both wings of Pakistan. Ayub Khan, who had been in power since the coup d'état of 1958, resigned in March 1969. But stalemates and sabotage around the 1970 national elections led to further upheaval in East Pakistan. The Pakistani military was mobilized to quell a nascent, national liberation movement, and against the army's most brutal efforts, the independent state of Bangladesh was declared on December 16, 1971. Ayub Nagar was renamed Sher-e-Bangla Nagar. Kahn's unfinished parliament complex, which was reputedly appropriated as a munitions storehouse for rebel *Mukti Bahini* (freedom fighters) during the war, was completed in 1982 and became the Jatiya Sangsad Bhaban, a national parliament for South Asia's newest state.

The 1970s were thus properly transformative for Pakistan. The liberation of Bangladesh amounted to a loss of more than half of Pakistan's population, a huge swathe of territory, and a considerable reserve of resources and labor for which West Pakistan had benefited in its imbalanced, pre-1971 extractive relationship. The civilian leader of this new, shrunken Pakistan, Zulfikar Ali Bhutto, had risen to power on the momentum of the anti-Ayub movement. His Pakistan People's Party deployed a populist rhetoric of anti-imperialism, Third World solidarity, and Islamic socialism, marking a shift from the pro-Western, technocratic paternalism of the Ayub Khan era. But the early years of the PPP in power were characterized by a crackdown on student activists, trade union militants, and progressive intellectuals, stopping short of any truly disruptive social or economic transformations. Furthermore, rather than approaching the disastrous rupture with East Pakistan and the atrocities committed by the military as an opportunity to reflect on Pakistan as a project and idea, Bhutto doubled down on his nationalism and reasserted Pakistan's desired status as a leader among Muslim nations.

The populism of the Bhutto era—replete with a hostility to foreign influences, an assertion of national pride, and an agenda of self-sufficiency—created a conducive climate for the new generation of Pakistani architects. A surge in public and private commissions provided these architects the opportunity to experiment with some of the questions mentioned in the previous section. The fact that the country was now more territorially coherent did not necessarily make the problem of what a Pakistani architecture could or should be easier to resolve. Many

Louis I. Kahn's Jatiya Sangsad Bhaban (National Parliament House), Dhaka, 2020

architects grappled with the variations in style, climate, and material evident across Pakistan's regions, from what were then known as the Northern Areas and Frontier Provinces through to Punjab, Balochistan, and Sindh.[14]

Yasmeen Lari, whose family had lost money and property as a result of Bhutto's nationalization policies, recalls that the new President (and, from 1973, Prime Minister) did a great deal to encourage her work as the first accredited woman architect in Pakistan.[15] Bhutto invited Lari to the President's Residence in Murree in 1972 and offered to support her growing interest in mud brick housing. He even suggested she build something in Naudero, in his family's ancestral district of Larkana. While ultimately nothing came of this, Lari was commissioned by the People's Housing Programme to design an expansive new housing scheme in Lahore, the innovative Angoori Bagh project, for which her studies of the old Walled City would be put into use. Lari's plan for a low-rise, high-density residential neighborhood used cheap and widely available local materials like brick, allowing for easy maintenance, and was laid out to facilitate social interactions among residents and cultivate community. These efforts captured a certain spirit of the Bhutto era and its concern for 'housing the poor.' This era was short-lived—Bhutto was deposed in a military coup in 1977—but for Lari it marked a beginning, an impulse to experiment that would soon characterize her protean practice as an architect in Pakistan.

V. Islamabad, 1980

Pakistan's capital city, nestled into the foothills of the Himalayas, is a showcase for international architects. Envisioned by the Greek planner and architect Doxiadis, Islamabad boasts ministerial buildings by the Italian Gio Ponti and a Parliament House by the American Stone. During the 1980s, Turkish architect Vedat Dalokay's iconic Faisal Masjid would join the landscape, followed years later by Japanese architect Kenzo Tange's Supreme Court. But on November 16, 1980, Yasmeen Lari was in the city to appraise General Zia-ul-Haq—Pakistan's new martial ruler—of the struggles facing Pakistan's own growing body of professional architects. She did so in her role as the newly-elected President of the IAP. The absence of any official register of standards or legal recognition of qualifications had led to an anarchic building industry susceptible to all manner of opportunists. Out of this meeting, a committee was formed, and in 1983—after much lobbying and internal politicking—the Pakistan Council of Architects and Town Planners (PCATP) Ordinance was promulgated. This ordinance provided for the recognition and regulation of architectural and town planning professions, requiring all practitioners to be licensed through the PCATP.[16]

14 Kamil Khan Mumtaz, *Architecture in Pakistan* (Singapore: Mimar, 1985).

15 Lari's father, husband and other family members were leading figures in the powerful Khyber Insurance Company and Khyber Textile Group, one of the industrial conglomerates targeted by Bhutto's reforms. See Moffat, "Lahore After the Modern: Architecture, Equality and Community in Yasmeen Lari's Anguri Bagh," 8.

16 Yemeen Zuberi, "PCATP completes eight years," *Archi Times*, November 1990.

Within the worlds of Pakistani architecture, Lari is celebrated for this accomplishment, even if the PCATP is often the subject of criticism and frustration, a fate common to many a bureaucratic professional body. In bestowing the architect authority as a qualified and trained expert, Lari and the IAP did much to protect the profession from the competing interests of other builders and designers, particularly engineers, whose own professional organizations lobbied fiercely against the Ordinance. Lari was, by this point, well established as one of Pakistan's foremost architects, the author of large-scale housing projects, hotels, and offices, primarily in Karachi. But even as Lari had done so much— through the IAP, PCATP, and her professional and educational work—to give status and respect to architects, the 1980s was also a period when she was actively questioning the role and responsibility of architects in Pakistani society. Specifically, Lari began to contrast ideas of the architect as 'expert problem-solver' with notions of the architect as listener and facilitator—less as someone who comes from outside with a set of preformulated approaches, but as a figure who strives to be embedded in their place of work, who engages in acts of translation, who is open to learning and having their authority challenged.

The seeds of this approach were, arguably, evident in the Angoori Bagh Housing Scheme, where Lari sought to involve future residents in the process of design. But it was given clear focus when, in 1980, Lari established the Heritage Foundation of Pakistan with her husband, Suhail. Through this Foundation, Lari carved a space to study and learn from the historic built environments of her country. While Lari's research and documentary work has been prolific in Sindh, especially in Thatta

Detail of Vedat Dalokay's Faisal Masjid, 2019

and Karachi, the Foundation has been involved in projects across the country, from Khyber Pakhtunkhwa to Punjab. An engagement with history becomes the necessary foundation for meaningful architecture in the present. In this work, Lari actualizes an impulse common across her generation—a group of architects who had lived through the tumult of two partitions, military coups and regime changes, periods of sectarian and ethnic violence, and the collapse of many of the progressive postcolonial aspirations for what type of country Pakistan could be. Rather than pursuing some abstract future, a key concern for this generation has been the work of *grounding:* an expansive ethic of place and belonging. Lari's work with the Heritage Foundation would evolve, over the decades, into the applied practice of barefoot architecture explored elsewhere in this volume. But for now, in this 1980s moment, under the shadow of an increasingly repressive dictatorship, Lari appears as an architect in motion, grappling with questions of hierarchy and authority. Designing, building, making, but also learning, unlearning, walking, drawing, thinking.

'Construction' as an idea is infused with notions of progress and linear development. But what does it mean to think of building and design outside of a clear trajectory toward the future? The spirit of return and renewal evident among Lari's generation is worth reflecting on. As suggested above, it has something to do with the particular worlds these architects inhabited, and specifically the cognitive-political space of 'postcoloniality,' shaped by a desire to recover histories of local agency and knowledge against histories of colonial (and neocolonial) domination. Today, this generation is eminent and

Construction scene, Lahore, 2019

celebrated, even if the vast majority of building practice in Pakistan does not resemble their own. So, what is their inheritance? How should younger architects trace a career like Lari's in the twenty-first century? On the one hand, it may be misleading—Lari and her contemporaries entered architecture from a position of privilege, supported by wealthy families and so able to find that space for experiment and exploration. The profession is much more open and democratic in today's Pakistan, where there are now tens and tens of architectural schools. But the capacity to reflect on one's practice, and to think critically about questions of responsibility and authority, does not rely on socio-economic advantage. It is, arguably, all the more crucial in today's Pakistan, where the Gulf state example of spectacular glass and steel architecture has become a desirable model for new construction, in spite of growing environmental crises and pervasive inequality. That resilient sense of possibility echoing across Lari's generation—the idea that architecture might still be a tool for creating a better and more just world—is one that must be affirmed and insisted upon, against the darkening shadow of an uncertain future.

All photographs: Chris Moffat

The Blossoming World of Yasmeen Lari

Helen Thomas

The powerful voice of a compelling living subject can be a useful historical tool when reflecting on the nature and meaning of their work, especially when embodied in its nature is a clear and urgent message. Situating the voice of Yasmeen Lari outside its echo chamber, giving it meaning in a larger perspective, is one of the intentions of this chapter. A framing of selected fragments from Lari's writing and speaking over the years includes other voices, notably that of her husband Suhail Zaheer Lari. While these two perspectives of Lari's professional life do not contradict each other, they provide different remembered facts that intertwine, within the caveat of the fallibility and self-censorship of reported memory. Recollections of others are interwoven where possible to add a little more density to specific moments.

The way that Lari practices architecture today—strategically and enacted through responsive and evolving networks—provides one apt and useful prototype for the profession of architecture going forward into a post-carbon, post-anthropocentric world. Although this way of being an architect seems to be defined by her twenty-first-century disaster relief work, it has deep roots in methods produced and reproduced in relation to the contingent realities of her professional life from the beginning. Lari's trajectory moves from UK-trained Brutalist architect reflecting twentieth-century western models of material technology and mass production, through national heritage campaigner and activist, to the development of zero-carbon disaster relief solutions drawn from local vernaculars, which today and into the twenty-first-century suggest organizational and construction technologies of global relevance. Dating from the time when she first started practicing, the motivating ethical intent underlying her work has been formed, developed, and shared through her presence, active participation, or initiation and coordinating of organizations and associated events. These identifiable bodies authenticate, give authority to, and define an identity for the multiple and varied activities of her practice, connecting their physical outcomes to larger issues of architecture and its responsibilities. This strategic enlacing of abstract norms and questions with tangible craft-based, material, and constructional responses to lived situations stands in lieu of more conventional discursive, intellectual, and conceptual discourses of architecture.

Through Lari's example, we discover that the architect can be a conduit, a catalyst, a pathway transforming authorship, where strategic control embodies the work of others, from individuals to large groups, including village communities as well as large organizations. The imaginative act, previously defined as creativity, now involves the initiation of ephemeral constellations. Their potential outcomes no longer rely on a formal canon of material intervention for their authority and meaning, and a continuous theme in Lari's method is the multiple and collective nature of the production, ownership, and implementation of knowledge. In her current work this is expressed, for example, in the training networks initiated within the Heritage Foundation of Pakistan (HF) that bloom across rural areas of Pakistan.[1] Lari also talks about instrumentalizing the communication between women in the isolated locations in which she is working. Their shared work, as well as their individual expression, is essential for the mobilization and adaption of Lari's zero-carbon solutions to large-scale disaster relief and rural dwelling challenges, such as the Pakistan Chulah, devised in response to flooding.

This co-production of intention, knowledge, and its operation can be traced back to origins that lie in the overlaps of three realms of action and participation: The first is the supranational and includes Lari's engagement with intergovernmental organizations such as the United Nations (UN) and its agencies UNESCO and UNICEF. It also embodies groups that represent regional interests, such as the Architects Regional Council of Asia (ARCASIA), the Council of Architects and Planners of Islamic Countries, and the Aga Khan Award for Architecture. Next, in terms of scale of influence, is the national. This refers to organizations such as the Institution of Architects, Pakistan (IAP), and the Pakistan Council of Architects and Town Planners (PCATP), in which

---

1 Yasmeen Lari's Zero Carbon Channel, accessed August 4, 2022, https://www.youtube.com/c/YasmeenLarisZeroCarbonChannel/videos.

Lari took a leading role at various times. The third is the specific, or the personal, and embodies the organizations that Lari herself founded or co-founded in her hometown of Karachi. In 1965, a year after she established Lari Associates, she found her public voice within the forum of the Karachi Artists' Gallery (KAG). This was the first contemporary art gallery in the young Islamic Republic of Pakistan (then just eighteen years old), set up at the home of Lari and her husband in 1964, a year after they returned to Pakistan from the UK. Her talk was titled "Some Thoughts on House Design," perhaps inspired by the KAG manifesto.

Floors, Tables, and Other Surfaces

The Laris' family home moved to a bespoke house that she designed in 1973, and remained a convivial club, as well as an occasional place of refuge, for a wide variety of locals and visitors to Karachi. It was also a social and professional resource. Carrying on a tradition that they had begun during their student years in Oxford, a large, furniture-free floor space was kept for informal meetings and suppers. Suhail Lari reports on their time in Oxford: "To accommodate so many people we cleared our flat of all furniture, to the delight of my landlady, and invited everyone to sit on the floor. My neighbour anthropologist Senayake Bandaranayake (later Professor and High Commissioner of Sri Lanka to India and France) loved to sit at the feet of Sir Isaiah Berlin, and used to say he felt that he was in the presence of a guru."[2] Lari herself recalls their Karachi home: "It was an open house. Anyone could drop in during the evening and on Sundays we had an open house lunch so anybody could come in. This tradition went on for many years, we stopped maybe only a decade or so ago."[3] KAG existed within this milieu, with walls and floors generously given over to artists and craftspeople to use as studio space, a legacy of which is the mural by Shakir Ali that still adorns the house.

In architects' understanding of architecture, the floor, the empty floor, is often merely a side effect of the plan. In Lari's work, this cleaned and cleared ground has a vibrant social potential, it creates a potential communal nexus. This principle underlies the platform of the Pakistan Chulah, for example, which serves as kitchen, storage, refuge, and meeting place for the women who inhabit it. The raised platform is analogous to the table, around which a common agenda can be defined. When the Laris created the HF in 1980, they set up its informal headquarters in their home, where it remains today. In her article "How Karavan was Born," the journalist Shanaz Ramzi recalls sitting there. "Venue: Mrs. Yasmeen Lari's office. A room with a huge table and a curious combination of people seated all around it Director of British Council, Richard Hardwick, Amina Sayed of OUP, Talat Rahim of PTDC,

[2] Suhail Zaheer Lari, "Oxford," Suhail Lari Pakistan, accessed July 28, 2022, https://www.suhaillari pakistan.com/chapters /Oxford/.

[3] Yasmeen Lari in conversation with the author, August 4, 2022.

journalists, industrialists, actors, designers, etc. As an animated discussion takes place, with everyone contributing their views vociferously, more people keep trickling in, offering to volunteer their services." This meeting around a table soon blossomed into a full-blown street festival.[4] At the same time, a program of cleaning and washing the walls of heritage buildings as a means to social investment was established that grew to involve young people from local schools and colleges in Karachi, Lahore, Bahawalpur, and Taxila.[5]

The nature of the street surface, whether in a village or in a city, which when clean becomes an inhabitable floor, has been a continuous preoccupation for Lari, which she uses as a mechanism for generating communal consensus. When she speaks of her "Zero-Carbon Street," 2021, she talks of the handmade terra-cotta tiles that cover its permeable surface. "It starts with cleaning the clay and removing all impurities through a series of screenings. The clay goes through a laborious process of kneading, balls are prepared, and then pressed into Plaster of Paris moulds by women artisans"[6] from settlements near Lari's Zero Carbon Cultural Centre at Makli. In conversation, she reports on a new project for 2022—a Zero-Carbon Crossroad, also in Karachi, as "another very good example of how people will join in… There's a lot of encroachment in the city and here there was a big mosque that had taken over and enclosed a large area. With the help of old maps, we persuaded them that they should give up the land, which we are making into a garden. The shopkeepers have voluntarily demolished their own encroachments and they're going to put money into making the pavement with terra-cotta tiles. Everybody is with me, they all want to be part of it."[7]

Each of these examples—the furniture-free floor, the raised platform and the table, the cleaned walls, the street as a theatrical arena, the terra-cotta-paved heritage route and the crossroads garden—defines a meeting place that is hospitable and conducive to speaking out and being heard, where together a common agenda is defined. Creating such situations in the simplest way possible, and then leveraging them, is one of Lari's skills. By framing them within organizations, from KAC to the HF and the Zero Carbon Cultural Centre, Lari not only enables a conduit for funding but also generates authority and meaning out of an established identity.

The Global Governance of Housing and Other Contexts

Lari's active and motivating concern for the people of Pakistan, the majority of whom are impoverished and disenfranchised, has a long personal history that is embedded in the global and national narratives in which she operated. The presidency of Zulfikar Ali Bhutto (1971–73)

[4] Shanaz Ramzi, "How Karavan was Born," Heritage Foundation of Pakistan, accessed August 16, 2022, https://www.heritagefoundationpak.org/Page/1585/How-Karavan-Started-How-Karavan-was-Born-by-Shanaz-Ramzi-Karavan-to-Somewhere-by-Sahar-Ali-The-Lady-%C2%B4.

[5] Farheen Abdullah, "Karavan Karachi Streetfest and Cleaning of Historic Facades," *Youlin Magazine*, May 10, 2019, https://www.youlinmagazine.com/article/karavan-karachi-streetfest-and-cleaning-of-historic-facades/MTQ3MQ, and, Suhail Zaheer Lari, "Heritage," Suhail Lari Pakistan, accessed July 28, 2022, https://www.suhaillaripakistan.com/chapters/Heritage/.

[6] Natasha Levy, "Yasmeen Lari works with impoverished villagers to re-pave Karachi's old town," *dezeen*, November 5, 2021, https://www.dezeen.com/2021/11/05/yasmeen-lari-heritage-foundation-pakistan-terracotta-tiles/#.

[7] Yasmeen Lari in conversation with the author, August 4, 2022.

initiated changes in Pakistan that transformed the architectural climate of the country in a way that endured beyond his short term in power. He had won the election through the slogan *roti, kapra, aur makaan*— food, clothing, and shelter—and low-income housing became a priority. "This was the heyday of activism and addressing issues related to the ground realities of the majority—the poor people of Pakistan."[8] Lari, along with peers like Habib Fida Ali and Arif Hasan[9] who had also set up their offices in the 1960s, flourished. She was commissioned to work on various schemes in Karachi, some supported by the UN alongside national funding. It was her assignment to the social housing development at Angoori Bagh in Lahore in 1975, however, that brought her onto the global stage. Nominated for the first Aga Khan Award for Architecture in 1978–80 and featured in the second Venice Architecture Biennale in 1982,[10] for example, it identified her outside Pakistan as an expert in the field of housing for the poor.

Honoring the right to housing enshrined in the 1948 Universal Declaration of Human Rights, the global governance of housing began with the UN, "the central site of action in the post-war [post-partition] era,"[11] The networks set up at large-scale events hosted by the UN and its subsidiaries enabled the development and sharing of research, norms, standards, and funding[12] that could be used to direct national policy as well as provide a supportive framework outside it at times of local complexity. In 1976, Lari was in Vancouver at the first UN Habitat Conference on Human Settlement, where she attended the Forum for NGO representatives. This was her earliest encounter with Hasan Fathy, she says, whose work introduced her to mud as a viable building material.[13] A directive published afterwards details the event: "More than 5,000 participants from 90 countries took part in plenary sessions, workshops, film and slideshows... Among the principal topics of discussion were: self-help and low cost housing, land policy, participation, appropriate technology... [with] attention to the fact that 'the world's resources are limited and need care and maintenance; they have to be distributed more equally among and within nations.'"[14]

Against this backdrop, Lari's work for low-income groups became the subject of study at the Aga Khan Program on Architecture at MIT, and she was invited to lecture there in 1981.[15] Prior to that, her presence had been requested at an important meeting in France, held in April 1978. "I suspect it was due to the design of the Angoori Bagh Housing that I was invited to the first Aga Khan Award seminar which was held at Aiglemont. I recall that there were only 30 odd participants who had been invited to discuss the state of architecture in Muslim countries. The group of luminaries included Hasan Fathy, Nader Ardalan, Charles Correa, Professor Oleg Grabar (Harvard) and Bill Porter (MIT) ..."[16] At the meeting, Lari proposed that the first Aga Khan Award

8 Fauzia Qureshi, "Lahore, Architecture and Architects of the 1970s," in *Pakistan's Radioactive Decade*, eds. Niilofur Farrukh, Amin Gulgee, John McCarry (Oxford: Oxford University Press, 2019), 67.

9 Niilofur Farrukh, Amin Gulgee, John McCarry, eds., *Pakistan's Radioactive Decade* (Oxford: Oxford University Press, 2019), 57–58.

10 See Paolo Portoghesi, *Architettura nei Paesi Islamici* (Venice: La Biennale de Venezia, 1982), 146.

11 Joshua K. Leon, "The global governance of housing: 1945–2016," *Planning Perspectives* 36, no. 3 (2021): 475–95.

12 Ibid., 481.

13 In conversation with the author, August 4, 2022.

14 *Report of Habitat: United Nations Conference on Human Settlements, Vancouver, 31 May– 11 June 1976* (New York: United Nations), 182, accessed July 21, 2022, https:// digitallibrary.un.org/ record/793768.

15 Suhail Zaheer Lari, "Slums," Suhail Lari Pakistan, accessed July 28, 2022, https://www.suhaillari pakistan.com/chapters /Slums/.

16 Yasmeen Lari, "Part II: My Un-learning Phase and the Angoori Bagh Project," *Architecture Design Art* VIII, no. 32, ed. Maria Aslam (Karachi: ArchWorks, 2015): 51.

for Architecture ceremony be held in Pakistan at the Shalimar Gardens in Lahore in 1980.

Defining the Profession

"After the award ceremony, as President of Institute of Architects Pakistan (IAP), along with Suhail, I had the privilege of hosting a dinner in honour of His Highness, Princess Salimah and the Aga Khan entourage," recalls Lari.[17] The same year, 1980, Lari enacted two campaigning positions through the mechanisms of two different institutions. The first was the HF, which she founded with her husband, initially to document and promote awareness of Pakistan's built heritage, and the second was the IAP. Appalled by the low status of architects in Pakistan and concerned about corruption and the abuse of the title of architect, she took on several executive roles: "Beginning my forays into establishing architects' status was by being elected as President of the Institute of Architects, Pakistan and Deputy Chairman of ARCASIA (Architects Regional Council of Asia). Later, I mounted a struggle for the creation of the Pakistan Council of Architects and Town Planners (PCATP), which earned me abiding foes among engineer-architects, non-architects and even architects."[18] In order to push through the legislation that would control the status and recognition of the titles of architect and town planner, and also claim for these titles a Pakistani as opposed to western education and character, she became a member of General Zia's Majlis-e-Shura (parliament).

Her move was ultimately successful, and in 1983 she became the inaugural Chairperson of PCATP.[19] In that capacity, she organized the first Conference of Architects and Town Planners of Islamic Countries in Lahore, in 1984, which was attended by 350 delegates. A persistent theme throughout the papers was what Lari described as a striving "for the creation of a built environment which is representative of our cultural and ideological roots and the nation's aspirations" as, in her welcome address, Lari outlined the themes of the conference: "Conservation of our architectural heritage, the adaption of this heritage to current needs and the challenge of town planning in Islamic countries."[20]

Return to Heritage Concerns

"I had hardly any interaction with UNESCO until 2002, the same year that HF was given the UN Recognition Award for promotion of a culture of peace. In 2000 I had decided to retire from architectural practice and concentrate on research and writing. […] When I received an email from the UNESCO Islamabad Office inviting me to discuss a project on

17 Ibid.

18 Yasmeen Lari, "Making of a Legend," *Architecture Design Art* VIII, no. 32, ed. Maria Aslam (Karachi: ArchWorks, 2015): 17.

19 Yasmeen Lari, ed., *Challenges to Transformation. Built Environment in Islamic Countries* (Lahore: Pakistan Council of Architects and Town Planners, 1985).

20 Yasmeen Lari, ed., *Challenges to Transformation. Built Environment in Islamic Countries*, 12.

Cultural Tourism in Lahore and Peshawar, I was both unsure regarding my own availability and also hesitant knowing the usual fate of reports that mostly gather dust on shelves."[21]

In the end, this invitation led to Lari becoming National Advisor for the World Heritage Site of Lahore Fort in 2003, a job which took her out of Karachi and into the field. "It was a very interesting period in my life, I was there for about three years, more or less. There was an amazing woman there who was the director, Ingeborg Breines, a great feminist, we hit it off very well. I went and it was very, very fruitful, I learnt a lot. [...] Working at the Fort helped me later, especially with the use of lime, which I learnt there—I had no idea before that. What I learnt I took to the earthquake area."[22]

Lari was still at the Fort when a massive earthquake in the northern mountains created a national disaster in 2005, to which she felt compelled to respond. Drawing together the knowledge and deep experience gained over forty years she traveled far, to the Siran Valley and into the heart of a completely new environment, which she read, as always, from what seem like first principles. In doing so, she intuitively marshaled her architectural knowledge of vernacular materials and construction techniques gained through her heritage work, her ability to mobilize people, those on the ground and those holding influential positions, through her administering and managing of various organizations, and the means to develop and apply a vision through a charisma sharpened on stages ranging from the global to the intimate.

[21] Ingeborg Breines and Hans d'Orville, eds., *60 Women Contributing to the 60 Years of UNESCO. Constructing the Foundations of Peace* (Paris: UNESCO, 2006), 134.

[22] Yasmeen Lari in conversation with the author, August 4, 2022.

Recognition for Built Heritage: A Continuing Struggle

Anila Naeem

Introduction

Heritage recognition and protection have remained an undermined aspect in the overall management of built environment in Pakistan. Defined through its constitution as 'The Islamic Republic of Pakistan,' the national ideology is framed around principles that reflect Islamic practices and Muslim cultures. However, within the geographic boundaries forming Pakistan today, there exist a diverse range of ethnicities, socio-cultural traditions, and varying religious practices based on deep-rooted historic influences. Within the realm of this diversified mosaic of cultural and historic traditions, it is impossible to achieve a unified vision for heritage recognition on the basis of religious and socio-cultural values, reflecting an identity that could be unanimously acceptable by the entire nation. Even after seven decades of Pakistan's creation, the policymakers still struggle with the challenge of defining the scope and framework of heritage management, unable to ascertain what should be acknowledged, and what would be politically incorrect to be given its due recognition. Nevertheless, the overwhelming legacy of historically dominant religious and political influences, left behind in the form of an incredibly rich and valuable built heritage, simply cannot be denied their rightful recognition as historic sites of national significance. Within this paradox, an often-ignored component is the built heritage of the colonial period, particularly in the urban centers of Pakistan.

Karachi, being a city that grew to become an economic hub under colonial rule, suffers from a lack of attention and intention to protect its historic fabric, perhaps due to an association as a reminder of colonized suppression. This perception, however, has been redefined in current interpretations and narratives that campaign for the need to protect Karachi's rapidly vanishing heritage legacy. In this context, the contributions of the not-for-profit organization, the Heritage Foundation, led by architect Yasmeen Lari, are considered as groundbreaking initiatives—bringing in a perspective that played a vital role in getting the city's historic center under the radar of heritage preservation consciousness at the provincial and local government level.

A Signature Architect cum Heritage Conservation Icon

A discussion on heritage protection practices in Pakistan would not be complete without the mention of Yasmeen Lari, perhaps the most celebrated and internationally recognized architect from the country. Among the many feathers in her cap are: the first foreign-qualified woman architect of Pakistan graduating from the Oxford School of Architecture (now Oxford Brookes University) in 1963, the first Chairperson of the Pakistan Council of Architects and Town Planners (PCATP) in 1983, the Sitara-e-Imtiaz (The Star of Excellence) in 2006, the Hilal-e-Imtiaz (The Crescent of Excellence) in 2014, etc.; her contributions in the field of heritage conservation are widely recognized, fetching her the UN Recognition Award 2002 for the Promotion of Culture and Peace and the Fukuoka Prize for Asian Art and Culture in 2016.

Contributing to the profession as a practicing architect, Yasmeen Lari designed many landmark projects in Karachi, including the Taj Mahal Hotel, the Finance and Trade Centre, the PSO House, and the ABN Amro Bank. After over a decade of thriving architectural practice, her focus gradually shifted to heritage protection, when she and her husband co-founded the Heritage Foundation in 1980, undertaking heritage research and conservation projects. Ever since, she has had the privilege of being appointed as UNESCO's consultant on various projects at World Heritage Sites, including Mohenjo-daro, Makli Hills, and the Lahore Fort. Even though she had officially declared her retirement from practice in 2000, her enthusiasm and zeal for heritage have never diffused. Through the Heritage Foundation platform, several initiatives have been consecutively launched for raising public awareness towards the safeguarding of heritage and promoting vernacular building materials and construction techniques. Among these, the most noteworthy and impactfully visible are the KaravanKarachi Street Festivals (2001), KaravanPakistan (2004), disaster relief and rehabilitation initiatives (2005, 2010, 2020, 2022), the promotion of zero-carbon construction, the LOC Lari OctaGreen, etc., that received continuing support by national and international agencies. Since then, the Heritage Foundation has enjoyed an uncontested status as a well-recognized and trusted organization, receiving financial support for its various projects from UNESCO, the US Ambassador's Fund, German government funds, the Prince Claus Fund of the Netherlands, Spiritual Chords (South Africa), Republic of Korea Funds-in-Trust, INTBAU, and many others.

Among Yasmeen Lari's numerous contributions in the domain of heritage conservation, the initiation of the National Register of Historic Places may be seen as a pioneering work that raised awareness for recognizing the urban historic areas of Karachi as worthy of preservation. The process started by first bringing the Sindh Cultural Heritage Preservation Act 1994 to the table; following the enactment of this law, the Heritage Advisory Committee received notification and the process of heritage enlistments took place. The roles of the Heritage Foundation and Yasmeen Lari remained instrumental in these developments, as she served as a member of the Heritage Advisory Committee, as well as the Director of the Heritage Foundation.

Monuments to Urban Heritage—A Paradigm Shift in Heritage Recognition

For almost three decades now, the Sindh Cultural Heritage Preservation Act (SCHPA) 1994 has remained a key piece of legislation for the province of Sindh, Pakistan, providing a legal base for heritage protection. This provincial legislation proved to be a turning point in the identification and recognition of culturally, historically, and architecturally significant properties and sites, establishing a precedent for heritage enlistments to progress beyond monument-centric notifications at a national level under the Antiquities Act 1975, except for a few properties representing colonial period urban development in Lahore that were given protection under the Punjab Special (Premises) Ordinance 1985.[1]

The Enactment of SCHPA 1994 in Sindh Province led to extensive heritage listings in Karachi; the first round being undertaken by the Heritage Foundation in 1995–97, covering around six hundred properties. The process further extended in 2011–18 through the efforts of the Heritage Cell at the Department of Architecture and Planning, NED University of Engineering and Technology, Karachi (HC-DAPNED). The enlistments of the 1990s followed identification through random spot listings, leaving a series of discrepancies and inconsistencies in

[1] Anila Naeem, "The Conflict of Ideologies and Ambiguities in Conservation Policy: A Legacy of Shared Built Heritage in Pakistan," in *Asian heritage management: Contexts, concerns and prospects*, eds. Kapila D. Silva and Neel Kamal Chapagain (London: Routledge, 2013), 87–104.

the decision-making process. To overcome these issues, a systematic mapping and inventory compilation methodology was developed in 2009,[2] which was then used for developing comprehensive heritage mapping and database compilation, including not just landmark heritage sites and historic buildings within the city center, but also urban elements and open spaces for protected heritage designation,[3] extending the enlistments to over 1600 properties in Karachi, largely concentrated within the city's historic core. A substantial number of these have government (provincial or federal) ownership or belong to various trusts; however, a much larger percentage are private properties owned by (single or multiple) individuals.

The enlistment process involved an inductive approach based on historical and archival research, combined with the collection of empirical data through field surveys. The listing criteria incorporated architectural, historical, environmental, locational, and group values derived from the urban context, clearly identifying the merits considered for enlistment: architectural features, plan typology, craftsmanship, construction materials and building technology, as well as cultural expressions or associations. The detailed inventory forms also attempted to address deficiencies of the system through the inclusion of analytical aspects, thus adding value to heritage inventories as a tool for heritage management. Two important analytical outputs included 'value-based grouping' (allowing similar properties grouped together) and the identification of a 'threat level' based on the correlation of data on present usage and physical condition to help prioritize financial support and the urgency of conservation initiatives. The compiled inventory database offered possibilities to advance into another level of heritage management and monitoring;[4] however, owing to the limitation of professional capacities and management systems, the concerned government department and organizations failed to utilize this resource in its full spirit.

An underlying objective of heritage enlistments, as required by SCHPA 1994, was to enact a cooperative arrangement between the government and property owners. Evidence indicates that this desired outcome could not be achieved. An absence of mechanisms to facilitate owners on aspects of technical and financial support, further impaired by the administration's inability to prioritize heritage protection over market forces and overly commercial gains, led to neither a rigorous implementation of the law nor a willing acceptance of heritage designation status by the stakeholders. Meanwhile, forces negating the objectives of heritage protection often succeed in derailing any progressive advancement, pushing the process back to shaky grounds.

2 The Heritage Cell – Department of Architecture and Planning, NED University (HC-DAPNED) undertook the research project "Karachi Historic Buildings Re-survey Project" (KHBRP), in collaboration with the Culture Department, from 2006 to 2009. The 'criterion for listing' was developed under this research project, see Anila Naeem, "Recognising Historic Significance Using Inventories: A Case of Historic Towns in Sindh, Pakistan" (PhD diss., Oxford Brookes University, 2009); idem., "Inventory of historic places: A systematic method for their identification, evaluation and determining significance – Part I: Core data and inventory form," *NED Journal of Research in Architecture and Planning*, 10, no. 1 (2011): 1–23; idem., "Inventory of historic places: A systematic method for their identification, evaluation and determining significance – Part II: Case studies," *NED Journal of Research in Architecture and Planning*, 10, no. 1 (2011): 24–34.

3 The HC-DAPNED inventories are available as an open resource for administrators, researchers, and heritage practitioners at the weblink https://www.neduet.edu.pk/arch_planning/Heritage/webpages/KHI-Enlt-Qtrs.html.

Beyond Recognition—A Deadlock of Defined Directions

Safeguarding the urban heritage of Karachi through the notification of individual properties within the historic districts required an integrated planning approach, keeping in consideration the original essence of mixed land-use, i.e., having commercial activities at ground level (shops, warehousing, storage) and residential apartments, or, in the case of the business district, offices and other commercial and institutional activities on upper floors. Increased commercialization pressures and loosened administrative controls on land-use changes subsequently led to an environmental degradation. The original balance of activities got severely disturbed, with a drastic decline in residential usage and an extensive infiltration of warehousing. A high percentage of properties now remain underutilized or have vacant upper stories left in a state of disrepair. Disorganized and chaotic activities at the street level (parked vehicles, trolleys, pushcarts, street vendors), created by years of ad-hoc and unregulated developments, obstruct the right of way for pedestrian and vehicular traffic flow, making the visitors' experience traumatic and unpleasurable. Four primary areas necessary to be addressed for any environmental level uplift in the historic areas include infrastructure and services, street space management, street profiles and façades, and the imbalanced activity pattern. These aspects are way beyond the scope of current heritage legislation and thus require other administrative linkages and support systems to be plugged into the heritage management framework.

Besides the larger environmental and area-level complexities, issues pertaining to individual properties also range over varied aspects, including those related to ownership and occupancy rights, physical

4 The inventory process, particularly in Karachi and Shikarpur, was comprehensive and well-published; see Anila Naeem, *Shikarpoor: historic city, Sindh, Pakistan: Inventory and mapping of heritage properties – Vol. I & II* (Karachi: Endowment Fund Trust for Preservation of the Heritage of Sindh, 2013); idem., *Urban traditions and historic environments in Sindh: A fading legacy of Shikarpoor, Historic City* (Amsterdam: The Amsterdam University Press, 2017); Heritage Cell – Department of Architecture and Planning, NED University, *Karachi Heritage Buildings Re-survey Project* (Karachi: Heritage Cell – Department of Architecture and Planning, NED University, 2006–2009). This series of unpublished reports, produced as separate volumes for each historic quarter, was taken up as a collaborative effort between a public sector university and the Government of Sindh.

The Thaker Laljee Lakhmidass Cloth Market located on Fakhr Matri (Newnham) Road, Bunder Quarter, Karachi, enlisted since 1997, has undergone a property subdivision resulting in a portion of the original building being replaced with a ghastly new construction. A picture of the building from the HC-DAPNED Archives dating from 2011 (left). A recent picture dating from September 2022 (right).

upkeep and maintenance, property subdivisions for inheritance, incoherent alterations, and insufficient revenue generation, which all impact their longevity and stability. The SCHPA 1994 and its implementation have unfortunately remained focused on a one-sided emphasis on control—only imposing restrictions without offering any compensational packages or incentives to benefit heritage owners. There has been an absence of initiatives to raise awareness of existing heritage law, clearly defining its objectives, and providing channels for the guidance and facilitation of potential economic and financial gains for property owners through heritage conservation initiatives. Growing resentment against the heritage designation status of private properties prevails, with an inclination and a desire of owners towards delisting, demolition, and eventual redevelopment. Many misconceptions generally predominate, leading to an attitude that, due to the notified status, all responsibility for maintenance lies with the government, and the owners cannot make any changes or sell their property.

Inapt administrative mechanisms have become a cause for the rapid loss of Karachi's historic fabric; properties suffer from lacking maintenance, vandalism, defacing alterations, illegal demolitions, unauthorized constructions, structural failures, damages due to inappropriate usage, etc. Rampant violations are in practice; even though penalties exist in the law, their strict implementation is not followed. The overall 'State of Conservation' indicates ad-hoc changes without seeking the required 'No-Objection Certificate' (NOC) from concerned authorities. The alterations broadly fall into three categories: haphazard additions or removals, the replacement of original materials and finishes, and changes in the original internal layout. These are often inconsistent due to multiple ownerships or occupants, impacting the overall coherence of the urban environment. Lapses in regulatory control manifest negligence and purposeful vandalism, resulting in a substantial number of listed properties undergoing partial or complete demolitions. Prolonged abandonment leading to collapse and the consequent inclusion in the Sindh Building Control Authority's (SBCA) 'Dangerous Buildings' list leave another lacuna for possible demolitions and new construction, particularly in cases where delisting appeals are clearly rejected.[5]

Properties under private single or multiple ownership or managed by a trust, predominantly have occupancy terms on a goodwill basis *(pugree)*—a primary root cause of the decaying historic fabric. *Pugree* occupancy allows occupants to retain their residence or business at a negligible monthly rent, after having paid a handsome, one-time amount of goodwill money to the owner. In the long run, the property does not generate enough revenue and economic benefits; thus investments in its maintenance and repairs are neither done by the

5 Anila Naeem, "Evolution and Repercussions of Heritage Designation Process in Sindh: Lessons from Karachi and Shikarpur" in *The Routledge Handbook on Historic Urban Landscapes in the Asia-Pacific*, ed. Kapila D. Silva (London: Routledge, 2020), 131–48.

owner, nor the occupant. Legislative reforms are required to eradicate or officially abolish the *pugree* system, enforcing a changeover to standard rental agreements based on a 'fair rental' value deed. Long pending court cases on such tenancy-related disputes require facilitation for early settlement.

A change-maker, crushing all hopes for urban heritage preservation, is the Sindh High Density Development Board Act 2010, allowing high-rise constructions, which tremendously disturb the Floor Area Ratios (FAR) within historic areas—originally ranging between 1:4 to 1:6, now increased to sixty stories and beyond. The optimum utilization of such excessively increased FARs has opened a race for speculative real estate that leaves no room for a respectful heritage integration in the development process. The only workable option is a compromise between heritage preservation and new development, where owners are bound to maintain only the outer shell, i.e., keeping only the protected road-facing façade(s) intact and incorporated in the new design—an approach of the fake imposition of a hollowed façade where the spirit of heritage preservation is completely lost. A possible rescue from such a commercially constraining situation was the possibility of exercising Transferable Development Rights (TDR) through Section 15–3.2 of the SBCA's Building and Town Planning Regulations 2002, which were

The Kanji Building on Belasis Street, Serai Quarter, Karachi, remained abandoned and neglected for a long time, and eventually got demolished from inside in 2018 without acquiring any prior NOC from the concerned authority. A picture dating from 2007 from the HC-DAPNED archives (top left). The current situation from inside (top right). Only the façade of the building remains on site as of October 2022 (bottom).

unfortunately removed through amendments in 2005 and 2008 that excluded all details of its four subsections, and limited the option for utilization of unused FAR by allowing construction on available open spaces around heritage buildings within the same property limits—leaving no possibility of a convincing bargain with heritage property owners.

The Department of Culture, Government of Sindh (GoS), is the primary custodian for SCHPA 1994, responsible for the implementation and monitoring of properties designated as protected under this law. Considering the multidisciplinary nature of urban heritage conservation and management, it is essential to do capacity building through the recruitment of appropriately qualified staff and officers, including professionals having technical know-how of heritage conservation works. A permanent technical wing must be established, with trained heritage conservation professionals having the capacity to advise and guide heritage owners. Closer coordination and cooperation between relevant government departments is also desired. The current working mechanism under an overbearingly bureaucratic system needs a changeover to a technocratic, performance-based approach aimed at facilitating heritage protection. Often causing financial losses, indefinite delays in decision-making on restoration and rehabilitation project proposals frustrate even the well-intending owners who face difficulties in acquiring the required No-Objection Certificates (NOCs) and the appropriate technical or administrative support.

The key to a successful formula for heritage preservation is community involvement; this calls for proactive advocacy and convincing dialogue with stakeholders—making them realize that an

The case of Lloyd's Bank building on I. I. Chundrigar Road, Karachi, has remained controversial and under debate for the high-rise redevelopment on this site (ongoing), retaining only the shell of the historic building.

approach to urban conservation is not just an uplift of the physical environment and creating visually appealing streetscapes. If approached with appropriate measures, it trickles down to a positive impact on the economy and well-being of resident communities.

Yearning for a Way Forward

For a meaningful change to happen, moving beyond mere listing notifications and fragmented individualistic efforts is most crucial. There is dire need to invest in establishing systems and mechanisms that could sustain themselves with continuity and progressive growth. Strategies need to be developed for facilitating heritage owners in gaining benefits from the enlistment process, particularly in terms of their economic sustenance. Taking a lead from the Walled City of Lahore Authority (WCLA), radical decision-making needs to be done—such as establishing a 'Karachi Historic District Authority' with clearly demarcated boundaries, within which the application of the Sindh High Density Act 2010 is prohibited. A customized set of regulations for the historic district should ensure sensitivity towards retaining its original character, relieving this less than ten percent of Karachi's metropolitan area from the pressures of commercialization and uncontrolled development.

To regain the charisma of historic districts, an action plan is required for two distinct levels: environmental and individual property, first attempting street reorganization through community support, and secondly facilitating restorations for viable usage through technical and financial support. The lost balance of activities can be regained by widening the spectrum of commercial activities from just wholesale businesses to include retail shops, neighborhood stores, and recreational outlets such as eating facilities, cafés or tea shops that remain open until late at night; and most importantly reinjecting the declined residential usage in vacant upper floors (bachelor residences, youth hostels, motels, short-stay B&Bs).

To encourage the willing participation of stakeholders, financial support programs should be launched, offering grants, rebates, and loans for repairs and restorations, either through public sector financing institutions (House Building Finance Corporation, National Bank of Pakistan, etc.) or public-private partnerships. Competitions, awards, and exhibitions, organized by the Municipality or Culture Department, GoS, on an annual or biennial basis, recognizing the best practices in accordance with internationally established standards, can also become attractive incentives. In collaboration with concerned departments and organizations (Water and Sewerage Board, Electric Supply Corporation, Land Revenue Department), schemes for subsidies (grants/aid), loans (low interest or interest-free) and tax relief (VAT/property tax) should be launched. Governmental patronage through revolving funds and endowment funds should also be made available.

Historic façades have a public and social ownership in addition to their rightful legal ownership. Conforming to this concept, the Culture Department should develop a module for a façade easement agreement signed between the heritage owner and the sponsor/easement donor, allowing maintenance and repairs of façades. These should be prioritized for areas with officially recognized, contiguous heritage streetscapes. The Department should develop an online portal for the easy tracking and follow-up of applications to acquire NOCs for restoration, renovation, or rehabilitation projects, and other objections or complaints, ensuring a smooth, transparent, and consistent decision-making process.

Engaging community volunteers for effective monitoring, by providing them with basic training to deal with the primary issues at the local level, can create self-sufficiency and long-term continuity. Active community groups for 'heritage watch' can be mobilized to report illegal acts of vandalism or demolition. Public access to heritage inventories and easy recognition of protected properties through the installation of 'heritage plaques' or 'commemorative plaques' can be effective, ensuring visibility for heritage protection.

Building political support, ensuring continuity in initiated processes, developing systems to ensure the strict implementation of policies and regulatory controls, encouraging public-private enterprise and collaborations for financial support, and, above all, involving community participation through interactive programs are some key success factors for heritage preservation. The responsibility lies with the profession, its associated professionals, and concerned public sector departments and organizations to collaborate and make collective efforts for the desired change.

All photographs: HC-DAPNED Archives

Karachi: Neoliberal Infrastructural Decisions and Development Crisis

Marvi Mazhar

Aspiring skyline of decay: I took this picture during my early morning long walks along the urban coastal periphery in Karachi; everyday solid waste of the city washed its course on the edge, accumulating and forming a layer of ruptured governance and lack of civic responsibilities.

Photograph: Marvi Mazhar, 2022

In recent years, the global South has witnessed some major urban development projects under the public-private partnership mechanism, which has led to a dysfunctional planning infrastructural status. This imbalance has created an unnatural disparity void, which has led to an unsustainable methodology where the power of attorney of projects lies with corporate companies, and access to the public is limited. Focusing on Karachi, a city by the coast/a port city, the Government of Sindh announced, in 2015, its intention to make "Karachi the first Smart City of Pakistan with plans of introducing free Wi-Fi, solar streetlights, and CCTV cameras for a more innovative future."[1]

With top-down state infrastructural planning consolidated through public-private partnership—and reviewing recent cases of anti-encroachment eviction drives in Karachi—the beautification of public spaces, i.e., the neoliberalization of public spaces, means only a select few can have access to such spatial arrangements.

Karachi, a conglomeration of multiple religions, sects, and economic divisions with increasing stratification, has consequently restricted the emergence of social sciences, art, literature, and cultural activities to a certain spatial and economic demographic of the city. As the city expands horizontally, the wealth is unevenly distributed. This strong symbolic segregation, associated with space in the city, has led to a mindset amongst its inhabitants that generates a discourse of exclusion. It is critical, therefore, to discuss public-private partnerships in developing state projects, a form of outsourcing through corporate mechanisms.

[1] Rizwan Anwer, "Sindh government intends to make Karachi Pakistan's first smart city," TechJuice, July 13, 2015, https://www.techjuice.pk/sindh-government-intends-to-make-karachi-pakistans-first-smart-city/.

Urbanity in the Global South

In a city as dynamic as Karachi—the largest city of Pakistan with more than six city centers and a population of twenty million at 2.45 % growth—"one of the problems with the built environment now is that it is socially antagonistic to justify the economic principles it has come to represent,"[2] and this period in current times does not have the luxury to exhibit naïveté in understanding the complexities of the city's growth. Here, spatial activism would operate like facilitators, using design not as an end but as a means to pursue a specific object or vision in facilitating.

It is important to emphasize looking at public projects through a lens of facilitating/creating socially responsible experiences outside our proposed corporate projects. When do we start noticing/adjusting the height of entry/exit steps of a public bus used by all genders and age brackets? When do we talk about grassroots change and bring activism within our design practice? When do parallel, nongovernmental, small-

[2] Stephen Graham and Simon Marvin, *Splintering Urbanisms: Networked Infrastructures, Technological Mobilities and the Urban Condition* (London: Routledge, 2001).

scale projects in vulnerable communities get noticed by the state as a prototype and design solution, as opposed to projects imported from the West or the global North that lay claim to knowing us more intimately than we do ourselves?

In her essay *Power Politics,* Arundhati Roy writes, "What is globalization? [...] What is it going to do to a country like India, in which social inequality has been institutionalized in the caste system for centuries? A country in which seven hundred million people live in rural areas, in which eighty percent of the landholdings are small farms. In which three hundred million people are illiterate."[3] This essay forms an important base for an argument towards the corporatization and globalization of agriculture, water supply, electricity, and essential commodities, i.e., a way forward towards pulling the developing South Asian landscape out of poverty, illiteracy, and religious extremism. Is the dismantling and auctioning off of elaborate public sector infrastructure, developed with public money over the last fifty years, really the way forward towards national development? Will globalization narrow the gap between the privileged and the underprivileged, the working and the upper classes, the educated and the illiterate? "Or," as Roy says, "is it going to give those who already have a centuries-old head start a friendly helping hand?"[4]

The response to the question—Is globalization about 'eradication of world poverty,' or is it another form of colonialism, robotically operated as a form of prosperity?—is varied. It depends on the situation of whether they come from the villages and fields of rural regions, from the slums and informal settlements of urban centers, from the living rooms of the burgeoning middle class, or from the boardrooms of big business houses, seated over authority and governance.

Cities that have inherited colonial planning legislations borrow from the same template to shape current national planning laws and strategies. Global North planning ideas—highly influenced by Dubai's and Singapore's hyper-modernist city planning infrastructures—continue to block the local, regional methodology of 'thinking cities.' This perspective, rooted in top-down master planning, is highly disconnected from the reality of most South Asian cities where rapid growth, poverty, and informality are the norm. It is this top-down approach that leads to what we currently face: an obsession with creating 'world-class cities?'

Edward Said noted in *Culture and Imperialism* (1993), "a brilliant formulation of how the production of a particular kind of nature and space under historical capitalism is essential to the unequal development of a landscape that integrates poverty with wealth, and industrial urbanization with agricultural diminishment."[5] Said's commentary orients us towards confronting an unequal development

[3] Arundhati Roy, *Power Politics* (Boston: South End Press, 2001), 14.

[4] Ibid.

[5] Edward Said, *Culture and Imperialism* (New York: Knopf, 1993), 225.

of the global economy, with its burgeoning extremes of wealth and poverty, and an accelerating pace of urbanization and environmental degradation.

Modern Mechanism of Socio-Economic Framework for the Reconstruction of Karachi

The 'smart city' discourse has become a container for many dimensions of the relationship between technology and cities. In Pakistan, to clear the way for 'development projects,' the government is constantly amending the present Land Acquisition Act (which, ironically, was drafted and conceptualized by the British in the nineteenth century to promote the commercial interests of the British for the presidencies in the East India Company) and continues making it more draconian than it already is.

A decontextualized 'best practice' in a form of transfer from north to south carries with it labels like world-class, eco and/or smart cities. This kind of placeless generalization of knowledge and application raises important issues when the parallel reality is the eviction and uprooting of submissive/subservient voices along with the aspiration to make Karachi a 'world-class city' because it pays the highest taxes. In the words of Samir Khalaf, "when the landscape goes […] it destroys the past for those who are left: people have no sense of belonging anywhere."[6]

"Cities are living entities. They do not wait for formal plans to acquire what they need. True, they acquire it in an ad hoc manner, shaped by the limitations of the financial and planning capabilities and capacities of their informal planners. And if the planning does not accommodate and support this informal process, the city bursts and eats up that which was formally planned."[7] The fact is that what is happening in urban cities today is not a problem, and the issues that some of us are raising are not causes. There are huge governance, political, and social decisions that convulse the system. Such developments create a huge professional market for all kinds of 'expertise,' but, as quoted in *Power Politics,* "there's a lot of money in poverty."[8] Who makes a professional living off of expertise in poverty, despair, and fractured systems?

But why did Karachi's planners and politicians not plan for all that was required? It is likely that there was an absence of anthropological research on socioeconomic relations which did not feature in the planning process. As such, the planners were unable to understand the social dynamics of the city. The other aspect may be that the planners and the politicians were more interested in the form of the city than aspects of livability, the result of class biases in their education and

[6] Samir Khalaf, "Contested Space and the Forging of New Cultural Identities," in *Projecting Beirut: Episodes in the Construction and Reconstruction of a Modern City*, eds. Peter Rowe and Hashim Sarkis (New York: Prestel, 1998), 144.

[7] Arif Hasan, "City & Plans," *Dawn*, December 10, 2018, https://csud.climate.columbia.edu/sites/default/files/content/documents/Hasan-Karachi-City-_-Plans.pdf.

[8] Roy, *Power Politics*, 26.

society. The development of large-scale industrial estates was undertaken, but again, in most cases, without space for workers' homes and the informal support facilities that they required.[9]

Developing Karachi through Public-Private Partnerships

World Bank-funded studies are among the most quoted in the world. Is the World Bank a dispassionate observer of the global situation? Are these studies entirely devoid of self-interest? Karachi accounts for one-third of Sindh's population and one-fifth of the country's urban population. A highly complex political economy, highly centralized and fragmented governance, land contestation among many government entities, and a weak institutional capacity have made it difficult to manage the city's development.

Moreover, according to a recent press release by the World Bank, "the Board of Executive Directors approved US$300 million in financing for two projects in Pakistan—the Sindh Resilience Project and the Solid Waste Emergency and Efficiency Project. These investments will bolster Pakistan's efforts to build resilience to natural hazards such as floods and droughts in the Sindh Province and will strengthen solid waste management in Karachi to tackle recurrent urban flooding and public health emergencies in the city."[10]

To set the stage, public and amenity space ownership is vested in the federal, provincial, and local government, with several departments governing the city through KDA, LDA, MDA, KMC, KWSB, SSGCL, K-Electric, Port Qasim, KPT, Cantonments, and Pakistan Railways, to name a few. According to Article 9 of the Constitution of the Islamic Republic of Pakistan 1973, the fundamental right of the citizens is guaranteed as the right to life, since it covers all facets of human existence. According to the Karachi Development Authority (Sindh Amendment) Act, 1994: "no amenity plot reserved for the purpose mentioned in clause (1) shall be converted to or utilized for any other purpose."[11] Despite such strong laws, sometimes we get into a precarious situation with state authority or people who own or control (or they think they do) space. The first phase is a No-Objection Certificate (NOC) for any activity in public space, long-drawn-out processes of obtaining permissions, paying rentals for such public spaces (which are made for cultural exchange notions), intellectual open mics, entertainment, and unplanned experiences in the non-curated setting. Laws are so open-ended that differentiation between the corporate sector, social interventions, and independent artists, and nonprofit organizations all pay for the unpleasant bureaucracy. As a citizen of the city, it is important to question the (re)claim of public space and to counter the Rights of Admission; with limited public

9 Arif Hasan, "City & Plans," December 10, 2018, http://arifhasan.org/karachi/city-plans.

10 The World Bank, "World Bank Announces $300 Million for Pakistan to Build Resilience to Natural Disasters and Health Emergencies," The World Bank, December 8, 2020, https://www.worldbank.org/en/news/press-release/2020/12/08/world-bank-announces-300-million-for-pakistan-to-build-resilience-to-natural-disasters-and-health-emergencies.

11 Sindh Ordinance No. XIV of 1999: The Sindh Disposal of Urban Land Ordinance, 1999, http://sindhlaws.gov.pk/setup/publications_SindhCode/PUB-16-000039.pdf, 4.

spaces, who owns and uses such large or intimate neighborhood-level spaces, either encroached or gated? Let us not neglect the power of the image, and how producers of Karachi's rich visual culture are also a source of narration and renarration of the city.

What does privatization really mean? Essentially it is the transfer of productive public assets from the state to private companies. Productive assets include natural resources like earth, forest, air, and water; these are the assets that the state holds in trust for the people it represents. The population living in rural areas is dependent on natural resources. The idea of 'privatization' is the term defining the act of taking away and selling them as stock to private companies, enabling a process of dispossession and violence.

Karachi, with its complex political power division and sprawled spatial communities, continues to be imperiled by a set of overwhelming predicaments and unsettling transformations. General views about the development and renewal of progressive projects in developing countries often describe it as a violent process where imported modern patterns, created in Western industrialized countries, are imposed by force on local cultures, destroying their values and traditions. Karachi has gone through a similar approach, where instead of a rehabilitation process of existing infrastructure, new projects have constantly been implemented as part of the 'five-year fiscal progress' of any given political party. It is the same when political decisions and developers assimilated to postcolonial elites brainwashed by imported Western images—where Karachi is only dealing with all short-term imperatives of construction, instead of resolved urban planning.

Regional planning gives the broad directives of urban and rural development after which urban planning can be applied to coordinate these efforts throughout the country. Development is seemingly equated with victory and looked like an ambitious task over rehabilitation, rearranging, and organizing. And that is the main dilemma with Karachi's progress—where constant development projects are conceived and nurtured. Even in the first phase of the 2020 pandemic, construction was the first thing allowed to continue while healthcare infrastructure was collapsing.

Here, when the government announces an idea of a project addressing social and formal issues, it is most ambiguous—the project looks more like the framework for a financial transaction. Even the invitation to bid suggests that the present 'conceptual plan' can be altered at will by the developer or construction company in a public-private partnership. This makes the idea of development a very subjective matter, as it will be altered according to the laws, and regulations will be curtailed according to kickbacks and underlined corruption.

When case studies like public improvement projects in Barcelona, São Paulo, Istanbul, etc., were shared as precedents to South Asian cities as the way forward, the government took the form of projects rather than plans and thinking processes. All these locations remind us that urbanization is pervasive, occurring in many cities, but it does not mean that such strategies play out the same in these cities or the forms of 'unequal and heterogeneous cities.' And the issues and problems are the same.

Outsourcing and partnering as a form of privatization of what would otherwise have been public projects have been on the rise for some time in the United States and Europe and, in turn, key joint venture projects are pushing ahead in several parts of the developing world. It is important to discuss 'planning' and 'engagement' in the global South and understand reflections from 'outside' of the field. Also, consider 'process' in project developments rather than external implementation strategies after all; specific geography and deep engagement help in planning cities and regions including rural dilemmas, not just filling gaps and temporary solutions, but producing new knowledge on a regional level.

Karachi is constantly in the phases of building and construction. Large formal housing schemes have gained momentum, while poor and vulnerable communities have become denser in the existing informal settlements and keep spreading to new settlements. There is very little coordination between the landowning agencies in the city on planning and development as mentioned above since the departments are split into many smaller departments, which makes it more bureaucratic and layered. This makes the livability standards incredibly low; so much so that Karachi was recently ranked as the least livable major city in the world.

Eviction is the action of expelling someone from a property, expulsion—this act has angered, hurt, and horrified millions of vulnerable communities around the affected area. And the question is: How did we get to a place where evictions of the homes and commercial activities of the city's poorest residents are made possible in a democratic setting? This leads to understanding and planning. Planning comprises many actors: scholarly institutional analysts, public policy and public administration practitioners, and many disciplines of planners. But with such planning, there is an obvious representation of privilege. The Government of Sindh aggressively started an 'encroachment drive' in 2019. Encroachment means intrusion on a personal territory, rights, etc., an act of gradually taking away someone else's rights, or taking control of someone's space, time, etc.

The Government of Sindh established an Anti-Encroachment Force in 2010. Its logo on Twitter has a unique tagline: 'to grab the grabbers.'

An act called the Sindh Public Property (Removal of Encroachment) Act 2010 was passed by the Sindh Provincial Assembly.

"Karachi's informal structures are what has kept the city going—providing everything from water to housing and education."[12] According to the noted urban planner and architect Arif Hasan, Karachi's informal economy counts for 30 to 40 percent of its total economy. But for the last year, Karachi has quickly been stripped of its character. An anti-encroachment drive in the city led to the dismantling of markets and shops. The most significant of these was the Empress Market, which housed bazaars selling every item imaginable.

The nexus between poverty and wealth has been lost. According to Bauman, this is caused by the division of the world population between the globalized rich that dominate the time, and the localized poor that are stuck in the space.[13] Public space loses its sense of inclusion and becomes a non-place for the poor and is subject to a permanent attack (agoraphobia), to the extent that plazas are on the road to extinction. Meanwhile, the rich build their private spaces exclusively for themselves: the social club, the sports club, the supermarket, and the closed neighborhood. The dual city finds its new dimension.

Co-Learning the City

Learning matters—it is the fundamental right and process of learning, from and within the cities. How we may think we know the city from historical referencing, but as cities change from daily interventions and use, learnings transform and evolve. Learnings also have the potential to challenge and transform the way of knowing/seeing urbanism, a shift from inherited knowledge that is taken for granted. Colin McFarlane, citing Steve Pile, states, "'Knowingness and unknowingness are constitutive of the city: each clads buildings in layers of visibility and invisibility, familiarity and surprise.' Learning is a dialogue between what we know and don't know, a dialectic of learning and *un*learning that has the potential to be both transformational and mere reconfirmation of the status quo."[14]

The projects mentioned above are recent case studies that highlight the idea of top-down policies and perspectives of planning. The images from various open-source data support the core ideology of how the government conceptualizes and reimagines infrastructures in cities with short-term planning methods through external investments. "Planning should be understood as a practice concerned with linking knowledge about the environment of action to projects of change."[15] We are witnessing an era of neoliberal globalization; the local state promotes corporatization and external funding procedures towards planning and intervention. It is now important to look at urban

12 Saba Imtiaz, "An Elegy for Karachi's Empress Market," Roads and Kingdoms, January 9, 2020, https://roadsandkingdoms.com/2020/empress-market-karachi/.

13 Zygmunt Bauman, "Space in the Globalizing World," in *Theoria: A Journal of Social and Political Theory*, no. 97 (2001): 1–22.

14 Colin McFarlane, "Learning from the city: A politics of urban learning in planning," in *The Routledge Companion to Planning in the Global South*, eds. Gautam Bhan, Smita Srinivas, and Vanessa Watson (London: Routledge, 2017), 323.

15 Clive Barnett and Susan Parnell, "Spatial rationalities and the possibilities for planning in the New Urban Agenda for Sustainable Development," in *The Routledge Companion to Planning in the Global South*, eds. Gautam Bhan, Smita Srinivas, and Vanessa Watson (London: Routledge, 2017), 33.

Anthropocene's relation between different negotiated viewpoints that help shape the pathways through which future planning practices evolve.

Concluding the essay on the idea of The Power of Interruption (People's Project),, an opinion emerges where the implications of such heightened forms of spatial and communal solidarities for urban planning are clear and work is placed as a collective, communal process. Cities must reconsider moving away from distributive power to the ideology of collective power.[16] Collective power in this sense implies active planning where social and private actors work together as societal partners in co-producing cities' infrastructure. According to Sudeshna Mitra, "advocacy and interventions, which acknowledge rather than dismiss politicized terrains of planning practice, offer more grounded practices of hope, to engage with planning in the face of power."[17] It is important to acknowledge community dynamics to prevent 'offensible spaces'; it may happen through participatory processes, to prevent excluding the most vulnerable members of the society.

The more important benefits of regional planning, namely of preserving building diversity and enhancing it, of creating breaks and boundaries between the different towns and cities rather than merging them into single metropolises, of providing clear orientation for movement between places and not just building highways, and of using the natural setting to enhance adjacent settlements. Karachi, much like "the Indian city, is growing, but that growth is driven more by rents, land price, and speculation than by enhancing productivity capacity and the

[16] Michael Mann, *The Sources of Social Power. Volume I: A History of Power from the Beginning to A.D. 1760* (Cambridge: Cambridge University Press, 1988), 6.

[17] Sudeshna Mitra, "A 'peripheries' view of planning failures in Kolkata and Hyderabad in India," in *The Routledge Companion to Planning in the Global South*, eds. Gautam Bhan, Smita Srinivas and Vanessa Watson (London: Routledge, 2017), 88.

Photograph: Zahabia K M, Women March 2020 Demands.

sustainability of even this limited form of growth is threatened by massive failures of coordination and infrastructure delivery."[18] At the most basic level, planning in Karachi has failed to deliver basic public goods, from sewage to transport and public health. "Karachi being [a] megacity, suffers from politicians and bureaucrats who have a strong incentive to retain control over urban wealth and votes; efforts at decentralization have been systematically thwarted and urban 'governance' reduced to a patchwork of overlapping jurisdiction, fractured lines of command, uneven and highly contested forms of authorization and porous legality."[19]

[18] Patrick Heller, "Growth and inclusion in the mega-cities of India, South Africa and Brazil," in *The Routledge Companion to Planning in the Global South*, eds. Gautam Bhan, Smita Srinivas, and Vanessa Watson (London: Routledge, 2017), 39.

[19] Patrick Heller, "Development in the City: Growth and Inclusion in India, Brazil, and South Africa," *States in the Developing World*, eds. Miguel A. Centeno, Atul Kohli, and Deborah J. Yashar (Cambridge: Cambridge University Press, 2017), 314.

The Gendered Impacts of Climate Change in Karachi

Abira Ashfaq

This essay is based on conversations with two groups of rural women in the Malir District of Karachi in an effort to understand the significance of their day-to-day labor and everyday experiences to climate change. The first comprised Hindu Bagri women and their Sindhi Muslim Khaskheli neighbors. Bagri women migrated to Malir from a rural district to the North, Tando Allahyar, after floods devastated their village and destroyed their crops and homes ten years ago. Resilience or the "capacity to withstand and adapt to a disruptive event" is evident in their migration.[1] Although this migratory resilience got them out of one precarity, it landed them in another as they face continuing socio-economic marginalities. The second group comprised Muslim Baloch women from Gabol, Kalmati, and Jokhio tribes who have been settled in Malir for over seventy years and now face displacement, loss of livelihoods, and looming cultural erasure due to mega commercial projects.

    Malir District is one of Karachi's remaining rural areas inhabited by indigenous Sindhi and Baloch tribes who have cultivated this land for centuries. This green belt to the south of the Kirthar Range, however, is fast depleting in size as agricultural land is subsumed by unbridled commercial development. Elite housing projects like Bahria Town, Defence Housing Authority (DHA) City, and Education City have

[1] Sara Meerow, Pani Pajouhesh, and Thaddeus R. Miller, "Social equity in urban resilience planning," *Local Environment* 24, no. 9 (2019): 800.

encroached farmland and radically altered the area's natural landscape towards the northwest of the district. In other parts of Malir, factories operating in flagrant disregard of zoning laws and an anticipated thirty-nine-kilometer highway further threaten agricultural productivity and the delicate ecosystem that supported a variety of wildlife and vegetation.[2] The city, including its rural areas of Malir, has absorbed migrants from all over Sindh, especially the submerging Indus deltaic regions facing a combination of poor governance and climate change. Escaping bonded labor in farming, exploitative wage labor in contract-based fishing, climate- and state negligence-induced catastrophes and challenges in obtaining fresh water, health, and education, many of these migrants settle in peripheral urban areas and, without state support, they are likely to enter new, exploitative labor conditions and insecure housing.[3]

Rural women of Malir engaged in farm labor are not a monolithic category. Their day-to-day experiences are constituted along lines of class, ethnicity, customs, caste, religion, migration history, landlessness, vulnerability to climate change, adaptive capacity, and chances at social mobility. Feminist sociologist Dorothy Smith theorized the "everyday" as a fundamental site of experience, organized and determined by broader relations of power. It is the "mundane practices and everyday experiences" where power and politics are played out.[4] It is in the everyday life of women in Karachi's rural belt—their physical labor and its gendered nature and informality, relationships with landlords, norms regarding mobility, access to state apparatus, and control over natural resources—that power relations are visible and capacity to improve material conditions determined. While these women's everyday work is intimately connected to the rural landscape, they are excluded from any dialogue in the community or at the state level related to rural development and climate change. This procedural injustice is a form of recognitional injustice as it invisibilizes their identities, their experiences and vulnerabilities to climate change, their ability to access recourses and paid work, and their capacity to inform decision-making.[5]

Their paid and unpaid farm and field work are merged into the category of housework and, "naturalized, obscured or trivialized as nonwork,"[6] its economic value is obfuscated in discourse as private despite its connections to the market, and its subsidizing of business as unpaid or legally unprotected informal labor. And while benefiting from this undervalued, self-regulated work, neoliberal policies leave people in the lurch and, when they face shocks and stresses, expect them to adapt and mitigate, and be resilient citizens without altering social relations.[7]

[2] See "Pakistan: Supporting Public–Private Partnership Investments in Sindh Province, Sovereign Project | 46538-002," Asia Development Bank, accessed on September 25, 2022, https://www.adb.org/projects/46538-002/main.

[3] Abira Ashfaq, "Understanding Urban Resilience, Migration, Displacement & Violence in Karachi," International Committee for the Red Cross, May 2020: 20–22, http://karachiurbanlab.com/assets/downloads/Understanding_Urban_Resilience_Migration_Displacement_&_Violence_in_Karachi.pdf.

[4] Beth A. Bee, Jennifer Rice, and Amy Trauger, "A Feminist Approach to Climate Change Governance: Everyday and Intimate Politics," *Geography Compass* 9, no. 6 (June 2015): 4.

[5] Meerow, Pajouhesh, and Miller, "Social equity in urban resilience planning": 797.

[6] Jacklyn Cock, "The Climate Crisis and a just transition in South Africa: an eco-feminist-socialist perspective," in *The Climate Crisis: South African and Global Democratic Eco-Socialist Alternatives*, ed. Vishwas Satgar (Johannesburg: Wits University Press, 2018), 212.

[7] Georg Frerks, Jeroen Warner, and Bart Weijs, "The politics of vulnerability and resilience," *Ambiente & Sociedade* 14, no. 2 (2011).

The Everyday Life of Women in Karachi's Rural Belt

Women's experiences as local and migrant farmers in Malir are seldom recorded, yet they have historically done (and continue to do) the bulk of the work in the field. Some of the most tedious and detail-oriented farm work has been traditionally done by women at socio-economic margins—picking cotton, chili, fruits, and vegetables, harvesting and bundling wheat, preparing the soil for sowing, managing livestock, and collecting fuel and water. A historical gendered wage gap has been sustained despite a gradual increase in daily wages for men and women.[8] Women are presently paid 500 (USD 2.30) and men 700 (USD 3.20) rupees per day of grueling farm labor. With farming output drastically reduced by commercialization and related water shortages, Malir's rural women face a loss of income and increased economic marginality, while men generally have a higher adaptive capacity, as they can venture out and seek jobs.[9]

Bagri Women in Malir—Climate Change Refugees

The Bagri community live in a Baloch village, Ali Murad Goth, just outside Karachi, adjacent to the highway leading to Hyderabad. Most of these twelve families arrived ten years ago from Tando Allahyar after losing their homes in floods. Over the years, prompted by monsoon floods each year, more families arrived. Presently they comprise a network of sixty people who live in makeshift homes and cooperate in farming. Bagri, Bheel, Kohli, and Meghwar are lower caste Hindus who have lived in Sindh for generations and comprise about 90 percent of the six to eight million Hindus settled in the province. A majority of them do farm labor and, because they do not enjoy secure housing tenure and are poor, they incur debt and consequently enter into relationships of bonded labor with their lender landlords.[10] This and climate-related disasters have caused many of them to migrate out of their villages.

Local landlords in Ali Murad Goth (village) in Malir have contracted with these Bagri migrants and given them space to settle and cultivate in a joint farming arrangement for lemons and melons. This *hissa* (portion) farming involves Bagri families doing the labor, then buying the output from the landowner and selling it in the market for a small profit, thus avoiding costly retailer middlemen (*aartis*). They bear the costs for fertilizer and pesticide while the landlord pitches in for water. The work is hard and laborious; thorns in lemon trees require vigilance in the picking process; they spend hours squatting and clearing the fields of weeds and loosening soil so plants can grow in a healthy environment. An alternative arrangement is a lump sum payment of 300 rupees

---

[8] Gul Hassan Kalmati, *Malir ki Kahani* [The Story of Malir] (Lahore: Shirkat Gah Women's Resource Centre, 2009).

[9] Ibid.

[10] Jürgen Schaflechner, "Betwixt and Between: Hindu Identity in Pakistan and 'Wary and Aware' Public Performances," *South Asia: Journal of South Asian Studies* 43, no. 1 (2020): 152–68, https://doi.org/10.1080/00856401.2020.1692277.

(USD 1.40) for picking fifty kilograms of lemons, an arrangement that even the landlord agreed was unfair, as the work requires multiple family members picking for several hours a day.

Migrant Bagri women are at the intersection of multiple inequalities—their work is "informal" and not within the protective ambit of labor law and, unlike local Baloch and Sindhi women settled here for over seventy years, they have no livestock. Baloch certainly face displacement as well, but their families can at least claim formal or equitable land title linked to colonial era surveys giving their villages legal identity, and more, recently village regularization pushed by social workers like Parveen Rehman as an anti-eviction measure. Bagris, as migrants, have no such claim. Bagris are thus pushed into the most economically peripheral and physically arduous forms of farm labor. Their socio-economic precarities are compounded by municipal neglect. Their children do not attend school and Bagris have no gas or electricity connections. Despite embodying economic and environmental marginalities, they are not involved in any consultative process on disaster management or rural development. Their socio-economic and cultural status is constituted to prevent any redressive citizenship action, including participation in protests outside their premises or litigation to challenge the injustices that add to their vulnerabilities, unfair work contracts, and other disruptions of their livelihood systems like illegal sand and gravel from riverbeds.

Climate change has led to reduced agricultural productivity and environmental degradation. Khaskheli, Muslim women who live in the neighboring village from the Bagris, find themselves being pushed out of paid farming work. Their mothers and grandmothers farmed and still come out and cut grass as a matter of habit. Younger Khaskheli women said they do their own farming—they tend the handful of goats jointly owned by them and the landowner in an agreement where they keep their milk and divide the offspring with the owner.

Women farm workers and other rural women's lives are entwined with their physical environment, and they are profoundly affected by reduced farm work, depleting water supplies, and diminishing pastures. Their everyday lives involve "complex tasks and processes that ensure the production and reproduction of the population on a daily and on a generational basis." This includes "meeting caring and provisioning needs, including child rearing, producing and preparing food" for which they rely on farm work, water, and fuel.[11] Their "everyday" is laboring in nature, sowing, harvesting, herding, collecting firewood, and fetching water. Women collect firewood and make several one- to two-kilometer trips to a community tap for water every day. According to Devi, a fifty-year-old Bagri farmer "When you cook, you walk and get water and when you wash clothes, you fetch again."[12]

[11] Cock, "The Climate Crisis and a just transition in South Africa": 212.

[12] Interview with Devi on July 6, 2022.

Through the gendered division of labor, women face the "greatest burdens" caused by environmental degradation. But they "are also potentially powerful agents for change" and can find solutions to climate change, including mitigation, adaptation, and sustainability.[13] Devi expressed concern: "Melons get ten sprays of pesticide." She explains how spraying is done, shows how to make small dams to channel the flow of water to rows of melons while the landlord laments that heavy monsoons have caused lemon leaves to curl and wither. Devi's mother said they need plastic tarpaals to defend against the rains. Devi and she have farmed in multiple districts in Sindh and have diverse experience, including growing and harvesting wheat and vegetables, and are at the epicenter of climate change and possess knowledge of adaptation and mitigation strategies.

However, the Bagri clan's continuing capacity for adaptive resilience in climate change and economic precarity is undermined by uneven power relationships; their intersecting identities as constituted by historical injustices and structural inequities are not recognized and they are on the margins of recognitional, distributional, and procedural justice.[14] They do not get agricultural subsidies and social assistance from the state that could potentially enhance their adaptation to climate change and capacitate them as climate informants. Those whose rural livelihoods are most damaged by commercial projects run amok and bad infrastructure, and who are situated amidst experiential wealth on the environment, are the least likely to be involved in technocratic, top-down decision-making. Neoliberal actors benefit from informality and offer no social safety net for adaptation to climate injustice. Invisibilizing the experiences of Bagri women farmers is a form of epistemic injustice and is reinforced by the media's presentation of powerful real estate interests as "development" and hence "natural, objective and inevitable."[15]

Baloch Women—Displacement and Loss of Customary Livelihoods

Since 2013, an elite housing complex called Bahria Town Karachi Limited (BTKL) in Malir District has displaced residents of forty-three villages. The remaining nineteen goths are fighting for survival while Bahria continues to use multiple tactics to expand their occupation, including isolating and coercing bigger landowners to sell, occasional raids in villages, threats of arrest and false criminalization of those who resist, and the construction of strategic, carceral-like walls in and around the goths that vex villagers and inhibit their movement. In 2013, without following process, the builders relied on help from the police to unlawfully demolish homes and occupy land.[16] Through administrative

[13] Karen Morrow, "Ecofeminism and the Environment: International Law and Climate Change," in *The Ashgate Research Companion to Feminist Legal Theory*, eds. Margaret Davies and Vanessa E. Munro (New York: Routledge, 2016), 380.

[14] Meerow, Pajouhesh, and Miller: 797.

[15] Katharine T. Bartlett, "Feminist Legal Methods," *Harvard Law Review* 103, no. 4 (February 1989): 886.

[16] Fahim Zaman and Naziha Syed Ali, "Bahria Town Karachi: Greed unlimited," *Dawn*, April 8, 2019, https://www.dawn.com/news/1252809.

and judicial complicity, BTKL usurped around 22,000 acres of land across villages in Malir District; the latter involved the apex court retrospectively "regularizing" Bahria's irregular transactions by giving them 16,896 previously encroached acres for PKR 460 billion.[17]

This elite complex is replete with implanted palm trees, foreign food chains, a golf course, two mosques, a cineplex, an open-air cinema, and stadiums. American-style precincts and replicas of world landmarks such as the Eiffel Tower and musical fountains are intended to leave diasporic buyers in awe. Local activist Hafeez Baloch stated that they cut trees, shaved off Mahar Jabal, a local mountain, and built villas atop. They blasted and flattened the Pawaro mountains for their Grand Mosque. This mosque occupied a spot known as "Shah ka takya," revered as the resting place of the seventeenth-century Sufi scholar and poet Shah Abdul Latif Bhittai in his travels to Malir. BTKL's golf course has damaged the eighteenth-century shrine of revered Sufi Hussain Shah Bokhari in Haji Shafi Mohammad Kachelo Goth. Historian Gul Hassan Kalmati has documented several antiquities for state notification and preservation, including a historical cemetery near Lal Bakhsh Kachhelo Goth in Deh Kathore, and a number of square-shaped carved tombs, quadrangular (*chowkandi*) carved tombs, and stone carving sites. This erasure of cultural capital, especially of spiritually significant spaces, condoned by the state, is both physical and symbolic. The impact is the obliteration of rural Karachi's Baloch identity that has been entwined with the land for generations through folklore and communal arrangements for preservation and resource sharing.

In duplicitous attempts to expand their territorial reach, these builders have also brazenly targeted customary easements and local rights to renew agricultural leases. In October 2020, Bahria blocked a local pathway that had historically connected Gadap to Kathore and were only forced to reopen it when locals protested. According to Hafeez Baloch, local farmers in various ancient Dehs,[18] by custom, recognize their lands as wildlife support areas to Kirthar National Park and engage in sustainable, rain-fed agriculture from water flowing from the mountains.[19] Kirthar is known to host fifty-eight species of birds and twenty-seven species of mammals and reptiles. Baloch adds that they now find carcasses, as construction and gravel excavation have ravaged their habitat.[20] Women at Hadi Bux Bukhsh Goth said their agricultural lease from 1974 expired in 2021 and, although they have the first right to renew, Bahria tried to forcibly evacuate their ancestral land to build a road.

The damage caused by such commercial projects is multi-faceted and gendered, and encompasses cultural erasure, socio-economic disruption, and environmental degradation. Builders and extractors have violated water rights in multiple ways; excessive pumping of

[17] Justices Azmat Saeed, Faisal Arab, and Munib Akhtar, CMA No. 8758-2018 (Supreme Court of Pakistan, 2019).

[18] Impacted Dehs or districts include Deh Kathore, Deh Bail, Deh Bolari, Deh Udharwa, Deh Langheji in Malir District, Karachi, and Deh Mahal Kohistan in Jamshoro District.

[19] Hafeez Baloch, interview by Abira Ashfaq, June 16, 2022, Kathore.

[20] UNESCO-protected Kirthar was designated a national park by the Sindh Wildlife Department in 1974, (Government Notification No. 74, 993-WLRFT [SO-I-DCF]); *1975 United Nations List of National Parks and Equivalent Reserves*, IUCN Publications News No. 33 (Morges, Switzerland: International Union for Conservation of Nature and Natural Resources, 1975).

water has lowered the water table and unmitigated mining has damaged riverbeds and interrupted the natural flow in rivers;[21] they have illegally dammed Langheji River in four places, disturbed an interconnected system of rivers, and blocked water channels farmers relied on for rain-fed or barani agriculture.[22]

With farming becoming precarious because of the loss of land and water, women and girls are the first to lose out on paid farm work. Women's social production, which includes planning marriages and expansions to the family home, has also been thwarted. Hawwa Bibi, a resident of Haji Ali Mohammad Goth, incrementally built a two-room house over six years in preparation of her son's marriage and now fears its demolition. Women in Arbab Gabol village complained that there is less land to graze and their livestock is down to one-fifth of what it was a few years ago. The limited mobility they did have within quasi-tribal customs, for herding and fetching water and fuel, has been further circumscribed by walls and surveillance cameras. "Women are affected in so many ways. Not just our lives and mobility, but our mental well-being as well," reported a young Jokhio woman.[23] Many girls stopped going to school and college because Bahria has taken over the old paths they used to get to school.

Women have been at the forefront of resisting numerous attempts to forcibly evict people from surviving goths. They are home when the builders arrive while most men leave for work. In April 2021, the women of Kamal Khan Jokhio Village faced one such attempt. They told a delegation of women activists of the socialist organization Women Democratic Front that they live in constant fear that their lands will be occupied by Bahria. During the attack, eight women fought with police and retired members of the army who were sent to add pressure. These men pushed them, hit them with batons, and made sexually violent threats.

> "It was the thirteenth day of Ramzan. We were told to go in their jeeps and 'deal' in cash or otherwise. There were women, men, even children, who resisted. They have been coming here since 2017 whenever they intend to occupy a goth. It is hard to focus on our work and if one brother goes to work, the other will stay to protect lands."[24]

Besides the on-ground resistance by women and men, villagers and their organizations have filed lawsuits, staged formal protests, used social and print media for advocacy, and build alliances to sustain a movement. An organization of residents of the Malir Indigenous Rights Alliance (IRA) have continued to hold the builder and the state accountable on many forums but women do not actively attend IRA meetings, protest or participate actively as litigants and thus face a

---

21 Naziha Syed Ali, "Wasteland foretold," *Dawn*, March 22, 2022, https://www.dawn.com/news/1681242/wasteland-foretold.

22 Hafeez Baloch.

23 Excerpt from a focus group discussion held with women in a Jokhio village in January 2022.

24 Ibid.

double marginality as the state also makes no effort to engage with women in a gender- and custom-sensitive manner.

Conclusion

Women in Malir are paradoxically most situated to inform rural development and climate change policy but instead remain faceless subjects of top-down climate governance. Feminist scholarship challenges such disembodied and technocratic policies and masculinist, market-oriented approaches that dominate climate change discourse.[25] It emphasizes that broad, pluralistic forms of knowledge be "incorporated into epistemological, ontological, or political understandings of climate change."[26] Positionality, as a feminist method, relies on "reliable experience-based grounds for assertions of truth."[27] This would necessitate a feminist project of political inclusion both at the community and state level and the centering of gendered and classed marginalized voices and subjectivities. Ecofeminists argue that it is only "critical engagement with the multitude experiences" that helps address climate change, environmental degradation, and discrimination against women.[28] Rural women in Malir who embody these marginalities must be driving policy around the environment and climate change. Their inclusion would be a form of procedural justice that could lead to reimagining resilience within the parameters of social justice. Bagri women are climate refugees and farmworkers with no social protection. Baloch women interviewed are at the forefront of defending their villages, but court actions to protect land, attending false criminalization hearings of residents, representation in media, protests outside of village premises, and building coalitions with allies are the domain of socio-economically empowered men. Thus, in recognizing their everyday—their experiences of migration, labor and resistance—and seeing how historical injustices and structural inequities shape their experience, we have a better chance at inclusionary, equitable, and sound rural development and climate change discourse and policy.

[25] Bee, Rice, and Trauger, "A Feminist Approach to Climate Change Governance": 3.

[26] Ibid.

[27] Bartlett, "Feminist Legal Methods": 884.

[28] Amy E. Kings, "Intersectionality and the Changing Face of Ecofeminism," *Ethics & the Environment* 22, no. 1 (2017): 70.

The Right to Housing

An interview with Raquel Rolnik, a former UN Special Rapporteur on the right to housing, by Elke Krasny

EK Following from your work as UN Rapporteur on adequate housing as a component of the right to an adequate standard of living and on the right to nondiscrimination, you have elaborated an extensive analysis of the financialization of housing. Can you please explain the effects of the financialization of housing and how the international aid industry is implicated in it?

RR We are witnessing the financialization of housing everywhere. It is now hegemonic all over the planet. While it expresses itself in different ways in each country or city, there is a common trend, which s the takeover of the housing sector, its production, and debate, by finance. Finance has, of course, always been involved in the production of housing. Housing needs resources. The novelty is not the fact that we mobilize resources for housing. The novelty is that housing became a vehicle in the circuit of the financial appreciation of value, basically, an opportunity for the surplus capital which circulates all over the planet with the only aim to get more profit, to be bigger, to circulate, to get more profit, to be bigger. The built space became a very crucial part of this financial circuit with the hegemony of finance over all other types and forms of capital and capital accumulation. We witnessed the building of rent-seeking landscapes instead of building landscapes for promoting and protecting life. In this process, there was a creative destruction of all types of other schemes of getting access to land and housing.

In the center of capitalism, in Europe in the last century, housing became a significant social policy by capturing part of the wealth produced by society to provide access to housing and adequate homes for those who could not afford property or land. Public policies were able, for several decades, to provide this. Such public policy was largely destroyed. Everybody and every generation were pushed towards homeownership through credit and debt. This creative destruction in the center of capitalism also happened in the peripheries of capitalism, but not in the same form. In the periphery of capitalism, we never had a welfare state and we never had housing as part of a universal social policy. But what we did have, and that is my point here, were traditional ways of getting land for housing and of distributing and allocating housing and land, which was linked to traditional relationships with nature and the process of production. All these traditional ways were completely destroyed and blocked by modernization, and eventually criminalized, considered not adequate or barbarian. Many other types of stigmatizations were mobilized to destroy traditional ways of housing. The process of modernization includes a very acute process of dispossession. This dispossession, including the historical dispossession, in the peripheries of capitalism, in Latin America, where I live, but also in Pakistan, is enormous. Such dispossession blocks access to land resources in order to open them up for extractive operations of capital. It is also a dispossession in terms of knowledge, of savoir faire in the process of building homes, and building habitat, in general, not only homes. As a UN Special Rapporteur on the right to adequate housing, I was shocked to see the level of responsibility international aid and international cooperations have in this process of dispossession, as they impose a model which is centrally designed by the finance industry with the real estate industry. This is a very powerful agent of the financialization of space, and the capture of all territories.

EK There is a difference between the production of housing and the building of homes. Could you say something about this difference and expand on ways of working against dispossession?

RR It is very important to discuss morphologies and typologies of housing. It is not by chance that they mainly look like plantations. It is the same difference you have between agribusiness and rural life. Seeing food as a commodity is the same idea as housing as a commodity. If housing is a commodity, then the inadequacy of housing to the way people will live and organize their lives is very acute.

Every initiative everywhere that cut the links between the financialization of housing is very important for building alternatives. This can be done in very different ways. Today, this theoretical but also practical debate and struggle has a lot to do with the discussion of collective property or collective initiative. Housing is not a plantation; it is the construction of an environment that provides protection and promotion of life. When I was a Special Rapporteur on adequate housing, I always asked the following question: What is an adequate house? How many square meters minimum? What material? Is mud adequate for adequate housing? Is brick more adequate or is cement? These questions are absolutely wrong. The questions are not the material or the number of square meters, because housing is a portal to other human rights. It is a place from which the person, the community, the family, the household, can have access to other human rights, to the right to mobility, the right to work, to income, to a good environment, to transportation. So, it is very, very important if this house provides to this end. This includes not having to be in debt for the rest of your life and to be enslaved by the debt, the new forms of slavery that we have now.
So, I think that the questions of adequacy should include how housing will open or block the access to other human rights, including the right to culture, which is a very important part of human rights, economic, social, and cultural rights.

EK In your book *Urban Warfare: Housing under the Empire of Finance* you explain how important it is to translate human rights into public policy and urban planning. Can you explain the links between the frameworks of international human rights and local public policies?

RR The way housing is organized in the world is 100 percent linked to public policies. One of the most important lies that new liberals and neoliberalism have presented to us is that neoliberal policies are designed to get the state out of the business and open space not only to the private sector, but to society as a whole. And this is a big lie, a big, huge lie. States, including public resources, public lands, public funds, and public budgets, are highly mobilized to open space for financialization. Highly mobilized. I think that public policies are central to human rights. You can have all the big words, very well-written, in the local constitutions. But then, when you go there, you see that the situation has nothing to do with those declarations. The link is established by public policies. Public policies promote inequality. But public policies can also promote equality. I am talking about the state, as a public sphere, in which the wealth that is produced by society, the knowledge that is produced by society, is redistributed. Who is going to get what? Who is going to lose what? Public policies, housing policies, urban policies, territorial policies are crucial, because they define who gets what. They define who gets access to the best locations and the best resources. They define what is the center of the gains of the policy. When I was a Rapporteur, I saw how homes were produced in a post-tsunami recovery in the Maldives by Canadian corporations. They were built in a way that had absolutely nothing to do with the way people were living. The producers of those homes took the whole gains of the operation. I think we should take back this debate and focus on the grassroots and local experience of people who have completely reversed the center of policy and put the people at the center. Housing plantations are not the response to the housing crisis. This is absolutely clear; it only leads to the financialization of housing. So, then what is the model? There is no one and only model. We should start from that point: let localities, actors, social struggles, and social organizations invent the ways in which they want to organize their territories. Do not impose a single model. That is why all the different initiatives, and that they are very, very, very different, are so important. And perhaps, in a moment in the future, all those initiatives will connect in a way. And that will be the new model, probably.

EK The right to the city has been a powerful concept in your work. Can you think about the right to the city in relation to the rural and to nonurban territories?

RR The formulation 'right to the city,' maybe has a contradiction. Because the urban model is the hegemonic one. I mobilized the concept of 'right to the city' instead of 'right to housing' to oppose the idea that a house is four walls and a roof. It is not. Seeing homes and housing as a portal means that we are not talking about the number of rooms, but about a place, an urban territory, in which you can have access to everything. The same concept can be applied to the un-urban, the rural. We are talking about the right to territory; this means the right to organize life in the multiple needs and desires of life. And this is very important, because we are talking about the massive dispossession of the rural. The process of urbanization is based on that, and it is still going on. We should talk more about the right to territories rather than the right to the city to have a broader concept than the right to housing.

EK Historically, the home has been seen as the territory of women. What does this mean in relation to public policy and in relation to the struggles for the right to housing today?

RR White men designed housing policies. White men related to the construction industry, to finance, eventually to unions. This is a very good starting point to talk about housing policies in ethnic terms, in gender terms, and in terms of who is benefitting from this now. It is important to decolonize housing from finance. It is equally important to decolonize this historical, patriarchal model of public policies, so public policies can promote equality.

Today, women are incredible leaders of housing struggles everywhere. Everywhere. At the center of capitalism, the periphery. In the housing movement there is always a female leadership. That is not by chance. The idea of care, the idea of protecting life, the idea of promoting and protecting life, the experience of care and promoting life that is, is a real experience for most of the women in the world, who take care of everybody. I think they provide a very important base for the idea of housing and housing policies based on care, based on protecting and promoting life and not profit.

The interview was recorded on Zoom on May 6, 2022, and edited by Elke Krasny.

Care by Design
Women, Change, and
the Climate Crisis

Anne Karpf

When Yasmeen Lari responded to the devastating earthquake in northern Pakistan in 2005, she found that much of the professional knowledge she had acquired in her earlier career as a prestigious architect was of scant use. She had already begun to unlearn it,[1] but now she drew upon and developed a whole other suite of skills instead. By placing the lived experience of women as carers in a climate emergency at its heart, Lari was reshaping the role of architect. Is this feminist architecture by another name?

Indeed, is it possible to 'design in' care into architecture, and might design itself become a process of care for both people and the planet? The transformation of Yasmeen Lari from "starchitect" to activist-architect[2] provides an instructive and inspiring model.

Care Work: Hiding in Plain Sight

It is certainly possible to 'design out' care, to make the experience of caring and being cared for ever more marginalized and invisible. And this, surely, is by design, for the many caring activities that sustain human life (the care of children, people with disabilities and old people; the reproduction of daily life through shopping, cooking, cleaning, educating, nursing) also sustain production. In neoliberal societies

[1] Steph Wade, "Yasmeen Lari: Architecture for Equal Access," *Gestalten*, March 2021, https://gestalten.com/blogs/journal/yasmeen-lari-architecture-for-equal-access.

[2] Oliver Wainright, "The barefoot architect," *The Guardian*, April 1, 2020.

(among others), however, these activities are mostly not just taken-for-granted, private, and privatized but actually secret—clandestine work that, as the climate scholar Sherilyn MacGregor has observed, amounts to a free subsidy given to people in power.[3]

Those who complain about carrying out such tasks unsupported or find them impossible to do adequately without help, or, like the Wages for Housework movement, demand reasonable payment for them, are publicly shamed or ridiculed—in part, because they have exposed the (gendered) labor of reproduction to the public gaze, challenged its representation as innately female and contested the idea that it is purely a freely-given expression of love and compassion. Ecofeminists have gone further, linking the exploitation of human resources to that of natural ones: the idea of the Earth as an infinite and unlimited provider of goods for the benefit and use of humans, they argue, is paralleled by the idea of female labor as an infinite, cost-free, self-replenishing fund.

The dismantling of state support for care has served to push it even deeper into the private realm and away from the center of public life and consciousness. Indeed, psychoanalyst and climate writer Sally Weintrobe has argued that we now live in a "culture of uncare," an economic system based on disregarding the very people who provide food, services, and care, one that encourages us to ignore rising wealth inequality and environmental degradation and exhorts us to participate in the undermining of any reemergence of care and social responsibility.[4]

Public debate about care, therefore, insofar as it exists at all, is today almost always about failed care—the care that is not provided, or provided 'poorly,' rather than that which is carried out daily, quietly, efficiently, out of sight.

The Production of Reproduction

The marginalized status of care work is structured into the built environment: its existence at the fringes of debate and public consciousness is reflected in its physical banishment from the center. Old people, in American feminist Betty Friedan's words, are often "warehoused" in so-called care homes, removed from the rest of the community[5] in what can feel like age apartheid. Our cities, too, are zoned, since the Industrial Revolution separated sites of production and reproduction, creating the home as a private sphere where women's labor was free, and the office or factory as a public sphere where labor was paid.[6] This "spatial schism"[7] effaces the work done by women in the home, for whom it constitutes a workplace but is now represented as a place wholly of leisure.

---

[3] Sherilyn MacGregor, *Confronting the Climate Crisis: Feminist Pathways to Just and Sustainable Futures*, online webinar, The Consortium on Gender, Security and Human Rights, 2020.

[4] Sally Weintrobe, *Psychological Roots of the Climate Crisis: Neoliberal Exceptionalism and the Culture of Uncare* (London: Bloomsbury Academic, 2021).

[5] Betty Friedan, *The Fountain of Age* (New York: Simon & Schuster, 1984).

[6] Eli Zaretsky, *Capitalism, the Family and Personal Life* (London: Pluto, 1976).

[7] Leslie Weisman, "Women's Environmental Rights: A Manifesto," in *Gender Space Architecture*, eds. Barbara Penner, Iain Borden, and Jane Rendell (Abingdon: Routledge, 2000): 1–5.

It is a schism not confined to city and town planning but also reproduced within private dwellings, where the rooms in which domestic work is carried out (the kitchen, utility room/laundry) are usually cordoned off from the communal heart of the home.[8] Such spaces are gendered, the kitchen considered a female domain (when Virginia Woolf demanded a room of her own, this was not the one she had in mind). More recently, the labor associated with reproduction has been recast as a troupe of glamorous female aspirational leisure activities. Whipping up a gourmet meal, developing a clever cleaning or storage system, raising super-smart children: in the global North these have now been reinvented as quasi-professional, almost competitive endeavors—still unpaid, of course, except for those few whose recipes for food or calm domestic order bring them celebrity and riches.

The zoning of public and private space also effaces those aspects of reproduction and care that occur in the public realm. As Krasny has observed, "All types of cleaning, mending and repairing reproduce architecture on a daily basis."[9] As a micro act of resistance to the over-aestheticization of public space and the obliteration of the labor involved in maintaining it, look up at an award-winning, gleaming steel and glass tower and ask who cleans the windows and how. Or try taking a buggy or a wheelchair through a turnstile or up a flight a stairs—you instantly become a 'handicapped' person.[10] The built environment disables you;[11] despite some local improvements, it excludes those people with care responsibilities who do not conform to what Audre Lorde called "the mythical norm."[12] Doing care work in the public realm can therefore often seem like a sequence of private struggles.

Discriminated by Disasters

Nowhere are the links between gender, care work, and the disempowerment of women clearer than in the climate crisis, where gender inequalities act as "threat multipliers." Women's sole responsibility for children and elders and as food providers makes it much harder in a climate-induced disaster, for instance, for them to concentrate on saving themselves (one reason that women and girls are fourteen times more likely than men and boys to die in disasters like floods and drought).[13] Their role as carers-in-chief also places them squarely on the frontline in the aftermath of climate-induced disasters, often having to set up house in emergency shelters or makeshift dwellings salvaged from the remnants of their homes. And yet, in disaster planning, reconstruction, and climate policy, from the most local to international levels, they are consistently and strikingly excluded or marginalized.[14]

8 Marianna Janowicz, "Kitchen debate: where labour and leisure collide," *The Architectural Review*, January 6, 2022.

9 Elke Krasny, "Care," in *AA Files* 76, ed. Maria Shéhérazade Giudici (London: AA Publications, 2019): 38–39.

10 Weisman, "Women's Environmental Rights: A Manifesto," 1–5.

11 Anne Karpf, *How Women Can Save the Planet* (London: Hurst, 2021).

12 Audre Lorde, *Sister Outsider* (London: Penguin, 2019).

13 UNDP, *Gender and Climate Change* (New York: United Nations, 2016).

14 Karpf, *How Women Can Save the Planet*.

Activist Architect or Feminist Architect: Is There a Difference?

Lari does not identify as a feminist architect—she wants to democratize architecture and calls instead for "a new activism among architects"[15]—but her practice, with its respect for women's role as carers, can certainly be read this way. Like feminist practitioners, she has reconceived the role of architect, challenging the social relations of power in the architect-client relationship. Professions jealously guard their power, prestige, and mystery, seen as the reward for years of study. Feminist architecture asks designers and planners to freely relinquish this power and put their technical and creative skills at the service of another group, the client/s. Not international companies erecting totems to wealth or palaces of profit, or local authorities trying to maximize density while minimizing cost: Lari's clients, in the second, late iteration of her career, are marginalized communities and the earth itself.

This requires a new kind of architecture, one resting on what Barbara Thayer-Bacon has described as a "relational epistemology,"[16] an interconnectedness in which the self is not separated from the object, the known from the unknown. It means being receptive to what the Other has to say and an openness to listening to them with respect. It also calls for "an awareness of one's own contingent situatedness and how it has affected one's view."[17] Such de-privileging of the professional self is not always a comfortable experience: it needs to "problematize and unsettle [...] knowledge, therefore allowing for multiplicity, dissonance, and discord,"[18] yet it is one that Lari has embraced with gusto.

In this vision, the architect has to decolonize themself while decarbonizing architecture. Lari's designs, rather than award-winning displays of individual imaginative brilliance, are co-created with the client, with the limits and capacities of the earth always in mind. Her job, she has argued, is to "create a canvas in which communities can participate as equal partners, making every structure unique using their own innovations, and not to give them a finite product."[19] The aim, then, is less to fashion a startling and ingenious aesthetic (although, as she has pointed out, aesthetics should not be the preserve of the elite) than produce a participative architecture that supports thriving, resilient communities and enables nonliterate women to take control over their lives, making low-cost, quality products such as bamboo furniture and ceramic tiles, for themselves and others. "It means that you empower them to become more self-reliant. We need to share our knowledge with other people, to bring that accessibility to them."[20] The skills that they learn help them to regenerate their own communities but

15 Wade, "Yasmeen Lari: Architecture for Equal Access."

16 Barbara Thayer-Bacon, "The Nurturing of a Relational Epistemology," *Educational Theory* 47, no. 2 (1997).

17 Ibid., 327.

18 Ibid.

19 Shanaz Ramzi, "Retrospective: Yasmeen Lari," *The Architectural Review*, September 9, 2019.

20 Wade.

also to act as trainers themselves, so passing on what they have learned. Conceived through mutuality, reciprocity, and shared agency, this is a reparative architecture, suggesting that care in the design process can help produce buildings and objects that encourage and facilitate care and which in turn are themselves nurturing. Yet if architecture, as Krasny has suggested, can itself become a process of care, it will need to overcome traditional goals, styles, and priorities— "Architecture with a capital A" and all that this implies.[21]

This kind of feminist-activist architecture, instead of chafing at the constraints imposed by the need to build sustainably, embraces them as part of the project of climate and ecological justice.[22] So Lari makes use of vernacular styles and materials, such as lime (which absorbs carbon from the air), bamboo (that sequesters carbon), mud, and stone as cost-effective and eco-friendly resources.[23] Making bricks out of dung or sawdust, she notes, reduces the use of firewood by 50-70 percent.[24] The idea of the planet as client can seem a fuzzily romantic one, a pre-modern idyll blind to the harsh realities of the 'natural.' The even harsher reality is that living within the limits of the planet's natural resources, rather than despoiling them (what Kate Raworth calls "doughnut economics"[25]), has become essential to avert human annihilation in an unlivable world. Architecture has a major role to play in this, since 40 percent of all carbon emissions in the world come from the construction industry.[26] As the current crisis in care is both interpersonal and planetary, architects need to design for both social and ecological justice. It is a stance to which Lari is drawn, stressing as she does the need for low-cost (aspiring to zero-cost), zero-carbon, zero-waste design and degrowth[27]—values that most feminist architects hold dear and that respond to the kind of extreme weather events, such as earthquakes, flooding, and drought, that the climate emergency has intensified and made more frequent, and which first brought Lari to develop her new way of working.

Fueling the Status of Women

No single design of Lari's illustrates more vividly her twin commitment to the needs of the planet and female carers than her design of the Pakistan Chulah. The open-flame, wood-burning stoves traditionally used in Pakistan and placed on the floor can give rise to serious respiratory illness and burns, while also causing deforestation and pollution. Lari's response was to teach women to build hygienic, smokeless, low-cost mud and lime-plaster stoves. Placed on a podium, the Pakistan Chulah elevates women physically, while it also raises their dignity and status.[28] Beautifully and literally, it makes the care work they do visible.

---

[21] Elke Krasny, "Architecture and Care," in *Critical Care: Architecture and Urbanism for a Broken Planet*, eds. Angelika Fitz and Elke Krasny (Cambridge, MA: The MIT Press, 2019): 33–41.

[22] Natasha Levy, "Earthen stove by Yasmeen Lari lets women in rural Pakistan cook in an eco-friendly way," *dezeen*, November 5, 2021.

[23] Wade.

[24] Levy, "Earthen stove by Yasmeen Lari lets women in rural Pakistan cook in an eco-friendly way."

[25] Kate Raworth, *Doughnut Economics* (London: Random House, 2018).

[26] Levy.

[27] Yasmeen Lari, "'We need to do away with the prevalent colonial mindset and the desire to create imposing megastructure,'" *dezeen*, November 5, 2021.

[28] Levy.

Feminist architects have tried to design ways of reducing the isolation of women in the home, creating instead spaces that foster community, facilitate interaction between different households, and encourage new spatial relationships to challenge the binary of public and private. This is exactly what the Pakistan Chulah achieves: it is a good place to socialize. "The stove improves cooking efficiency by around 25 percent. It also becomes a focal point in the village where women from neighboring houses could meet and interact, strengthening social ties."[29]

Scaling Down

Lari's work is visionary, in that, as other precedents in the history of radical and community architecture have done, it works for a non-commodified public good. What makes it vital and fresh, though, is that, like the many innovative projects now being developed around the world, it specifically addresses the needs of women and the planet too. In Gujarat, for instance, the Bhungroo, a pioneering water management system, has raised the income, power, and status of low-caste women, while Solar Sister supports African women to start clean-energy businesses in off-grid communities.[30] Initiatives like these show how effectively, if the needs of women and the planet are prioritized, gender inequalities and the climate crisis can be addressed simultaneously through simple but sophisticated design and technologies.

When planners and architects think about public space and private needs in these more holistic ways, they generate exciting ideas, in both the global North and global South. One interesting experiment that attempts to reduce dependence on motorized transport, but which also challenges spatial schisms, is the 15-minute city. Currently being trialed in parts of Paris and other cities around the world, this aims to enable residents to meet all their needs (for work, shopping, health, education, and leisure) within a quarter hour by foot or cycle from their doorstep. My own fantasy, meanwhile, is cities, towns, and villages designed with a carer on every block, available for the times when additional emergency or respite support is needed. We live in cultures that have fetishized independence, obscuring the fact that we are all dependent at some stage in the life cycle,[31] and thus requiring us to invent personal, rather than collective, solutions. Activist or feminist architects, by contrast, acknowledge our interdependence and try to build it into our physical and social structures.

This makes economic sense too. The Women's Budget Group have found that investing one percent of gross domestic product in the care sector creates 2.7 times as many jobs as the same sum invested in construction and is 30 percent less polluting. Care jobs, it turns out, are green jobs. What, they ask, would a society look like that prioritized care

29 Ibid.

30 Karpf, *How Women Can Save the Planet.*

31 Anne Karpf, *How to Age* (London: Pan Macmillan, 2014).

(paid and unpaid), rather than economic growth? That recognized the value of unpaid care, and gave men and women equal legal entitlement to paid caring leave, in which people have "time to care, as well as time from care"?[32] These questions, and others sketched out in various feminist Green New Deals, might seem marginal, if not irrelevant, to mainstream architecture, but the whole point of what Joan Tronto calls "an architecture of care"[33] is to place them center-stage and make them visible.

The scale of the transformative changes now required to avoid planetary destruction and create equitable, sustainable communities can feel so overwhelming (as I write, one-third of Pakistan lies beneath flood water and Somalia is experiencing catastrophic drought) that it almost inevitably encourages a kind of gigantism. Yet instead of fetishizing 'scaling up,' Lari's work could be called 'scaled down'— co-creating designs based on the local, sometimes hyper-local needs, of communities, in response to local cultures and environmental conditions and risks. Call it activist architecture or feminist, or perhaps "humanistic, inclusive"[34]—whichever label you apply, this way of designing, instead of exploiting human and natural resources, harnesses, develops, and celebrates them.

[32] Women's Budget Group, *Creating a Caring Economy* (London: WBG 2020).

[33] Joan Tronto, "Caring Architecture," in *Critical Care: Architecture and Urbanism for a Broken Planet*, eds. Angelika Fitz and Elke Krasny (Cambridge, MA: The MIT Press, 2019): 26–32.

[34] Lari, "'We need to do away with the prevalent colonial mindset and the desire to create imposing megastructure.'"

A Building Becomes More Beautiful by Its Usage

Runa Khan

Good architecture evolves and is beyond just aesthetics. It is about functionality, harmony in its context, play of light and air flow, optimizing its environment and setting, the impact it has on the eye and on the soul. It has been acknowledged for ages that humans are a product of their natural habitat, nurturing themselves in nature and of their choices, both as individuals and as a collective. As humans have evolved, we have chosen to exert further exigency over the environment, over our own nature of nurturing, and embarked more on materialistic choices.

Therefore, when we think about architecture, the search for beauty needs to be guided by a deeper understanding of human development, mental well-being, and how everything in our environment connects to enhance the individual experience.

Human consciousness continues to be a mystery to modern science, as to how it arises, how it functions, and its constant osmosis with nature even though we may think the identity lives within our mind. We have all noticed how different we act in a formal environment as compared to being in the neighboring café or a prayer hall. The surroundings, be it scale, function, or atmosphere, seep into our being and guide our behavior.

I have tried harnessing this understanding in my twenty years of working for the most climate-impacted people in the world, working with Friendship, a social purpose organization that today serves seven million people a year in Bangladesh. I believed that the aesthetics of a built environment have to do with its relationship with the people who inhabit or use it. The relationships must enable us to live better, individually and in our communities, and bring peace to our minds and spirits. Here I take a utilitarian approach to beauty, rather than pure aestheticism. I try to illustrate my view with a specific example of how these principles come into play for all the adaptation solutions with architecture that we have implemented with proven success over the years.

What must environments give us to help us live better? My answer is the following:
1. Protection,
2. Healing and finding spiritual peace,
3. Learning,
4. Opportunity & dignity.

1. Protection: The first step is for one to get a sense of security. A fear of danger cannot be conducive to rest and growth. For example, when we build a Friendship Raised Plinth that hosts a cluster village in flood-prone areas, it fortifies the land in a way that it can act as a shelter during the floods for all of the community, while housing thirty poorer families there all year round. The whole area becomes part of the river, but this is a sanctuary. It fulfills the basic needs of the people; there are latrines, deep tube wells, and a freshwater pond in the middle so that people have access to fresh water even when flash floods cause contamination and many times impact the food supply of fish. We worked with the internationally recognized architect Kashef Mahboob Chowdhury on the design. It incorporated the existing know-how, an understanding of the people, and water current predictions to make the best solution possible. Ten such plinths are functional today in our working area, providing rescue, relief, and rehabilitation for thousands of families.[1]

Similarly, if we look at the Aga Khan Award-winning Friendship Centre in Gaibandha in Northern Bangladesh, the area is elevated in a way that it protects the arena without compromising the natural beauty of the locality, but instead enhancing it. An embankment has been constructed with a water runoff pumping facility, with a green garden on its roof. It is made in a way that the training participants have an atmosphere of deep meditation leading to concentration and the ability to harness thoughts and carry these back with them to their homes.[2]

While the architecture in the north protects river communities from floods, in the south, our cyclone shelter (also a work of Kashef) protects coastal communities from the Bay of Bengal's fierce cyclones. While the

[1] Abu Siddique, "Elevated homesteads give hope to flood-hit communities in Bangladesh," Mongabay, August 2, 2022, https://news.mongabay.com/2022/08/elevated-homesteads-give-hope-to-flood-hit-communities-in-bangladesh/.

[2] AKDN, "Aga Khan Award for Architecture – Friendship Centre," October 2016, https://www.akdn.org/architecture/project/friendship-centre.

Friendship Plinth.
Credit: Yann Arthus-Bertrand

Friendship Centre.
Credit: Wasama Doja/Friendship

plinths get their beauty from the lush vegetation and fertility of the river's silt, it is the strength and weight of concrete that give the cyclone shelter its aesthetic quality. The stone-like façade welcomes the weak, the vulnerable, and the endangered to enter, to bring their livestock and possessions, and seek refuge from the brute force of nature. The shelter was nominated for the Zumtobel Group Award in 2021.[3]

3 Zumtobel Group, "Zumtobel Group Award 2021 – Nominated in the Category Buildings: Cyclone Shelter," December 14, 2021, https://z.lighting/en/group/news-insights/group/zumtobel-group-award-2021-nominated-in-the-category-buildings-cyclone-shelter/.

2. Healing: The second step, I believe, is for the architecture to facilitate healing, both for the individual and the natural environment. We have seen in recent times how an imbalance in the ecosystem can make mutations and viruses get out of control, effectively halting all of humanity. The 'one health' approach makes us rethink our idea of health, where we need to take care of people, animals, and nature to ensure proper healing. When we first started off with the hospital ships, we not only fostered awareness and intervention for humans, but the

The strength and protection of fair-faced concrete give the cyclone shelter its beauty because aesthetics come from utility. Credit: Kashef Mahbub Chowdhury

establishment started the process of awareness about all healthcare. We adapted to the harshest conditions, where no permanent infrastructure could exist, to innovate a three-tier health system that enabled the community to be in harmony with their condition and seek healing. Here the ship, or the architecture in place, is a beacon of change that culminates in better healthcare practices and preparation for everyone in the community, including the people, animals, and nature. Today, the floating hospitals dock at the chars (nomadic islands) and stay for two months before moving on to another island. The ships are equipped to provide services ranging from primary check-ups to complicated surgeries that address burn wounds or disfigurement.[4]

For the RIBA Award-winning Friendship Hospital Shyamnagar, we built a natural environment reminiscent of the coastal region, with an interplay of water and brick infrastructure, ensuring stability and health. The rising seawater levels in Bangladesh are central to the hospital's design scheme, which explains the canal that cuts through the length of the site, separating the inpatients and outpatients. Every section of the complex is entirely drained of rainwater, which is then stored in a tank—an essential resource to prevent waterlogging as the saline groundwater cannot be used for practical purposes. This water channel also assists in microclimatic cooling during sweltering summer days, eliminating the need for energy-intensive air conditioners. The spirit of the design was to create an uplifting experience for visitors, patients, and healthcare professionals that was reflective of both physical and mental well-being. With the interplay of light, clay, air, and water, Friendship Hospital Shyamnagar comes more alive in beauty with the

[4] Karim Naimul, "In climate change-hit Bangladesh, hospital boats keep healthcare afloat," Reuters, May 22, 2019, https://www.reuters.com/article/us-bangladesh-climatechange-environment-idUSKCN1SS03U.

Lifebuoy Friendship Hospital. Credit: Ørjan F. Ellingvåg

Friendship Hospital Shyamnagar. Credit: Friendship

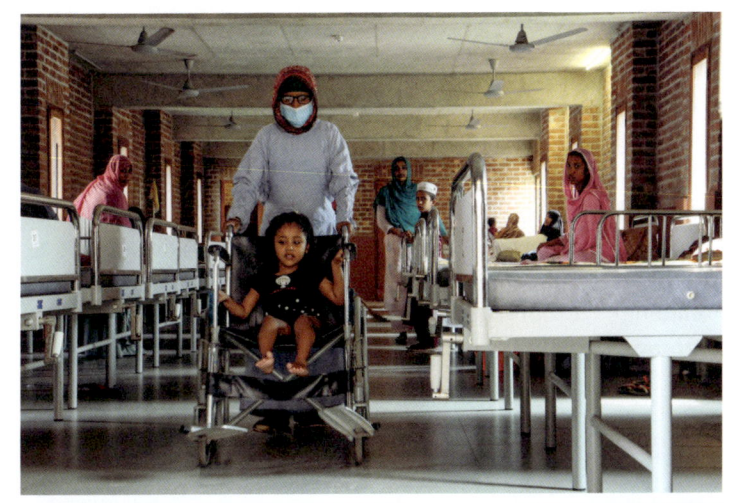

purpose it serves. It brings new hope of a better tomorrow to some of the most climate-impacted people on this planet.[5]

3. Learning: Our thoughts become our actions, and actions determine destination. Creating a better tomorrow thus sits on top of nurturing the right learning in people. Our interventions aim at producing the most conducive environment for learning in a proper environment. The Friendship Learning Centre in Cox's Bazar, hosting the world's largest refugee community, embodies an essence of aiming higher, in a playful environment for the Rohingya children. This two-storied bamboo structure in the Rohingya refugee camp in Cox's Bazar stands for learning and hope in an exiled community. Inside is a soothing and beautiful environment for the children to learn, and a respite from the harsh world outside. The Rohingya influx has led to the destruction of 6,000 acres of reserve forests. Many hills have been made barren in the area. So, instead of using metal and plastic, we built inspiring learning centers with bamboo for Rohingya kids to teach them the importance of saving nature and the environment.[6]

In the Friendship Centre Gaibandha, the local hand-made brick construction has been inspired by the monastic aesthetic of the third century BC ruins of Mahasthangarh, the earliest urban archaeological site yet found in Bangladesh. Structural elements are made of reinforced concrete and the finishes also include timber and stone. Offices, a library, meeting rooms, and prayer and tea rooms are included in pavilion-like buildings surrounded by courts and pools. It is an environment of remembrance, meditation, and team learning.

[5] Architecture.com, "RIBA International Prize 2021 – Friendship Hospital Satkhira," accessed September 6, 2022, https://www.architecture.com/awards-and-competitions-landing-page/awards/riba-international-awards/2021/friendship-hospital-satkhira.

[6] Shamsuddin Illius, "Eco-friendly learning centres built for Rohingya children," The Independent, June 27, 2019, https://www.theindependentbd.com/printversion/details/204916.

Friendship Learning Centre in Cox's Bazar. Credit: Md. Arifuzzaman/Friendship

4. Opportunity & Dignity: For dignity to be preserved where the need is, or to have it restored by our interventions, we must ensure that the right support is given at the right time. That it meets a true need of the recipient—as opposed to our availability of funds or donor wishes—and that the way in which we deliver the service is respectful. I believe that each of us has something to offer to this world, filled with extraordinary elements which we seem to take for granted, yet these are threatened with impending nonentity.

Once we take notice of these elements, work towards the realization of these gifts becomes a responsibility. This understanding flows through to everything we have built, keeping a familiar tone for the participants, so that they are not too uncomfortable in the architecture, yet feel elevated enough to aim for something better. The building materials are prominently sourced locally and brought together with natural elements. The technological inspiration carries with it the history of the evolution of a civilization and pride of generations of sailors on this unique delta of our planet.[7]

As we continue to build towards a world where everyone can live with dignity and hope, this article seeks to offer inspiration to work on architecture closer to the people, planet, and prosperity for everyone. Because only in the proper implementation and utility in a holistic sense, we find ultimate beauty of the mind, body, and spirit.

[7] Friendship Newsdesk, "A Winning Partnership," January 28, 2022, https://friendship.ngo/a-winning-partnership/.

Training at the Friendship Centre.
Credit: Friendship

The Stove Solution Yasmeen Lari and the Reclamation of Feminist Knowledge

Rafia Zakaria

In the summer of 2020, I was deeply immersed in research for my book *Against White Feminism.* One of the problems that I was looking at was why development projects whose ostensible purpose was to help the poor often failed dramatically in reaching their goals. One such particularly intransigent problem, it appeared, was the provision and adoption of clean cooking stoves in southern India and Pakistan. Various UN agencies and other development organizations had gotten together to identify this problem as one that existed at the confluence of environmental degradation, making women wage earners, and, of course, saving lives that were lost to stove fires in confined spaces.

Interestingly, women in China had also been provided the new clean stoves, ones that were not wood-burning and did not produce the smoke (and hence the respiratory problems) of wood-burning stoves. Those women had adopted the stoves, and while there is no proof to establish this, the fact that they had been provided by an authoritarian government could well have something to do with the lack of objections within that context. No such push was present within the South Asian context. An MIT study[1] that tasked itself with figuring out how successful the provision of clean stoves had been discovered, to the surprise perhaps of no one at all, that they had not been adopted widely. Households had failed to invest in upkeep, such as cleaning the chimney, so the more

[1] Rema Hanna, Esther Duflo, and Michael Greenstone, "Up in Smoke: The Influence of Household Behavior on the Long-Run Impact of Improved Cooking Stoves," MIT Center for Energy and Environmental Policy, July 2012, https://ceepr.mit.edu/working paper/up-in-smoke-the-influence-of-house hold-behavior-on-the-long-run-impact-of-im proved-cooking-stoves/.

time passed the less these stoves were used. Consequently, the respiratory advantages that would have resulted from proper use of the stove and from the absence of toxic smoke in confined spaces began to dwindle as the stove was either not used or used with a clogged chimney such that at the time of the study there was a statistically significant advantage to the health of the stove-using household.

Even more troubling was that stove-using households saw a decline in their living standards, and there was no evidence at all of a decrease in greenhouse gas emissions. Too much time was spent trying to repair the stoves, and the predicted improvement in rates of deforestation (because the clean stoves were not wood-burning) was also not seen. Other studies found that many aspects of the lives of the women using the stoves had been ignored by the development-industrial complex that had come up with the brilliant plan to save forests and women and the environment by the use of the stoves. Notable among these was the fact that the old stove could be made and repaired by the women themselves, that they enjoyed the daily outing to find firewood with other women in their village, and that many of the traditional dishes that they liked to prepare could not be prepared on the new stove. Finally, the forecast that the stove would free up women's time for wage labor was also controversial, because the jobs available to the women in most areas were low-skilled jobs like breaking rocks at a construction site. Given this option, women would much rather stay home and cook in their smoky kitchens instead of labor under the hot sun.

The Pakistan Chulah developed by Yasmeen Lari models the paradigmatic transformation that is required in the development community. Photograph: © Archive Yasmeen Lari

The story of how clean stoves failed is important because it highlights how development policy, dominated as it is by Westerners, fails to account for simple facts of life of those that it hopes to deliver from poverty, bad ventilation, pollution, and other kinds of catastrophe. When I made this critique, however, the solution of a locally informed and influenced collaborative project was a hypothetical one. I knew that locally informed and enacted solutions to problems like these could exist, but I could not point to one that would demonstrate the sort of intervention that freed development thinking into effective thinking.

Then I saw the new work done by the pioneering Pakistani architect Yasmeen Lari. To be clear, I have been aware of her architectural work as long as I can remember. Like Lari, I am from Karachi, in Sindh Province, where many of her architectural projects are located. I regularly drove past the imposing Pakistan State Oil building, a project that drew the curiosity of Karachiites for years before it was finally completed. I was also familiar with the Karachi Finance and Trade Centre near where I sat for my SAT exams years ago. I point this out to note just how significant an impact she has had on the aesthetic life of Karachi. In this sense, her work has endured political tumult, changing regimes, and natural disasters, to become deeply enmeshed in the identity of what is now a global megacity of over twenty million people.

These, however, are not the reasons why I find myself deeply indebted to and in awe of Lari's work. As she likes to state herself, the last decade or so has seen Lari move away from the corporate projects that took up most of her time, toward using her design genius to solve problems like those of clean, working stoves for the poorest of women in the most poverty-stricken areas of Pakistan and the world. In one recent interview from April 2020, when she was awarded the prestigious Jane Drew Prize, Lari bluntly admitted, "I feel like I am atoning for some of what I did. I was a 'starchitect' for 36 years, but then my egotistical journey had to come to an end. It's not only the right of the elite to have good design."[2]

Determined as Lari always has been—you cannot be the first female architect in Pakistan without such qualities—Lari has translated the transformation of her perspective into practice. Her exposure to the work of development agencies following various natural disasters in Pakistan had made her sensitive to how those who need help are infantilized by the development mindset. Outsiders come with an idea about what needs to be done and it is not always flexible enough to meet the needs of those who have been affected. Most crucially, Lari found herself skeptical of the 'universal solutions' offered by various development organizations in response to disasters or even as solutions to long-standing problems.

2 Oliver Wainwright, "The barefoot architect: 'I was a starchitect for 36 years. Now I'm atoning,'" *The Guardian*, April 1, 2020, https://www.theguardian.com/artanddesign/2020/apr/01/yasmeen-lari-pakistan-architect-first-female-jane-drew.

The clean stoves debacle, per which hundreds of millions of dollars were invested into clean stoves, was imagined as a universal solution for issues as varied as deforestation, to environmental degradation, to gender mainstreaming. What had happened with the stoves in China, it was assumed, would also be true of women in Indian Rajasthan or Pakistani Sindh. When this did not happen, the development-industrial complex, largely white, western, and upper middle class, could not understand why something that looked so good on paper and that had worked in other development contexts was failing so badly in South Asia.

Lari first came to this problem in 2014. Using her design acumen and combining it with her knowledge of local materials, she developed a different design for a clean stove that would also deliver women from the respiratory problems created by using wood-burning stoves inside confined spaces. Lari's eco-friendly design, which she named Pakistan Chulah, was designed to protect women from the many domestic house fires that injure women along with reducing the incidence of respiratory diseases. Using lime plaster and mud, the stove was easy to manufacture by local, nonliterate women.

Lari's stove was situated on a platform that is raised above ground level, providing access to better ventilation, and also giving women a physical iteration of being 'above' men when they are cooking. Unlike the other clean stove, this stove used agricultural waste that could be found easily in the area and varied from dung to sawdust bricks. These fuels are clean-burning fuels which reduce the carbon footprint for the cookstoves and do not necessitate women searching for logs for hours every day because of dwindling supplies. Since 2014, Lari has been able to create and supply seventy thousand such stoves. In addition to all the stated advantages, the stove project is knitted into the local structures because nonliterate women are trained as craftswomen and their knowledge of what is available locally is utilized to solve a problem that has been plaguing the community for a long time.

Lari's organization, Heritage Foundation of Pakistan, which has been producing the stoves, was awarded the UN Habitat Prize in 2018. The award recognized what had been theorized by development critics for quite a while: development solutions worked far better when someone from the community was able to deploy design acumen in a manner that included community members and their perspectives into the program. In this sense, the Pakistan Chulah represents not only a singular success to a single problem but also models the paradigmatic transformation that is required in the development community in general.[3]

One of the most egregious problems I witnessed when looking at how development programs were developed, almost always without local know-how or context-driven knowledge, was that the white and

[3] See Natasha Levy, "Earthen stove by Yasmeen Lari lets women in rural Pakistan cook in an eco-friendly way," *dezeen*, November 5, 2021, https://www.dezeen.com/2021/11/05/stove-design-eco-cooking-yasmeen-lari/.

western institutions that provided the funds for projects also wanted control over them. Those receiving the help, often Black or Brown women and their communities, were infantilized, if not literally then in what was expected or not expected for them. In this sense, the lack of resources faced by communities receiving aid translates to an impression of community members as incapable of solving their own problems and therefore inferior to the development professionals with their technocratic tools and expert-speak. As Lari put it in her manifesto, "We need to do away with the prevalent colonial mindset"[4] that this sort of thinking represents. Universal solutions, mega-projects that seek to solve problems all at once, are all examples of how communities in need of help are imagined as reductive and oversimplified such that the provision of one or another thing will suddenly transform their lives, free them from poverty, etc.

The Pakistan Chulah was one part of what Lari has called the Barefoot Architecture Project. In using local know-how to create innovative design solutions, this represented an epistemic as well as architectural project. This is key because unless the know-how possessed by local and nonliterate women was not understood to be as crucial to the success of a project as the charts, maps, and data that is the epistemic product of a professionalized development sector, there could not be a successful combination of the two. Lari understood this and the very idea of 'barefoot' architecture encouraged the paradigmatic transformation that put local knowledge possessed by nonliterate women at par with the knowledge base held by trained architects and development professionals looking to solve problems on the ground in contexts vastly different from their own western sensibilities.

Yasmeen Lari wants architects to be activists in this sense, using their design skills to create solutions for pressing problems rather than to simply build paeans to corporate excess. Her work is particularly relevant to a feminist movement that has seen the knowledge and capabilities of Black and Brown women in particular devalued against those of white women. As I have written in my book *Against White Feminism*, the structure of the feminist movement as it exists is centered around white women, their aspirations, sensibilities, and priorities. The consequence of this has been a one-size-fits-all feminism that is not unlike the one-size-fits-all development solutions that Lari has criticized in her manifesto.

Projects like Barefoot Architecture and the Pakistan Chulah in this sense also present a balancing of the feminist equation because they illustrate how Black and Brown women, whose expertise has been devalued or ignored completely, are once again recognized as having crucial clues to the solution of local problems. While Lari's platform cookstove is just one example, it is also the opening of a possibility and

[4] Yasmeen Lari, "'We need to do away with the prevalent colonial mindset and the desire to create imposing megastructures' says Yasmeen Lari," *dezeen*, November 5, 2021, https://www.dezeen.com/2021/11/05/yasmeen-lari-manifesto-dezeen-15/.

a vision that has implications far beyond just the provision of a clean cookstove that has health and environmental benefits. If anything, it demonstrates how knowledge and know-how need not come in the form of tables and charts and data alone, but exists in myriad other forms that involve knowledge of local materials, needs, potential, and so on.

Critics of colonialism have long pointed to how international development replicates the prejudices of old: white and western people making decisions about places they have never been. (Pakistan's borders were delineated by Sir Cyril Radcliffe, who had never been to the country.) Many of these critiques underscore the need for locally informed solutions that are developed through community collaboration so that the project will be successful. However, in too many contexts this effort (to the extent it even exists) is treated as perfunctory. Like any colonial enterprise, it is far easier to do things the way they have always been done and doubt the capacity of communities to have any useful information.

Yasmeen Lari and her work are important because it disrupts these hierarchies and beliefs. In this sense, her work serves as proof of just how wrong the colonial mindset which dominates development still is. The Pakistan Chulah project is evidence of what could have been done when the Clean Stoves Initiative began. At the same time, it is also an epistemic critique of what passes as feminist knowledge and what is excluded from it. If the actual provision of clean stoves is important, so too is this act of epistemic feminist rebellion. Knowledge is not simply what may be taught in textbooks for international development but also the knowledge of women who live difficult lives and are adept at solving complex problems. In this second sense, Lari's work redeems Black and Brown feminisms whose efforts have too often been omitted from the feminist empowerment conversation whatsoever.

Teaching Zero-Carbon Design Methodologies

Cassandra Cozza

Exhibition of the bamboo maquettes in scales 1:2 and 1:5 of the Lari OctaGreen and some joints made by the students participating in the workshop at LaborA. The group consisted of seventeen students—four men and thirteen women—from Italy, China, Iran, Turkey, and Japan. October 2021, Open spaces outside LaborA on Leonardo campus, Politecnico di Milano. Credit: Cassandra Cozza

A group of seventeen international students of the Politecnico di Milano attended a workshop on Yasmeen Lari's zero-carbon humanistic architecture, based on the mixing of advanced digital tools and maquette construction with Northern Italian-sourced bamboo. Students learned several of Lari's zero-carbon methodologies and had the opportunity to meet the architect and talk to her about ethical architecture and the future of architectural practice. Yasmeen Lari's Humanitarian Architecture workshop was one of the events organized to mark the awarding of the Honorary Degree in Architecture—Laurea Magistrale ad honorem in Architettura e Ingegneria Edile-Architettura—to Yasmeen Lari by the School of Architecture Urban Planning Construction Engineering (AUIC) in October 2021. The results of the workshop were exhibited at LaborA—a physical and digital modeling laboratory on the new Architecture Campus in Milan. The students participating in the workshop conducted the guided tours, transmitting what they had learned to other students, faculty members, and visitors.

On-field Experience at Politecnico di Milano

Lari's commitment to promoting changes in the world through architecture affects what she does and the way she does it at different levels and scales. Her architecture is a feat of activism, and she is establishing new trajectories of architectural practice based on important values that she translates into specific ethical design principles with an impact both on physical space and society. In fact, over time she has developed alternative ways of practicing and her zero-carbon humanistic architecture embodies the values of social and ecological justice. Teaching and disseminating—in and outside universities—are an important part of Yasmeen Lari's current work with two main focuses: educating future architects and training self-builders.

The idea to organize a workshop came up during a Zoom meeting between Yasmeen Lari, the former AUIC School Dean Ilaria Valente, and the author following Lari's suggestion to involve students of the AUIC School in activities representative of her zero-carbon approach.
The workshop was an important on-field experience for the in-depth teaching and researching of Lari's methodologies and for transmitting those principles underpinned to the conferral of the Honorary Degree. As Valente wrote in the Motivation for Conferment of the Honorary Degree in Architecture:

> "…it is the task of the school to define the model for these professionals of the future and the task they must perform.
> 'The role of universities is to identify the future and find the way to

get there,' Rogers added. And Lari's work is exemplary in this respect. Indeed, the form of her architectures echoes Rogers' belief in 'embodying the image of the aim to which makers aspire.'"[1]

Anyway, to convey Lari's methodologies in an architecture school—a 'Politecnico' of the global North—specific teaching strategies needed to be developed to properly impart values and methodologies in a different geographical, cultural, and technical context. For this reason, the definition of the activities to be carried out during the workshop and the selection of the case studies played an important role in teaching Lari's design principles and constructive features. Attentive research done prior to the workshop guided the choice of this teaching strategy that was meant to stimulate an active learning process where zero-carbon methodologies were tested in practice by working on digital and physical maquettes of paradigmatic prototypes. Different typologies of earthquake- and flood-resistant structures which can be reproduced several times, hosting variations, were designed through a composition of handcrafted modules—bamboo panels—that can generate various layouts and structures.

Knowledge was transmitted by accompanying the students in the creation of different kinds of replicas: digital maquettes with detailed constructive elements to understand the architecture in its relation between modular design and tectonics that, at the same time, perform as an aesthetical support, followed by on-scale bamboo maquettes to simulate prototype construction, its steps, and organization, and to know the technical behavior of a specific, i.e., the bamboo. Lectures were held to introduce the main topics of Yasmeen Lari's architecture, illustrate the safety instructions, and train the proper use of the machines and digital programs.

Digital modeling served as a tool for in-depth analysis in the first phase of the workshop to understand the construction process and its technical details. The reproduction of maquettes was based on technical drawings provided by the Heritage Foundation of Pakistan, adapted to the metric scale, and constantly compared with pictures of the built-up prototypes in their contexts. Some doubts emerged from this observation but were solved through a steady dialogue with Yasmeen Lari and her staff that accompanied us throughout the process. Moreover, a tutor and I watched the video tutorials published on Yasmeen Lari's Zero Carbon Channel[2] in advance to deepen the various aspects of the construction.

The multidisciplinary workshop teaching staff consisted of four professors of Architecture and Interiors from the Department of Architecture and Urban Studies who had been doing research on architect Lari since her nomination/candidature for the conferral of the

1 Ilaria Valente, "Foreword" in *Yasmeen Lari: An Architect*, eds. Fabrizia Berlingieri, Emilia Corradi, Cassandra Cozza, and Imma Forino (Milan-Turin: Pearson Italia, 2021), 12.

2 Yasmeen Lari and Heritage Foundation of Pakistan, "(LOC Lari OctaGreen House)," 2021. Playlist published on YouTube on *Yasmeen Lari's Zero Carbon Channel*, August 17, 2022, https://www.youtube.com/watch?v=YC5dm2Yl1EE&list=PLoCt7GwwhWNpzlKs3YVAnK1QRQF3ph0HY.

3 Fabrizia Berlingieri, Emilia Corradi, Cassandra Cozza, and Imma Forino are the authors and editors of the book *Yasmeen Lari: An Architect* (Milan-Turin: Pearson Italia, 2021).

4 Valente, "Foreword," 12.

Honoris Causa in 2020,[3] the scientific and technical heads of LaborA and their staff of experts in representation, digital skills, and maquette construction, as well as a group of tutors with diverse expertise.

We selected three case studies of humanitarian prototypes representative of different aspects of Lari's design methodology based on a zero-carbon approach where modular composition, tectonics, aesthetics, indigenous building materials, and appropriate technologies all contribute to establishing "a new concept of architectural beauty, pragmatism, and solidity"[4] open to co-design and participatory contributions.

The Lari OctaGreen Shelter and Guest House were chosen for the pragmatic use of the bamboo panels, and because they are exemplary prototypes for demonstrating various typological compositions based on a modular system and for learning the main technical features of construction. The Women's Centre at Darya Khan Sheikh was selected to explore a more complex bamboo architecture, where the composition of the roof combines tectonic and technical features with expressive and beautiful ones. The Pakistan Chulah clean stove was picked because it is a symbol of women's empowerment and is made of sustainable local materials such as earth, straw, and lime, where the original design is meant to take personalization, variations, and decoration into account, giving start to a co-design process.

The students were divided into four groups, each of which made a detailed digital reproduction of one prototype typology—the Lari OctaGreen Shelter and Guest House (one group), the Pakistan Chulah variations (one group), and the Women's Centre (two groups)—with different purposes. They initially did this to understand the design and constructive methodology through an in-depth study of the prototype in its composition, elements, modularity, constructive details, and materiality, as well as the digital maquette drawing. Subsequently, they made thoughts about how to show them both in the hologram room and the virtual theatre with their different potentialities. The former consists of a machine that projects a hologram, a three-dimensional visualization of a digital maquette that can be zoomed in and out, horizontally or vertically sectioned, etc., by the observer moving a specific joystick and wearing special glasses. The observer can interact with the hologram to better grasp the elements of hirs interest. The latter was an immersive experience in a circular room measuring seven meters in diameter, where images were projected onto the walls and the floor. An eight-minute-long video on the selected case studies was presented, illustrating them both in their technical-constructive and aesthetic characters through visual images, drawings, and pictures. We used it to better contextualize the architectures in their original places with pictures of built-up prototypes and show their materiality.

Hologram of a Lari OctaGreen guesthouse, viewed wearing specific glasses at LaborA's hologram room. The digital maquette can be seen in its whole, zoomed in and out, or sectioned both vertically and horizontally by using a specific tool and wearing special glasses. October 2021, LaborA on Leonardo campus, Politecnico di Milano. Credit: Cassandra Cozza

Yasmeen Lari visiting the digital exhibition of her humanitarian architecture with students and professors of the workshop at LaborA's virtual theatre: an eight-minute video projected on a curved surface of 360° and on the floor in a round theatre measuring seven meters in diameter. October 2021, LaborA on Leonardo campus, Politecnico di Milano. Credit: Lab Immagine Polimi

A maquette of the Lari OctaGreen shelter structure assembled with in-scale joints and bolts with two windows and a door mounted on a cardboard basement, scale 1:5. Bamboo is a natural material whose selection takes place at a delicate and crucial phase in which it is important to check the quality of each piece in terms of thickness, integrity, straightness, etc. September 2021, LaborA on Leonardo campus, Politecnico di Milano. Credit: Cassandra Cozza

The use of advanced digital tools allowed us to explore various typologies in the time at our disposal and analyze them from various points of view (tectonics, constructive features, materiality, aesthetics, etc.).

In the second part of the workshop, each group built one Lari OctaGreen Shelter on a scale of 1:5 and contributed altogether to the realization of a maquette on a scale of 1:2, testing the potentiality and the behavior of the bamboo: from the selection of the canes (straightness, diameter, thickness, etc.), their preparation for the cutting procedure (position of the inner joints, homogeneity, etc.), to the cutting itself (speed and heating, accuracy, inclination, the different cuts of edges according to the role they play in the construction, etc.). Moreover, students dealt with the assembly process: stacking all bamboo pieces into vertical posts, horizontal and diagonal lengths, and roof joists; organizing the elements for the panels according to their different types (standard, with a door, with a central window, or lateral window); marking the panels for the mounting sequence; testing the usage of *gutka* joints, bolts, nails, knots, and hinges; assembling the panels and the roof after having drawn the octagonal guideline on the ground. In this phase, they understood the importance of using zero-carbon and locally available materials in architecture, knowing their behavior, and trying to reduce waste production and lower the ecological footprint through a better design that integrates the constructive processes from the beginning.

In the end, all the students made different kinds of three-dimensional prints of the Pakistan Chulah, and prepared the exhibition in the virtual theatre, the hologram room, and the open spaces outside the LaborA. Students were enthusiastic and became more aware of the existence of inequalities and disadvantaged living conditions, and more sensitive to the importance of "democratizing" and "refashioning architecture."[5] They also were inspired by the message transmitted by Lari's specific way of practicing, where architecture contributes to the achievement of higher goals. In fact, she chose her clients, decided to use zero-carbon and local materials, developed low-tech and appropriate technologies[6] based on local wisdom, and updated vernacular methodologies. In this way, she established a building process aimed at empowering people, strengthening local identity, and reducing social inclusion. Humanitarian involvement in her practice is "an unequivocal choice, consolidated with her massive commitment in the field, which envisage inclusive projects and actions with two main aims, firstly to improve the living conditions of Pakistan's poorest and most vulnerable populations, and secondly to create low-cost, zero-carbon, zero-waste, sustainable architecture."[7]

---

5 Yasmeen Lari, "Yasmeen Lari: letter to a young architect," *The Architectural Review* 1474 (September 2020):41.

6 Cassandra Cozza, "Wanted: Architects to Change the World," in *Yasmeen Lari: An Architect*, eds. Fabrizia Berlingieri, Emilia Corradi, Cassandra Cozza, and Imma Forino (Milan-Turin: Pearson Italia, 2021), 43.

7 Ibid., 31.

Educating Designers

During the same period of the workshop at Polimi, in Karachi (and via Zoom), a zero-carbon workshop for universities called Empowerment and Dignity for Women through Built Environment Interventions—promoted by INTBAU Pakistan Chapter, Yasmeen Lari's Zero Carbon Channel and Heritage Foundation of Pakistan—was launched. Various universities from Pakistan and Bangladesh attended the training aimed at facilitating the fabrication of bamboo panels that can be used in various structures shaping different Lari typologies like the shelter, incremental urban housing, the guesthouse, as well as more complex ones. We were in contact via a WhatsApp chat with these universities, sharing info, videos, and images of the bamboo structures being made.

Yasmeen Lari's determination to support young architects and students—both in the global South and North—to design and think differently and develop new ways of practicing the profession led to the organization of various activities aimed at disseminating her knowledge and promoting a zero-carbon network, involving mostly women.

Zero-carbon architecture teaching in architecture schools can contribute towards stimulating a larger change in society. It is time to reorientate the profession by thinking, designing, and practicing in a way alternative to the mainstream. The collaborative "Laufen Manifesto for Human Design Culture" had already drawn attention to the need for more socially oriented design practices in 2013, underling the importance of educating designers and evolving design education and curricula, unfolding and identifying local beauty and constructive knowledge. Since then, many architects—Yasmeen Lari and others like Anna Heringer, Marina Tabassum, Architecture for Humanity, Anupama Kundoo, Tatiana Bilbao, etc.—have been demonstrating that thinking outside the box is possible by showing appropriate models of practicing and "affirming actions" that "convey an operative position about what is relevant in the world today."[8]

Architecture can provide spatial responses to "a condition of radical uncertainty" given by "interconnected forms of [territorial] fragility,"[9] tackling processes of impoverishment, planetary exhaustion,[10] human displacement, and climate migrations. In order to promote the practice of zero-carbon methodologies in architecture and, at the same time, intend it as an instrument for social and ecological justice, we need to deeply reflect upon its guiding design values and goals. Moved by ethical principles and inspired by activists and zero-carbon advocates, we need to reorient the professional practice and integrate the university curricula.

8 Paolo Tombesi, "Affirming Actions EPFL. Opening," May 29, 2021, Rolex Learning Center, Lausanne, Switzerland, video, 01:55, https://www.youtube.com/watch?v=Q8ku0XBSsRg&list=PL79IasEcK4rAMGlrlOboZil7eRGCv-PJS&index=1&t=115s.

9 Gabriele Pasqui, "Territori Fragili. Un progetto transdiciplinare per il paese," TF Giornale, no. 1 (2021): 3.

10 Marina Otero Verzier and Katia Truijen, "BURN-OUT. On Planetary Exhaustion and Alternative Public Infrastructures," Ardeth, no. 08 (2021): 18–29, https://doi.org/10.17454/ARDETH08.02.

WORKSHOP YASMEEN LARI'S HUMANITARIAN ARCHITECTURE
AUIC School, Politecnico di Milano | September 6–October 11, 2021

RESPONSIBLE PROFESSOR Cassandra Cozza

PROPOSING PROFESSORS Fabrizia Berlingieri, Emilia Corradi, Imma Forino

LaborA – PHYSICAL AND DIGITAL MODELLING LABORATORY
Cecilia Bolognesi, Renato Aiminio, Francesca Montaldo

TUTORS Simone Balin (holograms and digital modeling), Filippo Oppimitti (virtual theatre, 3D printing), Sara Anna Sapone, Arianna Scaioli, Andrea Sogja (digital modeling)

STUDENTS Tassnim Abdallah, Futaba Amano, Claudia Caccin, Niousha Doroudian, Ahmet Kayagil, Elaheh Nezafat, Giovanni Ossorio, Francesco Pauletti, Ilaria Pellegrini, Micaela Podestà, Federica Ronzitti, Mahsa Salek, Benedetta Tomasina, Guiqiang Yao, Siman Zhang, Jiayu Zhang, Yue Zhong

TECHNICAL SPONSOR Italboo

Building, Wounding, and the Future
On Planetary Care

Elke Krasny

'Building the New World': This expression is used as shorthand for global European imperialism with its beginnings in the late fifteenth century and its colonization of Abya Yala, commonly referred to as the Americas.[1] 'Building the new world order': This political claim was made by Russian President Vladimir Putin at the plenary session of the St. Petersburg International Economic Forum in 2022.[2] 'Building the new economy': People speak of building the new economy today to make claims to democratic data ownership and new ecosystems of data based on demands for restorative justice and ecological sustainability.[3] 'Building a new climate economy': This goal is currently being proclaimed by the International Monetary Fund or even portrayed as "the greatest economic opportunity in history" by "new corporate climate leadership."[4] Building as a metaphor for laying claim to the future can be found across the entire spectrum of different ideologies and political and economic regimes. Interested in the epistemological and ethical dimensions of the relations between metaphor and materiality, this essay is concerned with what it means that building is a central metaphor for the future when placed in relation to the ecological and social realities caused by building, in particular by modern building. Language contains a culture of metaphors that operate at the level of collective public and social imaginaries. A critical analysis of the

[1] See Valerie Fraser, *Building the New World: Studies in the Modern Architecture of Latin America 1930-1960* (London: Verso, 2001).

[2] Dimitry Sudakov, "Putin: Russia is building the new world order right now," Pravda.Ru, June 17, 2022, https://english.pravda.ru/russia/152411-putin_new_world_order/.

[3] See Alex Pentland, Alexander Lipton, and Thomas Hardjono, *Building the New Economy: Data as Capital* (Cambridge, MA: The MIT Press, 2021); New Economy Project, "Building a New Economy," accessed September 1, 2022, https://www.neweconomynyc.org/our-work/community-education/curriculum/.

materiality of metaphors requires one to look at how specific terms operating at the level of social imaginaries are entrenched in the material conditions of power inherent in the literal. Metaphors are constituted through the relations between the literal and the figurative. While the realities connected to the literal meanings of words can rapidly change, the metaphorical use of the same words often continues. Material realities connected to literal meanings seep into metaphors. I understand it as a social obligation of feminist cultural theory to work toward a more nuanced understanding of how the changes connected to literal meanings impact in epistemological and ethical terms on the figurative use of terms. Since the beginnings of industrialization, the realities of modern building have changed tremendously, and its effects are making the planet uninhabitable.[5]

Yet what it means that these realities of building are not reflected in the figurative use of building as a metaphor for the future has so far remained unquestioned. The metaphor of building as the imaginary for the future is ripe for critical analysis.

The continued use of building as a seemingly innocent metaphor capable of promising a different future has to be examined against the material and discursive realities of modern building. What I mean by this is lucidly expressed by the thinker on race and Pan-African civil rights activist W.E.B. Du Bois, who, as the anthropologist Elizabeth Povinelli stated, "argued that the material and discursive origins of European monumentalism, such as the gleaming boulevards of Brussels, were found in the brutal colonial regimes of the Congo."[6] Building joins "matter and meaning" in the words of the theoretical physicist and feminist theorist Karen Barad.[7] Building ties most firmly what the feminist epistemologist and historian of science Donna Haraway has called "material/semiotic nodes or knots."[8] Building materializes meaning. While the metaphor of building harnesses the power of building as the materialization of meaning not only as figurative, but effectively as prefigurative potential that promises to make the future real, the study of buildings as the canon of singular architectural objects has, for the longest time, avoided the modern colonial violence of their material and discursive foundations. Even though anti-colonial, feminist, queer, and race-critical investigations on the history of building are challenging canonical knowledge, the public history of buildings, as presented, for example, in the context of mass tourism or overview courses on architectural history, still lacks such critical narratives. This becomes obvious when placing the analysis given by W.E.B. Du Bois next to the hegemonic history of building. Therefore, the material and discursive realities of building have to be read back into building as a metaphor for future-making. As the realities created by modern building have resulted in foreclosing the future, building itself

[4] See IMF on Twitter, "Building a new #climate economy," March 11, 2021, 7:00 PM, https://twitter.com/IMFNews/status/1370072121989332998; Edward Cameron and Emilie Prattico, *The New Corporate Climate Leadership* (London: Routledge, 2021), 63–88.

[5] See David Wallace-Wells, *The Uninhabitable Earth. A Story of the Future* (New York: Crown Publishing, 2020).

[6] Elizabeth A. Povinelli, *Geontologies: A Requiem to Late Liberalism* (Durham, NC and London: Duke University Press, 2016), 4.

[7] Karen Barad, *Meeting the Universe Halfway: Quantum Physics and the Entanglement of Matter and Meaning* (Durham, NC and London: Duke University Press, 2007).

[8] Donna J. Haraway, *When Species Meet* (Minneapolis, MN: University of Minnesota Press, 2008), 4.

will have to be radically reimagined in order to become a meaningful metaphor for the future again.

In historical terms, the fact that modern building became the dominant form of building had far-reaching consequences. Informed by capitalist industrialization and entrenched in its value hierarchies of patriarchal supremacy characterized by ecological domination, racism, and sexism, modern building almost exclusively came to define what counts as building. Building that did not conform to modern building came to be viewed as backward, primitive, traditional, vernacular, or informal. To understand the realities produced by modern building, they would best be examined and studied through the largely invisible processes of how industries, policies, and technologies that organize financing, labor, land, and resources work together. Yet, the idea of building seems to have been much more defined by the visible presence created by building, by its style, scale, monumentality, and impressive command of materials, as well as by global dominance in modern urbanization and infrastructure.

While the complex processes behind building are largely rendered invisible, including examples such as the dependency of historical European building on colonial regimes in Africa, or the conditions created by China's colossal global infrastructure construction projects today, building, freed from its realities of domination, plunder, extraction, violence, and exploitation, represents the idea of the modern future as achievement. As a feminist cultural theorist, my interest is in examining the metaphor of building used to invoke a different and better future in relation to the realities of the future created by modern building. Responsibility to the future comes with the understanding that the aftermath of the modern future is "that which we [have come] to inherit."[9]

It matters that the meaning of building is used as a metaphor for future-making when we come to understand that modern building is co-responsible for the ongoing anthropogenic wounding of the planet. Understanding building as wounding the planet and buildings as the planet's wounds opens up a different understanding of building and thus completely different imaginaries connected to building. Wounding speaks to the ecological and social obligation of taking care of the wounds. Wounding imagines the future as care-taking. Therefore, modern building has to be more critically understood as part of the fast and "slow violence" that resulted in social and ecological planetary wounds.[10] And, building as future care has to be reimagined. The aim of this essay is not to argue for giving up on building as an imaginary for future-making. On the contrary, working through how modern building created highly uneven conditions of how bodies and minds are being supported and held together in their everyday lives, as well as

[9] Karen Barad, "Quantum Entanglements and Hauntological Relations of Inheritance: Dis/continuities, SpaceTime Enfoldings, and Justice-to-Come," *Derrida Today* 3, no. 2 (2010): 264. Quoted in Deboleena Roy, *Molecular Feminisms: Biology, Becomings, and Life in the Lab* (Seattle, WA: University of Washington Press, 2018), 176.

[10] See Rob Nixon, *Slow Violence and the Environmentalism of the Poor* (Cambridge, MA: Harvard University Press, 2011).

understanding how building is responsible for the exploitation and extraction of labor, land, and resources and the emission of carbon dioxide into Planet Earth's atmosphere, is seen as central to imagining building otherwise. For building to be future-enabling, we have to learn how to imagine building "otherwise" based on the decolonial notion of "worlds and knowledges otherwise," as introduced by the anthropologist Arturo Escobar.[11] Opening up to the horizon of building otherwise so that building can become a metaphor for care-full imaginaries of the future is rooted in understanding care as knowledge and based on feminist epistemologies of "critical care."[12] Critical care acknowledges the legacies of critical theory, specifically that the Frankfurt School simultaneously introduced a Marxian reinterpretation of Freud and a Freudian reinterpretation of Marx and thus joined together matter and meaning in discursive and materialist terms. Critical care introduces care as a way of knowing with a particular focus on how knowing relates to ecologies of interdependencies with all beings on Planet Earth dependent upon each other, upon infrastructural, material, and immaterial systems of support, as well as upon the planet as a whole. Care as knowledge brings into particular focus the ethical and political dimensions of how human beings respond to ineluctable interdependencies. Learning from the specific ways of knowing engendered by care, I suggest curiosity, worry, and hope as methodological approaches relevant to feminist epistemologies and ethics. The international relations scholar Cynthia Enloe has introduced "feminist curiosity," yet without making the link to its etymological root 'curiosus,' which connects to 'curare,' the Latin word for care.[13] Worry and hope as feminist methods are my suggestions. Curiosity, worry, and hope as ways of knowledge-making come from care as practice: one needs curiosity to find out what is needed for care; one finds oneself worrying when one cares; one tries to not give up hope when one cares, even when things seem desperate. Curiosity, worry, and hope are used as feminist approaches to building. Curiosity about why building is the metaphor constituting the imaginary of the future and worry about modern building as one of the main causes of a wounded planet leads me to think about how building can be imagined otherwise. This essay does not argue for giving up building. On the contrary, I am writing with hope that imagining building otherwise can lead to understanding the future as caring with the wounded planet.

Building the Future

Feminist curiosity leads me to ask why the metaphor of building has come to constitute the imaginary of the future. Imaginary is understood here as "an ethos," that is "a set of attitudes, dispositions and

[11] Arturo Escobar, "Worlds and Knowledges Otherwise," *Cultural Studies* 21, nos. 2–3 (2007): 179–210.

[12] See Angelika Fitz and Elke Krasny, "Introduction. Critical Care. Architecture and Urbanism for a Broken Planet," in *Critical Care. Architecture and Urbanism for a Broken Planet*, eds. Angelika Fitz, Elke Krasny, and Architekturzentrum Wien (Cambridge, MA and London: The MIT Press, 2019), 10–25.

[13] Cynthia Enloe, *The Curious Feminist: Searching for Women in a New Age of Empire* (Berkeley, CA: University of California Press, 2004), 4.

intuitions," as suggested by the globalization scholar and anthropologist of the future Arjun Appadurai.[14] Such a "social imaginary," following the feminist philosopher and public intellectual Judith Butler, "takes place at the level of a social ontology."[15] Interested in how "the materiality of metaphor" constitutes an ethos of social imaginaries and in how matter and meaning hold together in material/semiotic knots, the term building makes for an extremely interesting case.[16]

In order to approach building as a metaphor for the future, it is important to understand the literal meaning of building. A general and broad definition of building is helpful for this. Building brings something new into the world that has not been there before. Building takes up space, at it puts matter into place. All the parts and materials needed for building have to be procured, as well as the tools necessary for the builders who have the skills required so that the parts are joined together and take on a specific form and shape to fulfill their function. While all these dimensions of building, procuring materials, putting matter in place, taking up space, and fulfilling its function have implications for the future, they are, as I argue, not the main reasons why building has emerged as the central metaphor for future-making. Much more so, it is the power of imagination that is the imagined building that comes before the actual building. The imagination holds together the material process of joining its parts. This power of the imagination is crucial to building as an imaginary of the future. Building is practical and material imagination as the process of building creates the evidence of something imagined having been made material. This something that is being imagined can be imagined along the lines of how things have been built in the past. This something that is being imagined can also be radically different, not yet tested, never been done before, in short, new. In order to build this something, matter has to follow imagination. Building is the process of materializing what has been imagined; more specifically, building is the process that ensures that the materialization follows the imagination as planned. This suggests that building has the power to take command of organizing space, matter, and labor so that what has been imagined takes shape. Building literally makes the new fall into place according to plan. Building the future, metaphorically speaking, claims that the future will fall into place as imagined. Building unfolds the future according to plan. Building connects prediction and forecast and stands for predictable forecast, as well as the forecast of predictability. This reduces the ontological unknowability of the future and consequently its uncertainty. In my view, it is the distinct relationship between imagining and materializing that made building a perfect metaphor for making claims to the future. Building enabled a social imaginary that the future can be willed into existence as imagined.

[14] Arjun Appadurai, *The Future as Cultural Fact. Essays on the Global Condition* (London and New York: Verso, 2013).

[15] Judith Butler, *The Force of Nonviolence. An Ethico-Political Bind* (London and New York: Verso, 2020), 16.

[16] Donna J. Haraway, *When Species Meet* (Minneapolis, MN: University of Minnesota Press, 2008), 4.

Wounding the Planet

In historical hindsight, one comes to understand that building was central to making the future modern. Introducing this slight, yet important distinction between 'making the modern future' and 'making the future modern,' I argue that building gave shape to the idea that the future can be made forever modern. The notion of making the future modern was based on the paradox of changing everything at once so it would then last forever. Perfectly aligned with modernity's twin ideologies of progress and growth, modern building expanded Man's subjugation of space and time. Progress and growth underpinned the imperialist colonialist economies of limitless extraction and exploitation as modern building began to cover the surface of the planet and to scrape the sky. The modern future was Man-made. It was built according to Man's plan. "It is all part of the builder's plan," as it was proudly professed by a builder of skyscrapers in his monograph in the late 1920s.[17] The modern builder is heir to and incarnation of "the Enlightenment figure Man," to use the concept provided by feminist anthropologist Anna Tsing.[18] "He has a gender, a race, a religion, a theory of property and an idea about self," Tsing writes. To this one can add that modern Man also had an idea about building. He claimed the power to capital, land, resources, and labor to build the world according to His plan, as He colonized the future. Modern building understood land as resource and bodies as labor and established new resource and managerial ontologies based on expansion and replication. Tsing speaks of "machines of replication" and identifies the plantation as its modus operandi with the plantation being "the ecological simplification in which living things are transformed into resources."[19] The architect and urban planner Raquel Rolnik diagnoses modern housing and its morphologies and typologies as plantations.[20] Modern building thus has to be understood as transforming the entire planet into a resource always already assuming that its replication will expand not only over the entire planet, but also its future. Endless replication means sameness forever after. Endless expansion takes for granted that the resources for this replication will always be there. Viewed from these perspectives of replication, expansion, and extraction of resources, modern building did, in fact, make the future modern. The realities of modern building are largely co-responsible for the Man-made future, known today as the Anthropocene. In the words of the feminist anthropologist Elizabeth Povinelli, "the Anthropocene has meant to mark a geologically defined moment when the forces of human existence began to overwhelm all other biological, geological, and meteorological forms and forces and displace the Holocene. That is, the Anthropocene marks the moment when human existence became the determinate

17 Adrienne Brown, "Erecting the Skyscraper, Erasing Race," in *Race and Modern Architecture: A Critical History from the Enlightenment to the Present*, eds. Irene Cheng, Charles L. Davis II, and Mabel O. Wilson (Pittsburgh: University of Pittsburgh Press, 2020), 216.

18 Anna Tsing, "Earth Stalked by Man," *The Cambridge Journal of Anthropology* 34, no. 1 (2016): 3.

19 Ibid., 4.

20 See the interview with Raquel Rolnik in this volume, "The Right to Housing," 201–5.

form of planetary existence – and a malignant form at that."[21] The modern future resulted in wounding the planet's future.

As modern Man established the global economic system of patriarchal colonial capitalism overwhelming and dominating nature and bodies needed for replicating and growing the system, Man became a geological force and changed the condition of the planet. The future did not work out as planned. Making the future modern has resulted in climate catastrophe, extreme weather events, massive pollution, extreme inequities, and accelerating poverty. The hubris of forever replicating the modern as the future has put the planetary conditions essential to the continued existence and flourishing of human and other living and nonliving beings at risk. Building the modern future continues to wound the future.

Modern Man made Himself the scale of things: His life, His buildings, His history, His future. This has subordinated the scale of the planet to Man-centric imaginaries. It is still difficult to relate to the scale of the planet. One has to relearn that every breath we take, every drink of water we have, all the food we eat, every building we inhabit, is a part of planetary relatedness and interdependencies. In recent years, scholars have introduced new concepts to articulate the Man-made condition of the planet and to instigate new planetary relations. These concepts include "the damaged planet," or "the broken planet."[22] They raise the question of who caused such damage and breakage and also express the ongoing epistemological and ethical search for new ways of thinking with and feeling with the planet in the twenty-first century. Someone or something damaged or broken needs to be treated differently than someone or something undamaged and unbroken. To these concepts of the damaged planet and the broken planet, I want to add a third one: the wounded planet. Feminist worry and feminist hope lead me to imagine relating to the planet today and to the planet's future through wounding and woundedness. Wounding, like damaging or breaking, urges thinking about who or what causes the wounding. At the same time, wounding urges thinking about what it means that someone or something can be wounded. Ontological vulnerability is the condition of the possibility to become wounded by someone or something. A key lesson to be learned from the Anthropocene condition is that the planet, home to all living and nonliving earthly beings, is defined through ontological vulnerability. This means that the planet can be wounded. Making the future modern resulted in extreme planetary wounding. Modern building, with buildings literally the material interaction between humans and nature, saw land as an opportunity to be developed and resources ready for extraction. Understanding that the planet as a whole is constituted by relations is central to seeing how modern Man making Himself the scale of

[21] Elizabeth Povinelli, *Geontologies: A Requiem to Late Liberalism* (Durham, NC and London: Duke University Press, 2016), 9.

[22] See Anna Tsing, Heather Swanson, Elaine Gan, and Nils Bubandt, eds., *Arts of Living on a Damaged Planet* (Minneapolis, MN: University of Minnesota Press, 2016); Angelika Fitz, Elke Krasny, and Architekturzentrum Wien, eds., *Critical Care. Architecture and Urbanism for a Broken Planet* (Cambridge, MA and London: The MIT Press, 2019).

everything has neglected to take responsibility for the ontological vulnerability of the planet. Starting from the given that the planet is vulnerable and that relations are wounding, the planet requires decentering Man as the scale of everything in order to care with the wounded planet.

Caring with the Wounded Planet

Today, the harmed conditions of life and survival result from the effects of the future made modern. Facing the woundedness of the planetary future, modern building has to be understood as co-responsible for the ongoing wounding. In the language of policy and advocacy reliant on data and statistics, the situation of woundedness is expressed as follows today: "The built environment generates nearly 50% of annual global CO_2 emissions. Of those total emissions, building operations are responsible for 27% annually, while building materials and construction (typically referred to as embodied carbon) are responsible for an additional 20% annually."[23] While it is crucial to have accurate data on building as a cause of CO_2 emissions, there is, at the same time, work to be done so that one can understand and feel in epistemic and ethical terms what it means that the economic, political, and educational institutions globally do not prevent the continuation of building that wounds the planet. Without Planet Earth human beings cannot exist. Somehow this most obvious situation that being human means depending upon the planet for the very conditions of existence such as air, water, food, and shelter has not been central to the epistemic, cultural, and ethical traditions of Western modernity. Imagining building in ways so that the planet can be a good home to all its living and nonliving beings without wounding the planet has not been at the center of making the future modern. Working toward new imaginaries is crucial to building caring futures starting from the conditions of the wounded planet. This includes the building of homes for all those who are faced with the loss of their homes, who are displaced climate refugees, and who are confronted with extreme poverty because of ecological ruination and extreme weather events. "860 million people" are expected to be living in "extreme poverty" by the end of the year 2022, and they are, of course, in need of homes to provide for their continued existence.[24]

Caring with a wounded planet builds on the Tronto-Fisher framework of care. Care ethicist and political theorist Joan Tronto, together with educational scientist Berenice Fisher, provided a framework to examine care that, when first proposed in 1990, included four steps: "caring about, caring for, care-giving and care-receiving."[25] Much later, Tronto added the fifth step of "caring with." Caring with "centers

23 architecture 2030, "The Built Environment," architecture 2030, accessed September 30, 2022, https://architecture2030.org/why-the-building-sector/.

24 Annie Thériault and Jade Tenwick, "'Terrifying prospect' of over a quarter of a billion more people crashing into extreme levels of poverty and suffering this year," Oxfam International, April 12, 2022, https://www.oxfam.org/en/press-releases/terrifying-prospect-over-quarter-billion-more-people-crashing-extreme-levels-poverty.

25 Berenice Fisher and Joan Tronto, "Toward a Feminist Theory of Caring," in *Circles of Care: Work and Identity in Women's Lives*, eds. Emily K. Abel and Margaret K. Nelson (Albany, NY: State University of New York Press, 1990), 40.

responsibilities for care" assuming reciprocity over time, that is, that "we can trust over time, we will be able to reciprocate the care we received from fellow citizens, and that they will reciprocate the care we've given them."[26] The Tronto-Fisher framework is considered useful for imagining caring with a wounded planet for a number of reasons. This framework does not approach care solely from perspectives of affect and empathy, which, as evidenced in many everyday conversations, are still held to be the primary concerns for how good care can be achieved. It allows for a broader conception of care that includes bodily labors, built environments, and infrastructural support structures. Furthermore, the framework, though developed to examine human care interactions and how these are organized in societies, can be extended to understanding the planet as a whole as a set of relations of reciprocity and responsibilities. This extends the understanding of care as being given by the planet as much as by humans to their planet. This makes the planet, together with all living and nonliving beings, the givers and receivers of care as they are in relations of mutual constitution and interdependence.

Care is concerned with ensuring continued life-making conditions. Tronto observed that care always "starts in the middle of things."[27] Looking at the future from the perspective of care means that care always starts in the middle of things as they are in the here and now and that care is being continued despite given structures of inequity and carelessness. This is a very different approach to the future, which always begins in the middle of things as they are now and as we have inherited them from the past. Past care has resulted in the present conditions of life-making and death-making. Present care, together with the effects of past care, impact the conditions of future livability. Understanding buildings as the provision of care, therefore, has to relate the harmful and wounding effects of past and present building to future building.

If building—as caring with the wounded planet—were to start in the middle of things, then the diagnosis that building is responsible for half of the current climate ruination and the extreme weather events with all their effects on human and nonhuman life and the environment would be the starting point for reimagining building. The realities of building will have to change dramatically so building can become a social imaginary for caring futures. In order to understand these realities better, more public knowledge is needed on how modern building in the past actually wounded the planet. Basic questions for telling eco-materialist and social histories of modern building include, but are, of course, not limited to the following: Whose land has been built on? Which plants were killed because of building? Which animals were displaced because of building? Who are the human beings who have

[26] Joan Tronto, *Who Cares? How to Reshape a Democratic Politics* (Ithaca, NY and London: Cornell University Press, 2015), 15–16.

[27] Joan Tronto, *Who Cares?*, 4.

been displaced because of colonization or gentrification? Where did the materials for the building come from? What were the working conditions of the construction workers? Who financed the building? Did the building result in "mortgaged lives?"[28] How much CO_2 has the building emitted? Such questions are not only helpful to analyze buildings from the past, but to start imagining building as caring.

Caring with a wounded planet is concerned with enabling and maintaining life-making conditions as future-making. Such caring starts in the middle of things that are wounding the planet. Starting in the middle of things and enabling the continuity of care, including taking care of the wounds in the past, may seem a modest approach to the future. This is not the modern future that was imagined as a radical break, as breaking with everything that was given. This is not the heroic vision of building a new future, which will change everything at once. In my view, it is the most demanding and, at the same time, most realistic approach to the future provided by care as knowledge reliant on curiosity, worry, and hope. Curiosity: What is needed? Why is it needed? Worry: How can the needs be fulfilled so they do not inflict wounds, increase pain, or make existing inequities worse?
Hope: Working on ways of care that avoid wounding, increasing pain, or worsening inequities. Reworking ways of care constantly and continuously so as to become better at not wounding, causing pain, or deepening inequities. Building is seen as essential care for creating and continuing life-making conditions. Caring with a wounded planet requires becoming responsible for the historical and continued wounding caused by building and reimagining and relearning building so that it cares for existing planetary wounds and avoids continued wounding of the planet.

"We can't build what we can't imagine," writes the educator and activist Walidah Imarisha.[29] Understanding the consequences of what it means that what cannot be imagined cannot be built will require the hard and insistent work of emancipating the imagination, which has been eroded and colonized by capitalism, so that building can be imagined otherwise. This requires reimagining what building is and does in order to build in such a way that does not wound the planet. Far from proposing one way of building as the only way forward, which would only replicate the modern idea of one future dominating all other possible futures, which has led to the extinction of many different futures that would have been possible, building as caring with a wounded planet will need many different ways of building. Caring with the planet as future-making does not imagine the time that lies ahead through the idea of one possible future only. Caring with a wounded planet requires not giving up curiosity and hope despite worry, and, at the same time, not suppressing worry, as it is the best response to the

---

28 Ada Colau and Adrià Alemany, *Mortgaged Lives: From the housing bubble to the right of housing*, trans. Michelle Teran (Los Angeles, CA, Leipzig and London: Journal of Aesthetics & Protest, 2014).

29 Walidah Imarisha, "To Build a Future Without Police and Prisons, We Have to Imagine It First," OneZero, October 22, 2020, https://onezero.medium.com/black-lives-matter-is-science-fiction-how-envisioning-a-better-future-makes-it-possible-5e14d35154e3. Quoted in Jeanne van Heeswijk, Maria Hlavajova, and Rachael Rakes, "Introduction: Toward the Not-Yet," in *Toward the Not-Yet: Art as Public Practice*, eds. Jeanne van Heeswijk, Maria Hlavajova, and Rachael Rakes (Cambridge, MA and London: The MIT Press, 2021), 12.

ontological vulnerability of the planet. Caring with the planet in the least heroic and humblest ways possible begins by imagining that futures can be built in many different ways. Imagining building otherwise begins in the middle of the wounds of the present and conceives of the future as a time dedicated to planetary healing.

Acknowledgments
About the Authors
About the Editors
About Yasmeen Lari
Bibliography
Index

Acknowledgments

A book and an exhibition are always collaborative, their process and work shared by many. We are most thankful to the architect Yasmeen Lari, whose inspirational work makes it possible to claim that there is, in fact, 'architecture for the future.' We are humbled by her unwavering trust that has made this book possible, for opening her archives, for countless conversations, for her hospitality and tireless care. We are thankful to the authors, whose critical scholarship and whose reports on their activist practices contextualize Lari's work historically and politically, to the Architekturzentrum Wien with its dedicated and experienced staff, and, of course, to the core team working on the book and the exhibition. We thank Karin Lux, managing director at Architekturzentrum Wien, for her enthusiasm for this project since its nascent stages and for her wonderful support throughout.

Yasmeen Lari: Architecture for the Future had been in our minds for many years but was only in the making for the past year due to the Covid-19 pandemic. Already in 2019, we featured Yasmeen Lari's work in Sindh Province in the exhibition *Critical Care: Architecture and Urbanism for a Broken Planet* at the Architekturzentrum Wien, as well as in the accompanying book edited by Angelika Fitz, Elke Krasny, and the Architekturzentrum Wien, also published by The MIT Press in 2019. In the same year, together with the Museum of Applied Arts, we invited Yasmeen Lari to give a keynote address at the conference of the Vienna Biennale at the Architekturzentrum Wien. Back in 2019, we began to think about a book and an exhibition dedicated to Yasmeen Lari's work. Due to pandemic conditions, our research travel to Karachi had to be postponed until early 2022. For many months, our research process took the form of online meetings and conversations with Yasmeen Lari, through which we were able to learn and understand her work. We cannot thank her enough for making herself available so generously. During that period, architect Marvi Mazhar, a former member of staff at Yasmeen Lari's office, joined the editorial team, but it was not until February 2022 that we were all able to meet in person in Karachi. We thank Maria Falkner at the Architekturzentrum Wien for coordinating e-meetings, meetings in person, and for organizing our travels.

We thank the Heritage Foundation of Pakistan, founded by Yasmeen Lari and Suhail Zaheer Lari, and its staff, who responded swiftly to all our requests, especially Naheem Shah, Project Coordinator and Master Trainer, and Ashfaq Ahmed, Senior Architect. We thank everyone who opened their Yasmeen Lari-designed homes to us, Maheen Zia for a wonderful conversation in her garden, and Nayyar Jamil for an inspiring morning at her home, and both for sharing historical plans and publications. We thank Mohd. Rizwan ul Haque for an extensive guided tour of the PSO–Pakistan State Oil building, and Waseem Anwar Arain for leading us through the FTC–Finance and Trade Centre. We thank all the women artisans we met at the Zero Carbon Cultural Centre in Makli and Moomal Mumtaz for interpreting. A special thanks to Dani from Mirpur for demonstrating the construction of a Pakistan Chulah. We thank all the architects, activists, researchers, and urbanists who answered our questions, shared information, and deepened our understanding of urbanism and heritage in Karachi, especially Arif Hasan, Mariyam Nizam, Anila Naeem, Sheema Kirmani, Arif Belgaumi, Amber Alibhai, and Nazish Brohi.

Working with architecture students and thereby bringing about a change of direction in architecture is of great concern to Yasmeen Lari. We thank Andrea Rieger-Jandl, Professor at the Department of History of Architecture and Building Archaeology at the Vienna University of Technology, for hosting Yasmeen Lari as a visiting professor and for setting up a course on Lari's zero-carbon methods, which included having her students travel to Pakistan for research and learning.
We thank Yasmeen for accepting this visiting professorship and for initiating and organizing an exchange with the School of Architecture at the University of Lahore. We thank Harriet Wennberg of INTBAU for supporting this and other international workshops. Thanks to all the students who embarked on this journey with the goal of contributing to more sustainable architectural production in the future. And thanks for sharing their research and experiences in our exhibition. We thank Cassandra Cozza and her students at the Politecnico di Milano for lending us their bamboo models of the LOG–Lari OctaGreen.

We are deeply indebted to Yasmeen Lari for the generous provision of photographic and plan material. For additional material and rights of use, we thank the Aga Khan Documentation Center of the MIT Libraries, the Aga Khan Trust for Culture, Kazi Khaleed Ashraf, Rahul Aijaz, the UNESCO, and the nonprofit environmental communications centre GRID-Arendal. For filming at different locations in Karachi, we thank Imran Gill, and, for film editing, Wolfgang Haas. We thank Anna Livia Pugholm Vorsel for carefully transcribing our interviews and for digitizing historical slides from Yasmeen Lari's archive, and Iris Ranzinger for her expert guidance.

We thank all the supporters and funders who have made the exhibition and the book possible: the public funding partners of the Architekturzentrum Wien—the Cultural Affairs Department of the City of Vienna, the Urban Development and Planning Department of the City of Vienna, and the Arts and Culture Division of the Federal Chancellery of Austria—and all the members of the Architecture Lounge of the Architekturzentrum Wien. Many thanks to the dedicated staff at The MIT Press, and especially to Victoria Hindley for her interest, trust, and guidance, to Gabriela Bueno Gibbs for support, and to Kate Elwell for guidance on production. We are most grateful to all the contributors to this book: Abira Ashfaq, Cassandra Cozza, Anne Karpf, Runa Khan, Chris Moffat, Anila Naeem, Raquel Rolnik, Helen Thomas, and Rafia Zakaria. Working with the exhibition and book team has not only been inspirational, but it has also been rewarding and fun. We thank Agnes Wyskitensky for her smooth project coordination. We could not have found a better person to hold all the parts together. Brian Dorsey was always there for translations, language editing, and proofreading. Kimi Lum and Lisa Kusebauch-Kaiser supplemented the careful proofreading. We thank Andreas Kurz, the production manager of the exhibition, for his tireless search for local, feasible, and sustainable solutions, and Philipp Aschenberger for constructing prototypes and coordinating the workshop team. Thanks to the entire Az W team: Katharina Ritter for program coordination, Anne Wübben for education, Lene Benz for organizing the accompanying program, Ines Purtauf and Alexandra Viehhauser for communication, Maria Falkner, Sarah Hoogstoel, Ingrid North, and Christina Sorgmann for administration. We thank Alexander Schuh for his beautiful graphic design for the book and the exhibition. It has been a pleasure to work together with Alexandra Maringer on the exhibition design. Angelika, Elke, and Marvi are thankful for each other's friendship and support throughout. This book is dedicated to all those who use their imagination, energy, organization, and optimism for 'architecture for the future' that is a different architecture for a different future, a change of direction in architecture based on decarbonization and decolonization, as well as on social and ecological justice. Architecture for future-making is part of the continuous provision of care for all living and nonliving beings on this planet.

About the Authors

Abira Ashfaq

Abira Ashfaq is a human rights activist and legal educator based in Karachi, Pakistan. She is a visiting faculty member at the Institute of Business Administration (IBA) in Karachi, where she teaches feminist legal theory and international human rights. Before IBA, she worked at SZABIST in Karachi (2007–18), where she taught criminal law and jurisprudence and initiated a clinical project on gender-based violence and labor law. She was a Soros Justice Fellow and a clinical fellow at the Boston College School of Law. While in the United States (1999–2004), she defended people being deported from the US for criminal convictions. This work led her to write an essay for the book *Keeping Out the Other: A Critical Introduction to Immigration Enforcement Today* (Columbia University Press, 2008). She researched and wrote about natural resources rights and movements defending their rights to land, water, and minerals in Pakistan, as well as on urban resilience and communities forced to migrate because of the loss of livelihoods. In 2022, she partnered with Seema Maheshwary and the Institute of Development Studies (IDS) in Sussex, UK to write a paper on the forced conversions of Hindu girls and women, which is forthcoming. She has also worked in Karachi developing campaigns around housing rights and on highlighting gendered impacts of forced evictions, as well as challenging international financiers who have funded projects that are harmful to the environment.

Cassandra Cozza

Cassandra Cozza is Lecturer and Assistant Professor in Architectural and Urban Design at the Politecnico di Milano. She teaches at the School of Architecture Urban Planning Construction Engineering (AUIC). As an architect, she investigates architecture as a response to ongoing challenges, enhancing both spatial relationships and places. The recovery of the architectural and infrastructural heritage, zero-carbon methodologies and practices in architectural design and contemporary public spaces are the main topics of her research. She is a member of the scientific editorial board of the magazines *Territorio* and *Ardeth*. She co-edited the book *Yasmeen Lari. An Architect* (Pearson, 2021) published on the occasion of the Honorary Degree awarded to Yasmeen Lari by the Politecnico di Milano.

Anne Karpf

Anne Karpf is Professor of Life Writing and Culture at London Metropolitan University. She is a sociologist, writer, broadcaster, and award-winning journalist. Her wide research interests include gender, Holocaust studies, aging, orality, and the climate crisis. Her five books of nonfiction, which have been translated into thirteen languages, include an acclaimed family memoir, *The War After: Living with the Holocaust* (Heinemann, 1996), *How to Age* (Picador, 2014), and, most recently, *How Women Can Save the Planet* (Hurst, 2021). With Brian Klug, Jacqueline Rose, and Barbara Rosenbaum, she co-edited *A Time to Speak Out: Independent Jewish Voices on Israel, Zionism and Jewish Identity* (Verso, 2008).

Runa Khan

Runa Khan is the founder of Friendship, an international social purpose organization established in 2002, and Friendship International, operating from five European countries. Friendship works for the most vulnerable and remote communities in Bangladesh for saving lives, poverty alleviation, climate adaptation, and empowerment, bringing direct services to seven million lives a year. Her awards include the Green Award (2016), the IsDB's Social Entrepreneur Award (2008), the Rolex Award for Entrepreneurship (2006), the Ashoka Fellowship (since 1994), and the Schwab Foundation Social Entrepreneur Award (2012). She is also a board member of Global Dignity, an Advisory Council member of the British Asian Trust Bangladesh, the Honorary President of the One Sustainable Health Forum Approach, and an Honorary Trustee of the Duke of Edinburgh Award Bangladesh.

Chris Moffat

Chris Moffat is Senior Lecturer at the School of History, Queen Mary University of London. He is the author of *India's Revolutionary Inheritance: Politics and the Promise of Bhagat Singh* (Cambridge University Press, 2019). Chris's forthcoming, second monograph is a study of architecture, politics, and the philosophy of history in Pakistan, provisionally titled *Learning from Lahore*.

Anila Naeem

Anila Naeem is an academic and heritage conservation professional with over twenty years' experience involving research-based initiatives on historic environments and socio-cultural traditions. She is Professor and currently holds the position of Chairperson at the Department of Architecture and Planning, NED University of Engineering and Technology, Karachi, Pakistan. Graduating as an architect, Dr. Naeem pursued an academic career, attaining specialization in heritage conservation and management of traditional environments. Her significant contribution to the field is the development of a systematic method for assessing historic built-form traditions, published as a book titled *Urban Traditions and Historic Environments in Sindh: A Fading Legacy of Shikarpoor, Historic City* (Amsterdam University Press, 2017). She has to her credit various other book chapters and research papers in national and international publications. Naeem has been associated with the International Council for Monuments and Sites (ICOMOS) and served as the Secretary General, ICOMOS Pakistan (2005–20). She is also Editor-in-Chief of the *Journal of Research in Architecture and Planning* (JRAP), published biannually by NED University, and Book Review Editor for the *International Journal for Cultural Property* (IJCP).

Raquel Rolnik

Raquel Rolnik is a professor at the Faculty of Architecture and Urbanism of the University of São Paulo. She is an architect and urban planner, with over thirty-five years of scholarship, activism, and practical experience in planning, urban land policy, and housing issues. In her career, she has held various government positions, including Director of the Planning Department of the City of São Paulo (1989–92) and National Secretary for Urban Programs of the Brazilian Ministry of Cities (2003–07), as well as NGO activities such as Urban Policy Coordinator of the Polis Institute (1997–2002). In May 2008, Raquel Rolnik was appointed by the UN Human Rights Council as UN Special Rapporteur on adequate housing for a six-year mandate, which ended in June 2014. She is the author of several books, including *Urban Warfare: Housing Under the Empire of Finance* (Verso, 2019) and *São Paulo: o planejamento da desigualdade* (Fósforo, 2022), among others.

Helen Thomas

Helen Thomas is an architect, publisher, and writer with a PhD from the University of Essex in art history and theory. Attracted to all architecture that diverges from the canon, she has written on postcolonial architectural history and architectural drawing and takes an interest in the way that women practice as architects. Experience as an editor and senior lecturer at institutions including the Victoria & Albert Museum, Phaidon Press, Drawing Matter, the Architectural Association, and London Metropolitan University informs her construction of independent cultural products. Recent projects and publications include: Drawing Matter Reviews, www.womenwritingarchitecture.org; *Architecture in Islamic Countries: Selections from the Catalogue for the Second International Exhibition of Architecture Venice 1982/83* (gta Verlag, 2022); *The Hybrid Practitioner* (Leuven University Press, 2022); *Extracts 2: Women Writing Architecture* (Drawing Matter, 2021); *Architecture through Drawing* (Lund Humphries, 2019); *Drawing Architecture* (Phaidon, 2018); www.morethanonefragile.co.uk, 2016. With Adam Caruso she edited *The Limits of Modernism* series (gta Verlag, 2019–21).

Rafia Zakaria

Rafia Zakaria is the author of *The Upstairs Wife: An Intimate History of Pakistan* (Beacon Press, 2015), *Veil* (Bloomsbury Publishing, 2017), and *Against White Feminism: Notes on Disruption* (Penguin Books Ltd, 2021) She is a columnist for *Dawn* (Pakistan) and writes the Alienated column at *The Baffler.* She served on the Board of Amnesty International USA from 2009–15. She is a fellow at the African American Policy Forum at Columbia University.

About the Editors

Angelika Fitz

is the Director of the Architekturzentrum Wien. Since the late 1990s, she has worked as a cultural theorist and curator in the fields of architecture, art, and urbanism. Her curatorial and editorial projects include Austria's contribution to the São Paulo Biennial, Capital & Karma at the Kunsthalle Wien, the international traveling 'working exhibitions' *Weltstadt* and *Actopolis* and, with the Architekturzentrum Wien, *Assemble. How to Build* and *Downtown Denise Scott Brown*, the first comprehensive show on Scott Brown's work. Together with Elke Krasny, she edited *Critical Care: Architecture and Urbanism for a Broken Planet* (The MIT Press, 2019). She is co-editor of *Boden für Alle / Land for Us All* (Park Books, 2020) on land policies and the forthcoming book *Hot Questions–Cold Storage* (2023) on the new permanent collection of the Az W.

Elke Krasny

is Professor of Art and Education at the Academy of Fine Arts Vienna. She is a feminist cultural theorist, curator, and author. Krasny's scholarship addresses questions of care, ecological and social justice, critical memory work, and emancipatory practices at the present historical conjuncture marked by ecocidal and genocidal pasts. Together with Angelika Fitz, she edited *Critical Care: Architecture and Urbanism for a Broken Planet* (The MIT Press, 2019). She co-edited the 2022 volume *Radicalizing Care. Feminist and Queer Activism in Curating* (Sternberg Press, 2021). Her forthcoming book, *Living with an Infected Planet. Covid-19 Feminism and the Global Frontline of Care,* develops a feminist perspective on imaginaries of war and realities of care in pandemic times.

Marvi Mazhar

Marvi Mazhar is an architect and researcher whose practice combines visual culture, spatial advocacy, and interventions. She serves on several advisory boards in government and nonprofit organizations. Recently she completed her Master's at Goldsmiths, University of London (2021) and in 2022 started teaching at the Indus Valley School of Architecture (IVSAA) in the M.Phil Program, Pedagogies of Place. Her present ongoing research focuses upon the representation and production of Karachi's urban and rural coastal periphery, and its ecology.

Architekturzentrum Wien

The Architekturzentrum Wien is the Austrian museum of architecture. Located at MuseumsQuartier in the heart of Vienna, the Architekturzentrum Wien exhibits, discusses, and researches the ways in which architecture and urban development shape the daily life of each one of us. The broad program of the Architekturzentrum Wien is seen as a bridge between the specialist world and everyday experts. What can architecture do? This is a question of great relevance to all of us.
The program comprises more than 500 events per year, ranging from international exhibitions, symposia, workshops, and lectures to guided tours, city expeditions, film series, and hands-on formats. The museum's facilities include a unique collection on Austrian architecture of the 20th and 21st centuries and a public architecture library.

About Yasmeen Lari

*1941
born in Dera Ghazi Khan, Punjab, British India (now Pakistan)

1940–50s
Queen Mary's School, Adabistan-e-Soofia School, and Kinnaird College, Lahore, Pakistan

1963
Graduation from Oxford School of Architecture (now Oxford Brookes University), UK

1964
Founder of Lari Associates, Architects & Urban Designers
Co-founder, Karachi Artists' Gallery (KAG), the first permanent exhibition and studio space in Pakistan

1980
Co-founder and CEO of the Heritage Foundation of Pakistan

Selected Projects

1965
Mr. Parvaiz Bungalow, Karachi, Pakistan

1968
M. Ziaullah Khan House, Karachi, Pakistan

1969
Naseeruddin Khan House, Karachi, Pakistan

1969–70
Naval Housing, Karachi, Pakistan

1973
Lari House, Karachi, Pakistan

1975
Angoori Bagh Housing, Lahore, Pakistan

1978–87
Research project with Michael Jansen at the archeological site Mohenjo-daro, Pakistan

1979–89
Documentation of traditional wind-catcher houses, Thatta, Pakistan

1980
Lines Area Redevelopment Program, Karachi, Pakistan

1981
Army Mud Barracks, Bahawalpur, Pakistan

1982–89
FTC – Finance and Trade Centre, Karachi, Pakistan

1984–91
PSO House, Karachi, Pakistan

1997
ABN Amro Bank, Karachi, Pakistan

2000–
KaravanKarachi (later KaravanPakistan),
awareness program for heritage preservation

2003–05
Saving of Sheesh Mahal ceiling at the UNESCO World Heritage Site Lahore Fort, Lahore, Pakistan

2005
Post-earthquake rehabilitation, Siran Valley, Swat, Pakistan—development of the KaravanChar

2009
Community kitchens in Shaikh Shahzad Camp, Mardan, Pakistan

2010
Post-flood rehabilitation in Swat and Sindh, Pakistan—development of the Green KaravanChar

Green Women's Centre in Khairpur, Sindh, Pakistan

Beginning of damage assessment at Denso Hall, Karachi, Pakistan

2011
Damage assessment of Sethi House, Peshawar, Pakistan

Damage assessment and conservation of the UNESCO World Heritage Site Makli Necropolis, Sindh, Pakistan

Development of the smokeless Pakistan Chulah (Pakistani stove)

2016–
Zero Carbon Cultural Centre, Makli, Thatta, Pakistan

2019–

Rahguzar, walking street, Karachi, Pakistan

Cleaning of Denso Hall, Karachi, Pakistan

2020–

Zero Carbon Channel on YouTube

2022–

Post-flood rehabilitation in Sindh, prefabrication of Lari OctaGreens (LOG) at Zero Carbon Cultural Centre, Makli, Pakistan

Awards

2002

UN Recognition Award for promotion of culture and peace

2006

Sitara-e-Imtiaz, Star of Excellence, Pakistan

2011

First Wonder Woman of the Year Award

2014

Hilal-e-Imtiaz, Crescent of Excellence, Pakistan

2016

Fukoka Art and Culture Prize, Japan

2018

UN Habitat Award for Pakistan Chulah

2020

Jane Drew Prize of the Royal Institute of British Architects (RIBA), London, UK

2021

Honorary Degree in Architecture, Politecnico di Milano, Milan, Italy

Positions and Memberships

1969

Associate of the Royal Institute of British Architects (RIBA), UK

1974

Project Coordinator, Slum Improvement, Karachi Development Authority, Karachi, Pakistan

1975

Appointment by UNICEF to report on flood-affected areas of Pakistan

1980
Director, Heritage Foundation of Pakistan, Karachi, Pakistan

1980–83
President, Institute of Architects, Pakistan (IAP)

1981
Member, Expert Group of Government of Pakistan on National Housing Policy, Islamabad, Pakistan

1982–85
Member, Majlis-e-Shura (Federal Advisory Council), Islamabad, Pakistan

1983
Member, Selection Board for Headquarters of League of Arab States, Tunisia

1983–90
Member, Advisory Council, Ministry of Finance Pakistan

1983–85
Deputy Chairperson, Architects Regional Council of Asia (ARCASIA)

1983–86
Chairperson, Pakistan Council of Architects and Town Planners (PCATP)

1984
Coordinator, Council of Architects and Town Planners of Islamic Countries

Member, Board of Advisors and Keynote Speaker, First Asian Congress of Architects, Manila, Philippines

1987
Member, Pakistan delegation, South Asia Association for Regional Cooperation (SAARC) Conference on Women, Islamabad, Pakistan

1988
Member, Karachi Aesthetic Control Committee, Government of Sindh, Pakistan

Member, UN Habitat Group on Land Sharing, Bangkok, Thailand

1988–90
Member, Academic Council, NED University of Engineering & Technology, Karachi, Pakistan

1992
Member, Pakistani delegation to the Second International Symposium on Mohenjo-daro, Karachi, Pakistan

1992–93
Vice-Chairperson, National Institute of Public Administration (NIPA), Lahore, Pakistan

1992–94

Member, Board of Governors, National College of Arts (NCA), Lahore, Pakistan (also 2004–2006)

1993

Member, Sindh Chief Minister's Aesthetic Committee

Vice-Chairperson, Pakistan National Committee of the International Council on Monuments and Sites (ICOMOS)

1995–97

Member Syndicate, NED University of Engineering and Technology, Karachi, Pakistan

1996–99

Expert Member, Cultural Heritage Advisory Committee, Government of Sindh, Pakistan

2002–03

National Project Co-Coordinator, UNESCO

2002–05

Member, Board of Advisors, International Archive of Women in Architecture (IAWA), Virginia, US

2003–05

National Advisor at UNESCO Heritage Site Lahore Fort, Lahore, Pakistan

Board of Governors, National College of Arts, Lahore, Pakistan

2018

Founding Chair, International Network for Traditional Building, Architecture & Urbanism (INTBAU), Pakistan

2021

Trustee of Transparency International Pakistan

Conferences, Lectures, Teaching, and Exhibitions

1965

"Some Thoughts on House Design," presented at the Karachi Artists' Gallery (KAG), Karachi, Pakistan

1966

"Our Heritage in Muslim Architecture," presented at the Second National Seminar on Muslim Architecture, Islamabad, Pakistan

Lecturer, School of Architecture, Karachi, Pakistan

1968

"Architecture in West Pakistan—Islamabad," presented at the Third National Seminar on Muslim Architecture, Dhaka, Bangladesh

"Museum Architecture," presented at the All-Pakistan Museum Conference, Dhaka, Bangladesh

1975

"Slums and Squatter Settlements — Their Role and Improvement Strategy," presented at RCD seminar on Urban Development and Housing, Islamabad, Pakistan

1976

Speaker, Habitat Conference on Human Settlements, Vancouver, Canada

1978

"Housing — A Personal View," presented at the UN Regional Conference for the Economic Commission of Western Asia (ECWA), Amman, Jordan

Seminar for the Aga Khan Award for Architecture, Aiglemont, France

1980

Keynote Speaker, Aga Khan Award Seminar on Places of Public Gathering in Islam in Amman, Jordan

1981

"Lines Area Resettlement Project," presented at the seminar on Housing Design in Islamic Cultures at MIT, Cambridge, MA, US

"Search for Identity," presented at the Conference on Islamic Art, Architecture and Calligraphy, Peshawar, Pakistan

"Thatta: The Beginning of a Case Study," presented at the seminar on Architecture in Archaeology and History at Mohenjo-daro, Pakistan

Guest Faculty Member, MIT-Harvard seminar, Cambridge, MA, US

1982

"Identity and Heritage," presented at the All Pakistan Science Conference, Bahawalpur, Pakistan

MIT-Harvard seminar on Housing Design in Islamic Cultures, Karachi, Pakistan

Participation at 2nd Architectural Venice Biennial "Architettura nei Paesi Islamici," La Biennale di Venezia, Venice, Italy

1983

Chairperson, Planning Commission Working Group on Housing for Low Income Groups

1984

"Expanding Role of an Architect in the Asian Context," presented at the First Asian Congress of Architects, Manila, Philippines

MIT-Harvard seminar on Architecture in the Spirit of Islam, 2nd Session, Cambridge, MA, US

1985

Participant, WHO/UNEP Working Group on Environmental Health Aspects of Housing and Urban Planning, Moscow, Russia

"Women in Development," presented at the Conference of Women from Pakistan and Bangladesh, Islamabad

1986

Only architect invited to Conference of Intellectuals and Thinkers convened by the President of Pakistan, Islamabad, Pakistan

1988

"Professional Practice and Education of Architects in Pakistan," presented at the Conference on Development and Design in South and Southeast Asia, organized by the University of Hong Kong, Hong Kong, China

"The Lines Area Project: A Concept in Land Sharing," presented at the United Nations Group on Land Sharing Conference, Bangkok, Thailand

1990

"Architecture and Politics, and the Politics of Architecture," presented at the XVII World Congress of the International Union of Architects (UIA), Montréal, Canada

1991

Participant, UNDP & UNCHS Expert Panel on Karachi Masterplan — Beyond 2000, Karachi, Pakistan

2000

Speaker, International Conference of Architects, Mumbai, India

2001

International Conference "Heritage, Urban Space and Identity," Karachi, Pakistan

2003

Keynote Speech, UNESCO World Conference on Cultural Policy

2015

Invited to International Experts Meeting on Cultural Heritage Disaster Risk Management in Tokyo and Sendai, Japan

Chicago Biennial for Architecture, Chicago, IL, US

2016

Participation and Lecture at the Exhibition *Creation from Catastrophe*, Royal Institute of British Architects (RIBA), London, UK

Speaker, Oslo Architectural Triennale, Oslo, Norway

2019

Group exhibition *Critical Care: Architecture for a Broken Planet*, Architekturzentrum Wien, Vienna, Austria

Keynote Speaker, International Conference on Changing Values, Vienna Biennale for Change 2019, Architekturzentrum Wien, Vienna, Austria

2021

Impact Lecture, "Barefoot Social Architecture," National Centre of Competence in Research (NCCR) Digital Fabrication, ETH Zürich, Zurich, Switzerland

2022

The Mumford Lecture, "The Architect for the Poorest of the Poor," The Bernard and Anne Spitzer School of Architecture, The City College of New York, New York, NY, US

Talk, "Saving Humanity and Saving the Planet," RIBA, London, UK

Lecture, "Rights-based Development for Climate Migrants Through Barefoot Social Architecture," Nabeel Hamdi Human Rights Festival 2022, Oxford Brookes University, Oxford, UK

Sir Arthur Marshall Visiting Professor in Sustainable Design, Department of Architecture, University of Cambridge, Cambridge, UK

Inaugural Lecture, "Climate Migrants. Making Communities Self-Reliant After the Catastrophic Pakistan Floods," University of Cambridge, Cambridge, UK

Visiting Professor at the Department of History of Architecture and Building Archaeology, Vienna University of Technology, Vienna, Austria

2023

Solo exhibition, "Yasmeen Lari: Architecture for the Future," Architekturzentrum Wien, Vienna, Austria

Selected Publications by Yasmeen Lari

Lahore. Illustrated City Guide. Karachi: Heritage Foundation of Pakistan, 2003.

Karachi. Illustrated City Guide. Karachi: Heritage Foundation of Pakistan, 2000.

With A. F. Baillie. *Kurrachee: Past, Present and Future*. Oxford: Oxford University Press, 1998.

With Suhail Z. Lari. *The Jewel of Sindh. Sama Monuments on Makli Hill*. Oxford: Oxford University Press, 1997.

With Mihail S. Lari. *The Dual City. Karachi during the Raj.* Oxford: Oxford University Press, Karachi: Heritage Foundation of Pakistan, 1996.

Traditional Architecture of Thatta. Photographs by Suhail Z. Lari, Karachi: Heritage Foundation of Pakistan, 1989.

Challenges of Transformation. Built Environment in Islamic Countries, 1st Conference of Architects and Town Planners of Islamic countries. Papers. Karachi: Pakistan Council of Architects and Town Planners, 1985.

With Suhail Z. Lari. "Recreational and Tourist Complexes. An Overview." In *Architecture and Community. Building in the Islamic World Today. The Aga Khan Award for Architecture*, 52–54, edited by Renata Holod, New York: Aperture, 1983.

"The Lines Area Resettlement Project, Karachi." In *Designing in Islamic Cultures 2. Urban Housing*, edited by Margaret Bentley Sevcenko, 56–64, Cambridge, MA: Aga Khan Program for Islamic Architecture, 1982.

"Slums are not a Lost Cause." *Pakistan Economist*, 1975.

Reports and Documentation

Tombs of Sultan Ibrahim & Amir Sultan Muhammad at WHS Makli, Thatta. Progress Report, US Ambassador's Fund for Cultural Preservation, No. 2017/7–9, July–Sept 2017.

Revival of Ancient Kashi in Sindh. Research Document, UNESCO Project, Karachi, 3 June 2015.

Inventory of Cultural Property of the Province of Sindh, Pakistan. Vol. 1–4. Archive, Digital Database Media. Reiff, RwTH Aachen, Germany, 2015. http://rio-heritage.org/events-all/inventory-cultural-property-province-sindh/

Sethi House, Peshawar, Documentation, Damage Assessment & Conservation. Karachi: Heritage Foundation of Pakistan, 2014.

The Tomb of Jam Nizam al-Din. Documentation and Condition Survey, Karachi: Heritage Foundation of Pakistan and UNESCO, September 2011.

National Register. Historic Places of Pakistan. Vol. 1–11, Heritage Foundation of Pakistan, Directorate of Archaeology & Museums, and Government of NWFP, eds., Karachi, 1986–2010.

Shalamar Garden Master Plan 2006–2011. Islamabad: UNESCO Islamabad (with Pamela Rogers), 2006.

Lahore Fort Master Plan 2006–2011. Islamabad: UNESCO Office Islamabad (with Pamela Rogers), 2006.

Cultural Tourism in Lahore and Peshawar. Islamabad: UNESCO Office Islamabad, 2004.

Preservation Guide. Vol. 1–7. Karachi: Heritage Foundation of Pakistan, n.d.

Karachi Archival Records, City Survey Maps. Project of Heritage Foundation of Pakistan, Embassy of the Kingdom of Netherlands, and Consulate General of the Federal Republic of Germany, Karachi, 2012.

"Chat aur Chardiwari." Report on housing for the Prime Minister's Five Point Programme, 1987.

Report of Habitat: United Nations Conference on Human Settlements. Vancouver, 31 May–11 June 1976. New York: United Nations, 1976. https:// digitallibrary.un. org/ record/793768.

"Tharparkar and Sialkot after the War." Report commissioned by UNICEF and the Government of Pakistan, 1973.

"Housing for Industrial Workers." Report commissioned by the Federal Ministry of Labour Pakistan, 1969.

Disaster Risk Reduction Manuals

Green Shelters Project, Barefoot Social Architecture. Karachi: Heritage Foundation of Pakistan, 2018.

Community Forests Makli Villages. Pakistan, Report. Karachi: Heritage Foundation of Pakistan, June 2018.

DRR-Compliant Sustainable Construction: Build Back Safer with Vernacular Methodologies. Final Narrative Report. Karachi: Heritage Foundation of Pakistan, 22 June 2013.

DRR-Compliant Sustainable Construction: Build Back Safer with Vernacular Methodologies. DRR-Driven Post-Flood Rehabilitation in Sindh. Karachi: Heritage Foundation of Pakistan, 2011.

Green KaravanGhar GKG & Beyond for Disaster Risk Reduction. Darya Khan Shaikh & Uthero District Khairpur, Sindh. Karachi: Heritage Foundation of Pakistan, 2011.

Green Karavan Ghar, The Low-Carbon, Low-Cost Nucleus House. Implementation Report, District Swat, Khyber Pakhtunkhwa. Karachi: Heritage Foundation of Pakistan, Aug 2010–Feb 2011.

Revival of Women's Livelihood in Swat. Karachi: Heritage Foundation, June 2010.

Bibliography

Abdullah, Farheen. "Karavan Karachi Streetfest and Cleaning of Historic Facades." *Youlin Magazine*, May 10, 2019. https://www.youlinmagazine.com/article/karavan-karachi-streetfest-and-cleaning-of-historic-facades/MTQ3MQ.

Abel, Emily K., and Margaret K. Nelson. *Circles of Care. Work and Identity in Women's Lives*. Albany, NY: State University of New York Press, 1990.

AKDN. "Aga Khan Award for Architecture – Friendship Centre." October 2016. https://www.akdn.org/architecture/project/friendship-centre.

AKDN. "AKDN | Aga Khan Award for Architecture." Accessed September 28, 2022. https://www.akdn.org/architecture.

Ali, Naziha Syed. "Wasteland foretold." *Dawn*, March 22, 2022. https://www.dawn.com/news/1681242/wasteland-foretold.

Anwer, Rizwan. "Sindh government intends to make Karachi Pakistan's first smart city." *TechJuice*, July 13, 2015. https://www.techjuice.pk/sindh-government-intends-to-make-karachi-pakistans-first-smart-city/.

Appadurai, Arjun. *The Future as Cultural Fact: Essays on the Global Condition*. London and New York: Verso, 2013.

architecture 2030. "The Built Environment." Accessed September 30, 2022, https://architecture2030.org/why-the-building-sector/.

Architecture.com. "RIBA International Prize 2021 – Friendship Hospital Satkhira." Accessed September 6, 2022. https://www.architecture.com/awards-and-competitions-landing-page/awards/riba-international-awards/2021/friendship-hospital-satkhira.

Ashfaq, Abira. *Understanding Urban Resilence: Migration, Displacement & Violence in Karachi*. International Committee for the Red Cross, May 2020. http://karachiurbanlab.com/assets/downloads/Understanding_Urban_Resilience_Migration_Displacement_&_Violence_in_Karachi.pdf.

Asia Dvelopment Bank. "Pakistan: Supporting Public–Private Partnership Investments in Sindh Province, Sovereign Project | 46538-002." Accessed on September 25, 2022. https://www.adb.org/projects/46538-002/main.

Aslam, Maria, ed. "Making of a Legend." *Architecture Design Art VIII, no. 32.* , Karachi: ArchWorks, 2015.

Barad, Karen. *Meeting the Universe Halfway: Quantum Physics and the Entanglement of Matter and Meaning*. Durham, NC and London: Duke University Press, 2007.

Barad, Karen. "Quantum Entanglements and Hauntological Relations of Inheritance: Dis/continuities, SpaceTime Enfoldings, and Justice-to-Come." *Derrida Today* 3, no. 2 (2010): 240–68.

Bartlett, Katharine T. "Feminist Legal Methods." *Harvard Law Review* 103, no. 4 (February 1989).

Bauman, Zygmunt. "Space in the Globalizing World." In *Theoria: A Journal of Social and Political Theory*, no. 97 (2001): 1–22.

Bee, Beth A., Jennifer Rice, and Amy Trauger. "A Feminist Approach to Climate Change Governance: Everyday and Intimate Politics." *Geography Compass* 9, no. 6 (June 2015): 339–50. https://www.academia.edu/31037647/A_feminist_approach_to_climate_change_governance_Everyday_and_intimate_politics.

Berlingieri, Fabrizia, Emilia Corradi, Cassandra Cozza, and Imma Forino, eds. *Yasmeen Lari: An Architect*. Translated by A. Arnone. Milan-Turin: Pearson Italia, 2021.

Bhan, Gautam, Smita Srinivas, and Vanessa Watson, eds. *The Routledge Companion to Planning in the Global South*. London: Routledge, 2017.

Butler, Judith. *The Force of Nonviolence. An Ethico-Political Bind*. London and New York: Verso, 2020.

Cameron, Edward, and Emilie Prattico. *The New Corporate Climate Leadership*. London: Routledge, 2021.

Cheng, Irene, Charles L. Davis II, and Mabel O. Wilson, eds. *Race and Modern Architecture. A Critical History from the Enlightenment to the Present*. Pittsburgh: University of Pittsburgh Press, 2020.

Chung, Stephy. "These bamboo shelters are empowering communities displaced by Pakistan's floods." *CNN Style*, September 30, 2022. https://edition.cnn.com/style/article/pakistan-floods-bamboo-shelters-climate-intl-hnk/index.html.

Cock, Jacklyn. "The Climate Crisis and a just transition in South Africa: an eco-feminist-socialist perspective." In *The Climate Crisis: South African and Global Democratic Eco-Socialist Alternatives*, edited by Vishwas Satgar, 210–30. Johannesburg: Wits University Press, 2018.

Colau, Ada and Adriá Alemany. *Mortgaged Lives. From the housing bubble to the right of housing*. Translated by Michelle Teran. Los Angeles, CA, Leipzig and London: Journal of Aesthetics & Protest, 2014.

Daechsel, Markus. *Islamabad and the Politics of International Development in Pakistan*. Cambridge: Cambridge University Press, 2015.

Davies, Margaret, and Vanessa E. Munro, eds. *The Ashgate Research Companion to Feminist Legal Theory*, New York: Routledge, 2016.

Devji, Faisal. *Muslim Zion: Pakistan as a Political Idea*. London: Hurst, 2013.

Dhulipala, Venkat. *Creating a New Medina*. Cambridge: Cambridge University Press, 2015.

Enloe, Cynthia. *The Curious Feminist. Searching for Women in a New Age of Empire*. Berkeley, CA: University of California Press, 2004.

Escobar, Arturo. "Worlds and Knowledges Otherwise," *Cultural Studies* 21, nos. 2–3 (2007): 179–210.

Farrukh, Niilofur, Amin Gulgee, and John McCarry, eds. *Pakistan's Radioactive Decade*. Oxford: Oxford University Press, 2019.

Fisher, Berenice, and Joan Tronto. "Toward a Feminist Theory of Caring." In *Circles of Care. Work and Identity in Women's Lives*, edited by Emily K. Abel and Margaret K. Nelson, 35–62. Albany, NY: State University of New York Press, 1990.

Fitz, Angelika, Elke Krasny, and Architekturzentrum Wien. *Critical Care: Architecture and Urbanism for a Broken Planet*. Cambridge, MA/London: The MIT Press, 2019.

Franchini, Caterina, and Emilia Garda. *Women's Creativity since the Modern Movement (1918–2018): Toward a New Perception and Reception*. MoMoWo Symposium 2018, Programme and Abstract of the International Conference. Turin: Politecnico di Torino, 2018.

Fraser, Valerie. *Building the New World. Studies in the Modern Architecture of Latin America 1930–1960*. London: Verso, 2001.

Frerks, Georg, Jeroen Warner, and Bart Weijs. "The politics of vulnerability and resilience." *Ambiente & Sociedade* 14, no. 2 (2011): 105–22.

Friedan, Betty. *The Fountain of Age*. New York: Simon & Schuster, 1984.

Friendship Newsdesk. "A Winning Partnership." January 28, 2022. https://friendship.ngo/a-winning-partnership/.

Graham, Stephen, and Simon Marvin. *Splintering Urbanisms: Networked Infrastructures, Technological Mobilities and the Urban Condition*. London: Routledge, 2001.

Hahn, Jennifer. "Using 'ancient wisdoms and techniques' can lead to carbon-neutral buildings says Yasmeen Lari." *dezeen*, July 1, 2021. https://www. dezeen. com/2021/07/01/carbon-neutral-architecture-yasmeen-lari-interview/.

Hanna, Rema, Esther Duflo, and Michael Greenstone. "Up in Smoke: The Influence of Household Behavior on the Long-Run Impact of Improved Cooking Stoves." MIT Center for Energy and Environmental Policy, July 2012. https://ceepr.mit.edu/wp-content/uploads/2021/09/2012-008.pdf.

Haraway, Donna J. *When Species Meet*. Minneapolis, MN: University of Minnesota Press, 2008.

Hasan, Arif. "City & Plans," December 10, 2018. http://arifhasan.org/karachi/city-plans.

Heller, Patrick. "Development in the City: Growth and Inclusion in India, Brazil, and South Africa." In *States in the Developing World*, edited by Miguel A. Centeno, Atul Kohli and Deborah J. Yashar, 309–38. Cambridge: Cambridge University Press, 2017.

Heritage Cell – Department of Architecture and Planning, NED University. *Karachi Heritage Buildings Re-survey Project*. Karachi: Heritage Cell – Department of Architecture and Planning, NED University, 2006–2009. (unpublished)

Illius, Shamsuddin. "Eco-friendly learning centres built for Rohingya children." The Independent, June 27, 2019. https://www.theindependentbd.com/printversion/details/204916.

Imarisha, Walidah. "To Build a Future Without Police and Prisons, We Have to Imagine It First." *OneZero*, October 22, 2020. https://onezero.medium.com/black-lives-matter-is-science-fiction-how-envisioning-a-better-future-makes-it-possible-5e14d35154e3.

IMF on Twitter. "Building a new #climate economy." March 11, 2021, 7:00 PM. https://twitter.com/IMFNews/status/1370072121989332998.

Imtiaz, Saba. "An Elegy for Karachi's Empress Market." Roads and Kingdoms, January 9, 2020. https://roadsandkingdoms.com/2020/empress-market-karachi/.

Janowicz, Marianna. "Kitchen debate: where labour and leisure collide." *The Architectural Review*, January 6, 2022.

Justices Azmat Saeed, Faisal Arab, and Munib Akhtar, CMA No. 8758-2018. Supreme Court of Pakistan, 2019.

Kalmati, Gul Hassan. *Malir ki Kahani [The Story of Malir]*. Lahore: Shirkat Gah Women's Resource Centre, 2009.

Kapila, Shruti. *Violent Fraternity: Indian Political Thought in the Global Age*. Princeton, NJ: Princeton University Press, 2021.

Karim, Farhan. "Pakistan Papers: Louis Kahn's Designs of a Past and Future in Islamabad and Dhaka." *Comparative Studies of South Asia, Africa and the Middle East* 40, no. 3 (2020): 507–25.

Karpf, Anne. *How to Age*. London: Pan Macmillan, 2014.

Karpf, Anne. *How Women Can Save the Planet*. London: Hurst Publishers, 2021.

Khalaf, Samir. "Contested Space and the Forging of New Cultural Identities." In *Projecting Beirut: Episodes in the Construction and Reconstruction of a Modern City*, edited by Peter Rowe and Hashim Sarkis, 140–64. New York: Prestel, 1998.

Khan, Naveeda. *Muslim Becoming: Aspiration and Skepticism in Pakistan*. Durham, NC: Duke University Press, 2012.

Khwaja, Zahir-ud Deen. *Memoirs of an Architect*. Lahore: Self-Published, 1998.

Krasny, Elke. "Care." In *AA Files* 76, edited by Maria Shéhérazade Giudici, 38–39. London: AA Publications, 2019.

Kings, Amy E. "Intersectionality and the Changing Face of Ecofeminism." *Ethics & the Environment* 22, no. 1 (2017): 63–87.

Kulterman, Udo. *Architekten der Dritten Welt*. Cologne: DuMont Buchverlag, 1980.

Lari, Suhail. "Oxford." Suhail Lari Pakistan, accessed July 28, 2022. https://www.suhaillaripakistan.com/chapters/Oxford/.

Lari, Yasmeen, ed. *Challenges to Transformation. Built Environment in Islamic Countries*. Lahore: Pakistan Council of Architects and Town Planners, 1985.

Lari, Yasmeen. "In conversation with…Yasmeen Lari." Interview by Alison Cleary and Susie Ashworth, Parlour, August 31, 2018. https://parlour.org.au/series/in-conversation/in-conversation-withyasmeen-lari/.

Lari, Yasmeen. Interview by Angelika Fitz and Elke Krasny, Vienna, September 6, 2019.

Lari, Yasmeen. Interview by Angelika Fitz and Elke Krasny, Karachi, February 15, 2022.

Lari Yasmeen. *Karachi. Illustrated City Guide*, Karachi: Heritage Foundation of Pakistan, 2000.

Lari, Yasmeen. "Team work for cultural heritage preservation." In *60 Women contributing to the 60 years of UNESCO – Constructing the Foundations of Peace*, edited by Ingeborg Breines and Hans d'Orville, 133–39. Paris: United Nations Educational, Scientific and Cultural Organization, 2006

Lari, Yasmeen, and Mihail S. Lari. *The Dual City. Karachi during the Raj.* Oxford: Oxford University Press, Karachi: Heritage Foundation of Pakistan, 1996.

Lari, Yasmeen. "The Lines Area Resettlement Project, Karachi." In *Designing in Islamic Cultures 2. Urban Housing*, edited by Margaret Bentley Sevcenko, 56–64, Cambridge, MA: Aga Khan Program for Islamic Architecture, 1982.

Lari, Yasmeen. *Traditional Architecture of Thatta*. Photographs by Suhail Z. Lari, Karachi: Heritage Foundation of Pakistan, 1989.

Lari, Yasmeen. "We need to do away with the prevalent colonial mindset and the desire to create imposing megastructures." *dezeen*, November 5, 2021, https://www.dezeen.com/2021/11/05/yasmeen-lari-manifesto-dezeen-15/.

Leon, Joshua K. "The global governance of housing: 1945–2016." *Planning Perspectives* 36, no. 3 (2021): 475–95.

Levy, Natasha. "Yasmeen Lari works with impoverished villagers to re-pave Karachi's old town." *dezeen*, November 5, 2021. https://www.dezeen.com/2021/11/05/yasmeen-lari-heritage-foundation-pakistan-terracotta-tiles/.

Lorde, Audre. *Sister Outsider*. London: Penguin, 2019.

MacGregor, Sherilyn. *Confronting the Climate Crisis: Feminist Pathways to Just and Sustainable Futures*. online webinar, The Consortium on Gender, Security and Human Rights, 2020.

Malik, Anushay. "Narrating Christians in Pakistan through Times of War and Conflict." *South Asia* 43, no. 1 (2020): 6–83.

Mann, Michael. *The Sources of Social Power. Volume I: A History of Power from the Beginning to A.D. 1760*. Cambridge: Cambridge University Press, 1988.

Meerow, Sara, Pani Pajouhesh, and Thaddeus R. Miller. "Social equity in urban resilience planning." *Local Environment* 24, no. 9 (2019): 793–808.

Moffat, Chris. "Lahore After the Modern: Architecture, equality and community in Yasmeen Lari's Anguri Bagh." *Global Intellectual History* (June 2022). DOI: 10.1080/23801883.2022.2062419.

Mumtaz, Kamil Khan. *Architecture in Pakistan*. Singapore: Concept Media, 1985.

Naeem, Anila. "The Conflict of Ideologies and Ambiguities in Conservation Policy: A Legacy of Shared Built Heritage in Pakistan." In *Asian heritage management: Contexts, concerns and prospects*, edited by Kapila D. Silva and Neel Kamal Chapagain, 87–104. London: Routledge, 2013.

Naeem, Anila. "Evolution and Repercussions of Heritage Designation Process in Sindh: Lessons from Karachi and Shikarpur." In *The Routledge Handbook on Historic Urban Landscapes in the Asia-Pacific*, edited by Kapila D. Silva, 131–48. London: Routledge, 2020.

Naeem, Anila. "Inventory of historic places: A systematic method for their identification, evaluation and determining significance – Part I: Core data and inventory form." *NED Journal of Research in Architecture and Planning*, 10, no. 1 (2011): 1–23.

Naeem, Anila. "Inventory of historic places: A systematic method for their identification, evaluation and determining significance – Part II: Case studies." *NED Journal of Research in Architecture and Planning*, 10, no. 1 (2011): 24–34.

Naeem, Anila. *Recognising Historic Significance Using Inventories: A Case of Historic Towns in Sindh, Pakistan*. PhD diss., Oxford Brookes University, 2009.

Naeem, Anila. *Shikarpoor: historic city, Sindh, Pakistan: Inventory and mapping of heritage properties – Vol. I & II*. Karachi: Endowment Fund Trust for Preservation of the Heritage of Sindh, 2013.

Naeem, Anila. *Urban traditions and historic environments in Sindh: A fading legacy of Shikarpoor, Historic City*. Amsterdam: The Amsterdam University Press, 2017.

Naimul, Karim. "In climate change-hit Bangladesh, hospital boats keep healthcare afloat." *Reuters*, May 22, 2019. https://www.reuters.com/article/us-bangladesh-climatechange-environment-idUSKCN1SS03U.

Naz, Neelum. "Development of Architectural Education in Pakistan." *CBER 7*, no. 2 (2010).

New Economy Project. "Building a New Economy." Accessed September 1, 2022. https://www.neweconomynyc.org/our-work/community-education/curriculum/.

Ngũgĩ Wa Thiong'o. *Decolonising the mind. The politics of language in African literature*. Oxford: James Currey Ltd.; Portsmouth, NH: Heinemann, 2005.

Nixon, Rob. *Slow Violence and the Environmentalism of the Poor*. Cambridge, MA: Harvard University Press, 2011.

Pasqui, Gabriele. "Territori Fragili. Un progetto transdiciplinare per il paese," *TF Giornale*, no. 1 (2021).

Penner, Barbara, Iain Borden, and Jane Rendell, eds. *Gender Space Architecture. An Interdisciplinary Introduction*. Abingdon: Routledge, 2000.

Pentland, Alex, Alexander Lipton, and Thomas Hardjono, *Building the New Economy. Data as Capital*. Cambridge, MA: The MIT Press, 2021.

Portoghesi, Paolo. *Architettura nei Paesi Islamici*. Exhibition Catalogue, 2. Biennale Architettura, La Biennale di Venezia, directed by Paolo Portoghesi, 20 Nov 1982–6 Jan 1983. Venice: La Biennale di Venezia, 1982.

Povinelli, Elizabeth A. *Geontologies. A Requiem to Late Liberalism*. Durham, NC and London: Duke University Press, 2016.

"Profile: Yasmeen Lari." In *Mimar. Architecture in Development*, 2, edited by Hasan-Uddin Khan, 45–54. Singapore: Concept Media Ltd., 1981.

"Profile: Yasmeen Lari." In *The ideal city. Exploring urban futures*, edited by Robert Klanten, Elli Stuhler, and SPACE10, 80–85, Berlin: Gestalten, 2021.

Ramzi, Shanaz. "How Karavan was Born." Heritage Foundation of Pakistan, accessed August 16, 2022, https://www.heritagefoundationpak.org/Page/1585/how-karavan-started-how-karavan-was-born-by-shanaz-ramzi-karavan-to-somewhere-by-sahar-ali-the-lady-i.

Ramzi, Shanaz. "Retrospective: Yasmeen Lari." *The Architectural Review*, September 9, 2019. https://www.architectural-review.com/buildings/retrospective-yasmeen-lari.

Rolnik, Raquel. *Urban Warfare. Housing Under the Empire of Finance*. Translated by Gabriel Hirschhorn. New York, London: Verso, 2019.

Roy, Arundhati. *Power Politics*. Boston: South End Press, 2001.

Roy, Deboleena. *Molecular Feminisms. Biology, Becomings, and Life in the Lab*. Seattle, WA: University of Washington Press, 2018.

Rudofsky, Bernard. *Architecture without architects. An introduction to nonpedigreed architecture*. New York: The Museum of Modern Art: Distributed by Doubleday, Garden City, NY, 1964.

Said, Edward. *Culture and Imperialism*. New York: Knopf, 1993.

Schaflechner, Jürgen. "Betwixt and Between: Hindu Identity in Pakistan and 'Wary and Aware' Public Performances." *South Asia: Journal of South Asian Studies* 43, no. 1 (2020): 152–68. https://doi.org/10.1080/00856401.2020.1692277.

Siddique, Abu. "Elevated homesteads give hope to flood-hit communities in Bangladesh." *Mongabay*, August 2, 2022. https://news.mongabay.com/2022/08/elevated-homesteads-give-hope-to-flood-hit-communities-in-bangladesh/.

Siddiqui, Anooradha Iyer, and Vazira Fazila-Yacoobi Zamindar. "Partitions: Architectures of Statelessness." *e-flux*, March 2022. https://www.e-flux.com/architecture/positions/454156/partitions-architectures-of-statelessness/.

Sindh Ordinance No. XIV of 1999: The Sindh Disposal of Urban Land Ordinance, 1999. http://sindhlaws.gov.pk/setup/publications_SindhCode/PUB-16-000039.pdf.

Sudakov, Dimitry. "Putin: Russia is building the new world order right now," *Pravda.Ru*, June 17, 2022. https://english.pravda.ru/russia/152411-putin_new_world_order/.

Thayer-Bacon, Barbara. "The Nurturing of a Relational Epistemology." *Educational Theory* 47, no. 2 (1997).

Thériault, Annie, and Jade Tenwick. "'Terrifying prospect' of over a quarter of a billion more people crashing into extreme levels of poverty and suffering this year." *Oxfam International*, April 12, 2022. https://www.oxfam.org/en/press-releases/terrifying-prospect-over-quarter-billion-more-people-crashing-extreme-levels-poverty.

The World Bank. "World Bank Announces $300 Million for Pakistan to Build Resilience to Natural Disasters and Health Emergencies," December 8, 2020. https://www.worldbank.org/en/news/press-release/2020/12/08/world-bank-announces-300-million-for-pakistan-to-build-resilience-to-natural-disasters-and-health-emergencies.

Thomas, Helen, ed. *20th-Century World Architecture*. "Lari House," 79. London: Phaidon, 2012.

Tombesi, Paolo. "Affirming Actions EPFL. Opening." Rolex Learning Center, Lausanne, Switzerland, video, 01:55, May 29, 2021. https://www.youtube.com/watch?v=Q8kuoXBSsRg&list=PL79IasEcK4rAMGlrlOboZil7eRGCv-PJS&index=1&t=115s.

Tronto, Joan. *Who Cares? How to Reshape a Democratic Politics*. Ithaca, NY and London: Cornell University Press, 2015.

Tsing, Anna. "Earth Stalked by Man." *The Cambridge Journal of Anthropology* 34, no. 1 (2016): 2–16.

Tsing, Anna, Heather Swanson, Elaine Gan, and Nils Bubandt, eds. *Arts of Living on a Damaged Planet*. Minneapolis, MN: University of Minnesota Press, 2016.

UNDP. *Gender and Climate Change*. New York: United Nations, 2016.

United Nations List of National Parks and Equivalent Reserves. IUCN Publications News No. 33. Morges, Switzerland: International Union for Conservation of Nature and Natural Resources, 1975.

UN News. "Pakistan: More than 6.4 million in 'dire need' after unprecedented flood," September 2, 2022. https://news.un.org/en/story/2022/09/1126001.

Vandal, Pervaiz. "Architecture in the Post-Colonial Lahore." In *Portrait of Lahore*, edited by Pervaiz Vandal, 203–24. Lahore: THAAP, 2012.

van Heeswijk, Jeanne, Maria Hlavajova, and Rachael Rakes, eds. *Toward the Not-Yet: Art as Public Practice*. Cambridge, MA and London: The MIT Press, 2021.

Vergès, Françoise. *Decolonial Feminism*. Translated by Ashley J. Bohrer. London: Pluto Press, 2021.

Wainwright, Oliver. "The barefoot architect: 'I was a starchitect for 36 years. Now I'm atoning.'" *The Guardian*, April 1, 2020. https://www.theguardian.com/artanddesign/2020/apr/01/yasmeen-lari-pakistan-architect-first-female-jane-drew.

Wallace-Wells, David. *The Uninhabitable Earth. A Story of the Future*. New York: Crown Publishing, 2020.

Weintrobe, Sally. *Psychological Roots of the Climate Crisis: Neoliberal Exceptionalism and the Culture of Uncare*. New York: Bloomsbury Publishing, 2021.

Weisman, Leslie. "Women's Environmental Rights: A Manifesto." In *Gender Space Architecture*, edited by Barbara Penner, Iain Borden, and Jane Rendell, 1–5. Abingdon: Routledge, 2000.

Women's Budget Group. *Creating a Caring Economy*. London: WBG 2020.

"Yasmeen Lari's Zero Carbon Channel." YouTube, https://www.youtube.com/c/YasmeenLarisZeroCarbonChannel.

Zaman, Fahim, and Naziha Syed Ali. "Bahria Town Karachi: Greed unlimited." *Dawn*, April 8, 2019. https://www.dawn.com/news/1252809.

Zaretsky, Eli. *Capitalism, the Family and Personal Life*. London: Pluto, 1976.

Zeitoun, Lea. "'Lari Octa Green': Sustainable Bamboo Design for Flood Relief." *designboom*, October 26, 2022. https://www.designboom.com/architecture/lari-octa-green-emergency-bamboo-shelters-flood-relief-heritage-foundation-of-pakistan-10-26-2022/.

Zuberi, Yemeen. "PCATP completes eight years." *Archi Times*, November 1990.

Zumtobel Group. "Zumtobel Group Award 2021 – Nominated in the Category Buildings: Cyclone Shelter." December 14, 2021. https://z.lighting/en/group/news-insights/group/zumtobel-group-award-2021-nominated-in-the-category-buildings-cyclone-shelter/.

Further Literature and Media

Adnan, Jaudat. "Yasmeen Lari's Chulah Stoves." In *Pakistan in Resurgence of organicism*, edited by Sarah Bonnemaison, 40–43, Riverside Architectural Press & Dalhousie Architectural Press 2019.

Al Jazeera. *Rebel Architecture. Pakistan: A Traditional Future*. Film by Faiza Ahmad Khan, 2014. https://www.aljazeera.com/program/rebel-architecture/2016/4/27/pakistan-a-traditional-future.

Ashfaq, Abira. *Keeping Out the Other: A Critical Introduction to Immigration Enforcement Today*. Columbia University Press, 2008.

Bloom, Jonathan, ed. *The Grove Encyclopedia of Islamic Art and Architecture*. Yasmeen Lari, 93. Oxford: Oxford University Press, 2009.

Bordone, Simone. "Pakistan Chulah." *Domus*, Jan 3, 2017. https://www.domusweb.it/en/architecture/2017/01/03/the_pakistan_chulah.html.

Gillin, Jaime. "Q&A with Pakistan's First Female Architect." *Dwell Magazine*, July 2, 2012, https://www.dwell.com/article/qanda-with-pakistans-first-female-architect-d642fdb6.

Jeong, Da Hyung. "Anguri Bagh Housing." *The Project of Independence: Architectures of Decolonization in South Asia, 1947–1985*. Edited by Martino Stierli, Anoma Pieris, and Sean Anderson. New York: The Museum of Modern Art, 2022.

Karpf, Anne. *The War After: Living with the Holocaust*. Portsmouth, NH: Heinemann, 1996.

Karpf, Anne, Brian Klug, Jacqueline Rose, and Barbara Rosenbaum, eds. *A Time to Speak Out: Independent Jewish Voices on Israel, Zionism and Jewish Identity*. New York/London: Verso, 2008.

Moffat, Chris. *India's Revolutionary Inheritance: Politics and the Promise of Bhagat Singh*. Cambridge University Press, 2019.

Naeem, Anila. *Urban Traditions and Historic Environments in Sindh: A Fading Legacy of Shikarpoor, Historic City*. Amsterdam: Amsterdam University Press, 2017.

Nizam, Mariyam. "Lari House, Karachi, Pakistan." *SOS Brutalism. A Global Survey*, edited by Oliver Elser, Philip Kurz, Peter Cachola Schmal. In cooperation with Deutsches Architekturmuseum DAM and Wüstenrot Foundation, 322–23. Zurich: Park Books, 2017.

Piciocchi, Alice. "The Heritage of the Earth." *Abitare*, May 20, 2017. https://www.abitare.it/en/habitat-en/historical-heritage/2017/05/20/donne-custodiscono-tradizioni-terra/.

Rolnik, Raquel. *São Paulo: o planejamento da desigualdade*, São Paulo: Fósforo, 2022.

Shah, Sonal. "In Conversation with Yasmeen Lari." *Elle Décor India*, Oct–Nov 2014: 64–66.

Thomas, Helen. *Architecture in Islamic Countries: Selections from the Catalogue for the Second International Exhibition of Architecture Venice 1982/83*. Zurich: gta Verlag, 2022.

Thomas, Helen. *Extracts 2: Women Writing Architecture*. Drawing Matter, 2021.

Thomas, Helen. "'In architectural practice you are so isolated from the reality of the country:' Yasmeen Lari and self-sustaining architecture." *The Architectural Review*, March 9, 2020. https://www.architectural-review.com/ awards/w-awards/in-architectural-practice-you-are-so-isolated-from-the-reality-of-the-country-yasmeen-lari-and-self-sustaining-architecture.

Thomas, Helen. "Introduction to Yasmeen Lari." *Dwell Magazine*, July 20 2017.

Thomas, Helen. "Technology and architecture: from the Venice Biennale of 1982 to Yasmeen Lari's 'instant Islamic.'" *Domus*, 1050, October 25, 2020. https://www.domusweb.it/en/architecture/2020/10/22/alternating-currents-technology-as-cultural-expression.html.

Thomas, Helen. *The Hybrid Practitioner*. Leuven: Leuven University Press, 2022.

Thomas, Helen. "Yasmeen Lari: Drawn Closer." *Domus*, 1045, April 7, 2020. https://drawingmatter.org/yasmeen-lari-drawn-closer/.

Thomas, Helen, and Adam Caruso, eds. *The Limits of Modernism – A Forgotten Generation of European Architects*. Zurich: gta Verlag, 2019–2021.

Thomas, Helen, Desleay Luscombe, and Niall Hobhouse. *Architecture through Drawing*. London: Lund Humphries, 2019.

Thomas, Helen, ed. *Drawing Architecture*, London: Phaidon Press Limited, 2018.

Zakaria, Rafia. *Against White Feminism: Notes on Disruption*, London: Penguin Books Ltd, 2021.

Zakaria, Rafia. *The Upstairs Wife: An Intimate History of Pakistan*. Boston, MA: Beacon Press, 2015.

Zakaria, Rafia. *Veil*. London: Bloomsbury Publishing, 2017.

A

Aalto, Alvar, 95,
Abdullah, Farheen, 169n5
Abel, Emily K., 241n25
accessibility, 56, 209
activism, civic 73; zero-carbon, 63;
activist, 10, 14, 16, 17, 19, 89, 161, 167, 198, 199, 206, 209, 210, 211, 212, 224, 232, 235, 243, 246, 247, 249
Adabistan-e-Soofia School, 33, 255
advocacy, 73, 158, 180, 191, 199, 241
aesthetics, 209, 213, 214, 216, 231, 243n28
Afghan War, 147
Afghanistan, 97
Aga Khan, Award for Architecture, 13, 43, 92, 95, 95n2, 167, 170, 214, 214n2, 260; Group, 93; Trust for Culture, 61, 89, 92, 247
agency, human; shared, 12, 21, 164, 210
agents for change, 197
agriculture, 185, 198, 199
agrobusiness, 20
Ahed, M.A., 158
Ahsan, Syed Mohammad, 38, 44
Ahsan, Zafarul, 34, 157
Aiglemont, 92, 170, 260
air, bad, 115; conditioners, 216; flow, 213; fresh, 115
Aijaz, Rahul, 64, 247
aid industry; international aid complex, 10, 16, 97, 98, 99, 105, 147, 201
Alexandria, 92
Ali, Habib Fida, 159, 170,
Ali, Naziha Syed, 197n16, 199n21
Ali, Shakir, 168
Ali Murad Goth, 195
All-India Muslim League, 154
American University of Beirut, 159
Amritsar, 156
Amro Bank, 15, 57, 97, 174, 256
Angoori Bagh, 36, 37, 38, 39, 40, 45, 142, 143, 144, 162, 163, 170, 170n16, 255
Anthropocene, 191, 239, 240
Anti-Encroachment Force, 189
Anwer, Rizwan, 184n2
archeological site, 76, 256
architectural, canon, 74; education 16, 157, 157n11; history, 18, 27, 159, 235; monuments, 107; Pakistan's history, 159; styles, 59
architect, a catalyst, 167; activist-, 206, 209, 211; Brutalist, 166; as expert problem solver, 163; as listener and facilitator, 163; first female, 222; signature, 174
architects, engineer-, 171; feminist, 209, 210, 211; Pakistani, 56, 145, 158, 160, 161, 222; non-, 171;
Architects Regional Council of Asia ARCASIA, 167, 171, 258
architecture, as a profession in Pakistan, 156; barefoot, 164, 206n2, , 222n2, 224, 262; cultural values in, 73; democratize, 209; emergency, 16; feminist-activist, 210; for the future, 10, 12, 15, 17, 18, 21, 22, 234, 238, 256, 248, 262; Islamic 47, 50, 56, 92, 97, 160; of care, 221; Pakistani, 56, 146, 160, 161, 163, 227; pre-Mughal and Mughal funerary, 82; relief, 12, 66, 101; retire from, 97, 171; rural humanitarian zero-carbon, 70; traditional mud, 59, 102; vernacular, 16, 69, 73, 74, 76, 100, 122, 167, 172, 174, 210, 231, 236; zero-carbon humanistic, 227
Architecture Campus in Milan, 227
Architecture for Humanity, 232
Ardalan, Nader, 170
Appadurai, Arjun, 238, 238n14
army, barracks, 59, 62
artisans, 81, 103, 149, 150, 169, 247
Ashfaq, Abira, 19, 193–200, 194n3, 198n19, 247, 248, 249
Asia Development Bank, 194n2
asphalt, 115, 116
atmosphere, 31, 213, 214; Planet Earth's, 237
Awaran Earthquake, 102, 103
Ayub Khan, Muhammad, 160, 161
Ayub Nagar, 160

B

Bagri, 193, 195, 196, 197, 200
Bahawalpur, 58, 59, 60, 169, 256, 260
Bahria Town, 193, 197, 197n16
Baloch, Hafeez, 198n19, 199n22
Baloch, 193, 195, 196, 197, 198, 200
Balochistan, Province, 102, 162
bamboo, 12n4, 20, 59, 66, 67, 68, 69, 101, 102, 105, 107, 108, 113, 121, 122, 123, 124, 133, 136, 149, 209, 210, 218, 226, 227, 230, 231, 247; maquettes, 226, 228; prefabricated modules, 69, 108, 110, 122, 126, 127, 133, 134, 228, 229, 232; platforms, 116; shelters, 10,10n1, 15, 102
Bandaranayake, Senayake, 168
Bangladesh, 20, 66, 85, 119, 160, 161, 214, 214n1, 216, 216n4, 218, 232, 250, 259, 260, 261
Barad, Karen, 235, 235n7, 236n9
Barcelona, 189
Barefoot Architecture Project, 224
Barnett, Clive, 190n15
Bartlett, Katharina T., 197n15, 200n27
Bay of Bengal, 214
Bauman, Zygmunt, 190n13
beauty, local, 232
Bee, Beth A., 194n4
Begum, Shirin Amir, 59
Belasis Street, 179
Bengal, Subah, 160
Berlin, Sir Isaiah, 168
Breines, Ingeborg, 78, 80, 92, 145, 172, 172n21
Bhamani, Tajuddin, 158
Bhan, Gautam, 190n14, 190n15, 191n17, 192n18
Bheel, 195
Bhutto, Zulfikar Ali, 15, 37, 50, 142, 161, 169; Administration, 15, 37, 38, 59, 162; era, 161, 162, 169
Bilbao, Tatiana, 232
bodily, 21, 242
Bombay, 157
Borden, Iain, 207n7
bricks, bricklaying technology, 41, 63, 155; earth, 59, 61; sundried mud-, 67, 111, 123, 131, 133, 162; -out of dung or sawdust, 210, 223; used as weapons, 156
British, Antiquities Act, 90, 175; Council, 87, 147, 168; rule, 30, 57, 73, 77, 141, 174; soldiers, 47
Brown, Adrienne, 239n17
Brutalism, 15, 27, 28
building, as a metaphor, 234, 235, 238; cleaned the, 118; hegemonic history of, 235; historic, 63, 115, 118, 147, 150, 176, 176n2, 180; industry, 21, 162; local traditions, 62, 69, 74, 105; of homes, 20, 202, 241; knowledge of traditional, 69; materials, 12, 15, 17, 59, 60, 69, 174, 219, 229, 241; modern, 234; privacy, 47; self-help, 47, 66, 97; self-, 37, 66, 97, 97, 98; techniques, 71, 97, 100
builder/builders, self-, 227
business, 15, 15, 49, 115, 177, 178, 181, 194; agro-, 20; architecture as, 145

C

Café Al-Mehran, 157
Cairo University, 93
Cantonments, 187
canon, of singular architectural objects, 235
capabilities, 186, 224
capital, 27, 97, 201, 202, 239

capitalism, 12, 185, 202, 205, 207n6, 236, 240, 243; finance, 49

carbon, emissions, 210

care; critical 22, 22n6, 210n21, 212n33, 237, 237n12, 240n22, 246, 253; planetary, 18, 21, 234–244; Tronto-Fisher framework of, 241, 242; work

caring, activities, 206; with a wounded planet, 241, 242, 243; with the planet, 243, 244

caste, 13, 154, 185, 194, 195, 211

cement, 61, 64, 65, 97, 105, 122, 123, 149, 150, 176, 196, 203

Centeno, Miguel A., 192n19

Champa, 132

Chapagain, Neel Kamal, 175n1

Cheng, Irene, 239n17

children, Rohingya; women and 218, 218n6

Chowdhury, Kashef Mahboob, 214, 216

chowkandi, 198

chulah; Adhis, 130; Pakistan, 17, 95, 112, 121, 130, 131, 132, 150, 167, 168, 210, 211, 221, 223, 224, 225, 229, 231, 247, 256, 257; smokeless, 111

civil society, organizations, 16, 89, 90

class, lower, 16, 37, 89, 90; middle, 15, 27, 39, 44, 185, 223

clay, 41, 123, 126, 169, 216

Clean Stoves Initiative, 225

cleaning, 79, 87, 169, 169n5, 206, 208, 220

climate, change, 19, 63, 105, 106, 122, 149, 193–300, 208n13, 216n4; change discourse, 200; change policy, 200; corporate leadership, 234, 235n4; crisis, 20, 106, 194n6, 196n11, 206-212, 207n3, 207n4; destruction, 12, 15, 21; economy, 234, 235n4; emergency, 206, 210; -impacted, 12, 18, 213, 218; informants, 197; new economy, 234, 234n3; -related loss, 21; policy, 208; ruination, 12, 16, 18, 21, 242

Cock, Jacklyn, 194n6

Colau, Ada, 243n28

Colombo Plan, 159

colonial, anti-, 235; -era laws; heritage, 57, 146; mindset, 16, 22, 22n7, 210n27, 212n34, 224, 225, 224n4; rule, 30, 73, 77, 140; rulers, 57; times, 47; violence, 235

colonialist, 12, 74, 239

colonialism, neocolonial continuation of, 98

coloniality; patriarchal coloniality, 13

comfort, 75

commodity, 202

community, Bagri, 195; center, 63, 100; collaboration, 225; development, 221; international, 157n9, 159, 160n13, 225; involvement, 84, 180; kitchens, 101, 149, 256; meeting, 100

communities, coastal, 214; Muslim, 47; refugee, 218; river, 214

Complex La Cité, 51

concrete, reinforced, 28, 41

Conference of Architects and Town Planners of Islamic Countries, 14, 94, 171

conservation, 64, 73, 80, 81, 82, 84, 85, 171, 174, 175, 175n1, 176, 178, 180, 181, 198n20

construction, industry, 15, 98, 204, 210; sector, 21, 98, 105; simple methods, 47; under, 19, 154–165

cooking stoves, 20, 220, 220n1

cooling, passive, 74

Correa, Charles, 93, 170

CO_2 emitters, 105

Council of Architects and Planners of Islamic Countries, 167

courtyard, 27, 42, 44, 45, 47, 53, 61, 70, 143, 144, 145

Covid-19, 33, 114, 253

Cozza, Cassandra, 20, 226-233, 228n1, 229n3, 231n7, 240, 248, 249

craft, 59, 73, 84, 86, 87, 90, 127, 143, 167, 176, 220

craftspeople, 114, 168, 223

crisis, 12, 19, 20, 98, 106, 183, 194n6, 196n11, 204, 207n3, 207n4, 206, 208, 210, 211, 250

cultural tourism, 172

cyclone, 106, 214, 215, 215n3, 216

D

d'Orville, Hans, 172n21

Daechsel, Markus, 157, 160

Dada, Nayyar Ali, 159

Dalokay, Vedat, 162, 163

Dangerous Buildings, 178

Dani, 247

Darya Khan Sheikh, 66, 108, 135, 136, 229

Davies, Margaret, 197n13

de-privileging, 209

decarbonizing, 209

decolonial, decolonizing, 13n5, 16, 73, 237

decolonization, 12, 73, 69, 158

Defence Housing Authority DHA, 193

Delhi Polytechnic, 157

Delta, 219

Denso Hall, 87, 115, 118, 150, 257, 258

Dera Ismail Khan District, 63

design, ethical, 227; perspective, 59; spirit of the, 216; studios, 66; urban, 69, 143, 249, 255

destruction, 12, 15, 16, 21, 98, 148, 149, 202, 212, 218

developing countries, 43, 188

development, 44, 50, 51, 77, 158, 160, 164; agencies, 222; crisis, 19, 183–192; critics, 223; housing, 170; international, 98, 157n9 159, 160n13, 225; postcolonial, 157; rural, 188, 194, 196, 200; sustainable, 85, 167, 190n15; urban, 49, 175, 177, 181, 184

Deh Kathore, 198, 198n18

Devi, 196, 196n12, 197

Dhaka, 159, 160, 160n13, 161, 259, 260

digital, 17, 20, 105, 114, 134, 170n14, 227, 228, 229, 230, 231, 233

dignity, 12, 18, 20, 22, 105, 121, 150, 210, 214, 219, 232, 250; life in, 133

Dir, 68

Director of the Islamabad UNESCO Office, 78, 145

Directorate of Archeology in Sindh Province, 64, 84

Director General of the Archeological Survey of India, 64

disaster/disasters, natural, 66, 98, 105, 109, 114, 121, 125, 126, 149, 166, 167, 172, 175 187n10, 195, 196, 208, 222, 261, 264; planning, 196

displacement, 193, 194n3, 196, 197, 232

dispossession, 20, 188, 202, 204

Doxiadis, Constantinos, Associates, 27, 33, 46, 143, 159, 160, 162

Drought, 20, 187, 208, 210, 212

Du Bois, W.E.B., 235

Dubai, 49, 185

Dubaiization, 49

Duflo, Esther, 220n1

dwelling, units, 39, 42

E

Earth, 12n3, 207, 209, 235n5, 237, 239n18, 241

earthquake, 11, 16, 62, 68, 97, 98, 100, 102, 103, 105, 106, 122, 124, 127, 147, 148, 149, 172, 206, 210, 228, 256

East India Company, 186

East Pakistan University of Engineering and Technology, 159

Écochard, Michel, 159, 160

ecologies, zero-carbon, 62

economic opportunity, 234

economy, craft-based heritage, 87; doughnut, 20, 210, 210n25

economies, of resources, 59

Education City, 193

Eiffel Tower, 198

Electric Supply Corporation, 181

elite, 19, 38, 39, 157, 188, 193, 197, 198, 209, 222

emergency, shelters, 12, 16, 208

Emperor Shah Jahan, 39

mpowerment and Dignity for Women through Built Environment, 232 Interventions, 83, 187, 190, 191, 218, 219, 232
ncroachment, drive, 189, 190
ngland, 29, 30, 33, 73, 141, 157
nlightenment, 12, 239, 239n17
nloe, Cynthia, 237, 237n13
nvironment, 18, 20, 50, 91, 171, 171n19, 171n20, 173, 181, 184, 190, 193n1, 200, 200n28, 203, 208, 213, 214, 216, 218, 221, 232, 241, 242
nvironmental, degradation, 177, 186, 196, 197, 198, 200, 207, 220, 223
quity, social, 193, 193n1, 194n5
thical, 11, 12, 16, 17, 22, 59, 167, 227, 232, 234, 235, 237, 240, 241
thics, of dignity, 22
thnicity, 12, 154, 194
thos, 237, 238
pistemological/epistemologies, 237, 240
quality, 15, 37, 47n1, 157n10, 162n15, 203, 205
scobar, Arturo, 237, 237n11
ssentials, for life, 17, 121–136
thos, 237, 238
veryday, communal life, 44; life, 12, 29, 40, 115, 194, 195
xpansion, 109, 157, 199, 239
xperiment/experimenting, 15, 30, 54, 60, 62, 71, 109, 110, 130, 161, 162, 165, 211
xploitation, 12n3, 19, 27, 105, 151, 207, 236, 237, 239
xtraction, 12n3, 21, 239, 240
xtreme weather events, 10, 20, 102, 105, 106, 210, 240, 241, 242

F

Façades, historic, 151, 182
Faisal Masjid, 162, 163
Fakhr Matri, 177
Farmers, 195, 197, 198, 199
farm work, 19, 196, 199
Farrukh, Amin Gulgee, 170n8, 170n9
Fathi, Hassan, 15, 59
Fazal Mansion, 87
feminism, 13n5, 20, 197n13, 200n28, 220, 224, 225, 236n9, 252, 253
feminist, cultural theory, 235; curiosity, 237; empowerment conversation, 225; epistemic rebellion, 225; knowledge, 20, 220-225; method, 200, 237; solutions 18; theorist, 235
Fraser, Valerie, 234n1
Frere Hall, 57
finance, 19, 49, 201, 202, 203, 204, 205, 243, 253

Financialization, 19, 201, 202, 203, 204
Finance and Trade Centre, 15, 49, 50, 70, 145, 174, 222, 247, 256
firewood, 196, 210, 221
First Asian Congress of Architects, 94, 258, 260
First Conference of Architects and Town Planners of Islamic Countries, 14, 94, 171
Fisher, Berenice, 241, 241n25
Fitz, Angelika, 10–22, 22n6, 24, 26–35, 48–57, 89–95. 104–119, 120–136, 141–151, 208n9, 210n21, 212n33, 234–244, 237n12, 240n22, 246, 253
floating hospitals, 216
flood, disaster, 114; floods, 10, 10n1, 16, 20, 105, 106, 116, 121, 127, 128, 187, 193, 195, 208, 214
flooding, severe, 108
Floor Area Ratios FAR, 179
Ford Foundation, 46, 158
fossil fuel, 123, 130
Frankfurt School, 237
freedom, 37, 160
Frerks, Georg, 194n7
Freudian reinterpretation of Marx, 237
Friedan, Betty, 207, 207n5
Friendship, Centre Gaibandha, 20, 214, 218; Hospital Shyamnagar, 20, 216, 217; Lifebuyo Hospital, 217; NGO, 20; Plinth, 214, 215
Fulbright, Program, 158; Professors, 159
funding, 64, 147, 149, 169, 170, 190
future, 10–22, 27, 34, 55, 59, 60, 73, 89, 118, 121, 136, 149, 151, 155, 157, 160n13, 163, 164, 165, 184, 191, 204, 207n3, 227, 235n5, 234–244; care, 21, 236; -enabling, 236; -making, 10, 11, 12, 14, 235, 236, 238, 243; responsibility to the, 11, 236; modern, 236, 239, 240, 243

G

Gadap, 198
Gaibandha, 20, 214, 218
galis, 156
gender, inequalities, 208, 211
gendered, division of labor, 197
gigantism, 212
glass, 15, 17, 27, 49, 55, 59, 156, 165, 208, 229
global, North, 185, 208, 211, 228; South, 150, 184, 189, 190n14, 190n15, 191n17, 192n18, 211, 232
governance, urban, 169, 170n11, 171,183, 185, 186, 187, 192, 194, 200
Government School of Architecture, 157
Graham, Stephen, 184n2
granite, 49, 146
Great Britain, 16, 27

Green Women's Centre, 108, 135, 136, 256
Greening, 117
Greenstone, Michael, 220n1
grounding, 164
growth, 55, 181, 184, 185, 191, 192n18, 192n19, 212, 215, 239

H

Hadi Bux Bukhsh Goth, 198
Haji Shaif Mohammad Kachelo Goth, 198
Hanna, Rema, 220n1
Haraway, Donna J., 235, 235n8, 238n16
Hardjono, Thomas, 234n3
Hardwick, Richard, 168
Haris, 102
Hasan, Arif, 159, 170, 186n7, 187n9, 190, 247
Harvard University, 92, 236n10
Hassan, Mubashir, 38, 142
healing, planetary, 244
health system, 216
Heeswijk, Jeanne van, 243n29
Heller, Patrick, 192n18, 192n19
Heringer, Anna, 232
heritage, designation status, 176, 178; enlistments, 175, 176; inventories, 176, 182; management, 173, 175n1, 176, 177; management framework, 177; management and monitoring, 176; material, 59; preservation, 174, 175, 179, 180, 182; site, 16, 64, 73, 78, 84, 85, 89, 92, 109, 116, 145, 149, 172, 174, 176, 256, 259; training, 87; work, 63, 65, 73, 80, 145, 172
hierarchy/hierarchies, 164, 225, 236
Hilal-e-Imtiaz, 174, 257
Himalayas, 10, 68, 162
Hindu, traders, 80, 156
hissa, 195
Hlavajova, Maria, 243n29
Holistic, 20, 210, 211
Holl, Steven, 95
home, problem of, 37
homeless, 97, 107, 127
homes, building of, 20, 202, 241; makeshift, 195
Honorary Degree in Architecture – Laurea Magistrale ad honorem in Architettura a Ingegneria Edile-Architetettura, 227, 257
hope, politics of, 22
household, kitchens, 100; latrines 100
housework, 194, 207
houses; flood-resistant mud, 108; safe, 120
housing, adequate 37, 201, 202, 203, 253; collective, 44; crisis, 204; decolonize, 205; elite, 19, 193, 197; financialization of, 19, 201, 203, 204; for the poor, 170; industrialized, 20; is not a plantation, 203;

land for, 202; mass, 21; non-high-rise, 44; policies, 204, 205; problems, 43; production of, 201, 202; right to, 18, 19, 170, 201–205, 239n20; schemes, 189; sector, 201; social, 15, 38, 39, 122, 142, 144, 170; typologies, 20, 202
human rights, 19, 20, 89, 121, 144, 150, 170, 203, 207n3, 249, 251, 262
humanitarian, rebuilding efforts, 71; worker, 16, 97–103, 146
Hyderabad, 74, 157, 191n17, 195

I

icons, 15, 21, 49–56
imaginary/imaginaries, 14, 17, 21, 234, 235, 236, 237, 238, 240, 241, 242, 253
Imarisha, Walidah, 243, 243n29
imperialism, European, 234
Imtiaz, Saba, 190n12
India, 20, 27, 46, 64, 94, 97, 154, 157, 168, 185, 191, 191n17, 192n18, 192n19, 220, 223, 250, 255, 261
Indian Civil Service ICS, 34
Indus, 76, 194
industrialized systems, 97, 148
inequities, structural, 197, 200
informal, 19, 47, 53, 143, 168, 185, 186, 187, 189, 190, 194, 236
infrastructure, infrastructures, 15, 17, 20, 46; essential 10, 12, 18, 21; delivery, 192; vital, 134
injustice, epistemic, 197
innovation, 15, 16, 209
Institute of Architects, Pakistan IAP, 13, 93, 94, 157, 171, 258
Institutions, 13, 16, 89–95, 157, 171, 181, 224
INTBAU, 110, 175, 232, 247, 259
Interconnectedness, 209
intergovernmental organizations, 167
interiority, 50, 53, 70
internally displaced people, 142
International Monetary Fund, 234
International Organization for Migration, 107, 130
intersectional, 13, 200n28
Iran, 85, 226
Islam, Muzharul, 159
Islamabad, 27, 78, 80, 84, 92, 143, 145, 157n9, 160, 160n13, 162, 171, 258, 259, 260, 261
Islamic, building traditions, 89; Housing Design in Cultures, 47, 93; instant, 56, 97; socialism, 161
Islamic Republic of Pakistan, Constitution of the, 160, 173, 187
Istanbul, 189
Italy, 66, 85, 226, 257, 260

J

Jabbar, 98, 100
Jam Nizamuddin II, 83
Jane Drew Prize of the Royal Institute of British Architects, 95, 222, 257
Janowicz, Marianna, 208n8
Jansen, Michael, 76
Fukuoka Art and Culture Prize, 95, 257
Jatiya Sangsad Bhaban, 160, 161
Jensen, Vibeke, 84
Jokhio, 193, 199, 199n23
Jordan, 84, 260
Junejo, Rabela, 82
justice, ecological, 144, 210; ecological and social, 71, 210, 227, 232, 248

K

Kahn, Louis I., 95, 161
Kalmati, Gul Hassan, 195n8, 198
Kanji Building, 179
Karachi, Artists' Gallery, 89, 255, 259; Boulevard, 15, 49–57; Bunder Quarter, 177; first Smart City of Pakistan, 184; Historic District Authority, 181; Karavan, 86, 87, 90, 118, 146, 168, 169n4, 169n5, 175, 256; Malir District, 19, 193, 197, 198, 198n18; Press Club, 89; Public Work Department, 157; rural, 193, 194, 198; Serai Quarter, 179; US Embassy, 35
Karavan, Karachi, 118, 147, 175, 256; Pakistan, 86, 175, 256
kapda (cloth), 15, 37
Kareema Village, 62
Karpf, Anne, 20, 206–212, 248, 250
Kathore, 198, 198n18, 198n19
Khairpur, 66, 108
Khalaf, Samir, 186, 186n6
Khan, Rahimuddin, 60
Khan, Runa, 20, 213–219, 250, 252
Khyber Pakhtunkhwa, 63, 68, 97, 127, 164
Kings, Amy E., 200n28
Kinnaird College for Women, 33, 255
Kipling, Lockwood, 159
kitchen, 42, 101, 208, 208n8
Khwaja, Zahir-du, 158, 158n12, 159
Kirthar, National Park, 198, 198n20; Range, 198
Kohli, 195
Kohli, Atul, 192n9
knowledge/knowledges, 12, 13, 14, 16, 59, 60, 69, 73, 97, 101, 105, 109, 111, 114, 121, 164, 167, 186, 189, 190, 197, 200, 202, 203, 206, 209, 228, 232, 235, 237, 237n11; context-driven, 223; feminist, 20, 220–225; otherwise, 237
Kobe, 124
Kodar, 98, 99, 100

Korea, Republic of, 85, 175
Korangi township, 46, 143
Krasny, Elke, 10–22, 22n6, 24, 36–47, 58–71, 72–87, 96–103, 141–151, 201–205, 208, 208n9, 210n21, 212n33, 234–244, 237n12, 240n22, 248, 253
Kundoo, Anapuma, 232

L

labor, bonded, 19, 194, 195; farm, 194, 195, 196; female, 207; unskilled, 41, 63, 127; wage, 194, 221
Lahore, Deputy Commissioner, 34, 147, 157; Fort, 16, 73, 78, 79, 81, 92, 97, 145, 149, 172, 174, 256, 259; Walled City, 156, 157, 158, 162, 181; Walled City of Lahore Authority WCLA, 181
Lal Bakhsh Kachhelo Goth, 198
Land Acquisition Act, 186
Land Revenue Department, 182
landless, rural workers, 109
landlessness, 194
landlords, 194, 195
landowner, 102, 109, 195, 196, 197
Langheji River, 198n18, 199
Lari House, 28, 91, 159, 255; OctaGreen LOG, 119, 122, 126, 127, 149, 175, 226, 228n2, 229, 230, 247, 257
Lari, Mihail, 77
Lari, Suhail Zaheer, 13, 16, 29, 33, 33, 35, 64, 69, 73, 74, 82, 89, 90, 166, 168n2, 169n5, 170n15, 247
Lari Associates, Architects and Urban Designers, 13, 30, 57, 148, 168, 255
Lari, Yasmeen, accreditation from the Royal Institute of Architects 159; activism 20, 63, 73, 209; architect as expert-problem-solver 163; architect as listener and facilitator, 163; architecture for the future, 10; architecture is more than buildings, 89; Aga Khan Award, 12, 92; Aga Khan Group 93; bamboo, 15, 66, 101, 210; bamboo shelters, 102; bank building, 57; Barefoot Architecture Project, 224; barefoot entrepreneurs, 109; big buildings, 15; Black and Brown feminisms 225; Brutalism, 15, 27, 159; career 19; cement, 65; Chapter Chair of INTBAU Pakistan, 110; civil society 89, 95; clients 209; community meeting, 100; community spaces, 135; craft-based heritage-economy, 87; decarbonization, 12; decolonization, 12; decolonizing legacies, 16; degrowth 210; design(s), 41, 44, 60, 62, 209; design methodology, 229; earthquake, 206; eco-friendly design 223; education, 33; emergency architecture, 16; essentials, 17; essential needs, 99; experimentation, 71; experiment, 162; family, 34, 59, 162; family home, 168; final building with Lari Associates, 57; first woman to open an architectural office in

Pakistan 13; first female architect in Pakistan, 2 flood 103, 114; from "starchitect" to activist-architect, 206; guest-lecturer at MIT, 93; heritage 73, 77, 80, 85, 86, 90, 171, 175; heritage ethics, 82; historic Islamic architecture, 50; housing problem of the poor, 43; humanitarian, 62, 105, 107; Humanitarian Architecture workshop, 227, 233; Lahore, 157; landmark projects 174; large-scale buildings 49; lime, 15, 64, 101, 210; local needs, 40; local prefabrication and handmade seriality, 68; local workforce, 99; low-cost 210; manifesto, 224; material ecologies, 59, 63; materials, 15, 97, 101, 162; method, 167; methodologies, 228; modernism, 15; mud, 15, 101, 107, 108, 162, 210; Oeuvre, 11; office, 30, 38, 44, 78, 168; openness to learning more, 76; Oxford School of Architecture, 159; World Heritage Site, 92, 2003; Pakistan Chulah, 130, 210, 221, 223, 224; paradigm shift, 12; parliament, 94; PCATP (Pakistan Council of Architects and Town Planners), 163; People's Housing Programme, 162; politics of hope and an ethics of dignity, 21; president of the Institute of Architects Pakistan IAP, 94, 163; public space, 86, 115; Sitara-e-Imtiaz (Star of Excellence), 95, 257; retire from architecture, 97; 'scaled down', 212; social housing, 15; star architect/starchitect, 49, 222; stove solution, 20; tradition, 15; toilets, 133, 134; traditional technologies, 75; training center, 105; typologies, 232; UN Habitat Conference, 89, 170, 260; UNESCO, 79, 80; vernacular architecture, 78; wind 69, 70, 71; women, 20, 37, 39, 99, 136, 167, 206, 210; work for low-income groups, 170; zero-carbon, 17, 20, 105, 110, 111, 115, 122, 136, 210; Zero Carbon Channel, 114, 232; Zero Carbon Cultural Centre, 109, 169; zero-carbon houses, 133; zero-carbon humanistic architecture, 227; zero-carbon methodologies, 227; zero-carbon shelter program, 11, 67; zero-carbon solutions, 167; zero-carbon system, 109, 119; zero-carbon techniques 125; zero-waste, 210

Laufen Manifesto for Human Design Culture, 232

law, laws, 13, 16, 89, 91, 94, 109, 150, 175, 176, 178, 180, 185, 187, 188, 194, 196, 197n13, 197n15

learning, co-, 190; how to build, 12, 20, 61, 62; process, 60, 142, 228; shared, 112, 134; re-, 11, 141, 243; un-, 141, 164, 170n16, 190

Le Corbusier, 33

Levy, Natasha, 169n6, 211n22, 210n24, 210n26, 210n28, 211n90, 223n3

lime, 15, 16, 59, 63, 64, 65, 66, 67, 68, 69, 97, 99, 98, 101, 107, 121, 122, 123, 124, 126, 130, 131, 133, 148, 172, 210, 223, 229

Lines Area Redevelopment Program, 37, 38, 46, 143, 256

Lipton, Alexander, 234n3

livelihood; livelihoods, 12, 17, 18, 19, 21, 73, 98, 113, 121, 144, 193, 196, 197

local, building traditions, 16, 17, 63, 69, 74, 105; labor, 41; materials, 12, 66, 100, 121, 130, 162, 223, 229, 231; prefabrication, 15; timber, 41

Lodi, Sarosh Hashmat, 124

Lorde, Audre, 208, 208n12

low-cost, 105, 133, 149, 209, 210, 231

low-tech, 15, 73, 231

M

M. Ziaullah Khan House, 32, 255

MacGregor, Sherilyn, 207, 207n3

Mahar Jabal, 198

Mahasthangarh, 218

maintenance, 19, 63, 64, 71, 84, 162, 170, 178, 179, 182

makaan (shelter), 15, 37

Makli, Necropolis, 16, 17, 64, 65, 73, 76, 82–85, 87, 92, 105, 109, 113, 150, 256

Malir, Indigenous Rights Alliance IRA, 199

Manifesto, 22n7, 168, 207n7, 208n10, 224, 224n4, 232

Man, -made, 12, 13, 15, 105, 106, 239, 240; modern, 12n3, 239, 240

Manila, 94, 258, 260

Mann, Michael, 191n16

marginalized, communities, 39, 209; knowledge, 18

Marshall, John, 64

Marvin, Simon, 184n2

Marxian reinterpretation of Freud, 237

material; decolonization, 73; ecological thinking, 59; ecologies, 15, 58–71; technology, 167

materials, environmentally-friendly, 97; local, 12, 66, 100, 121, 130, 162, 223, 225, 229, 231

materiality, 59, 229, 231, 234, 235, 236

martial rule, 160, 162

Mayo School of Arts, 159

Mazhar, Marvi, 14, 19, 58–71, 96–103, 183–192, 246, 253

McCarry, John, 170n8, 170n9

McFarlane, Colin, 190, 190n14

Meerow, Sara, 194n5, 196n14

megacity, 192, 222

megalopolis, 18, 19

Meghwar, 195

mental well-being, 199, 213, 216

metal work, 144

metaphor, 234, 235, 236, 237, 238

migrants, 46, 154, 194, 195, 196

migration, history, 194

Miller, Thaddeus R., 193n1

military, Pakistani, 160; regime, 160

militarization, 49

mining, 199

Minoo, Mistri, 158

Mirpur Khas, 132

Mitra, Sudeshna, 191, 191n17

Mirza, Mehdi Ali, 157

MIT, 22n6, 37, 92, 93, 210n21, 212n33, 220n1, 220, 234n3, 237n12, 240n22, 243n28, 246, 247, 248, 253

Miyawaki, Akira, 117, 151

Moak Sharif, 67, 68, 102, 130

modern, future, 236, 239, 240, 243; Man, 12n3, 239, 240

modernism, European, 33; heroes of, 33

modernist, practices, 160

Moffat, Chris, 19, 37, 47n1, 154–165, 157n10, 162n15, 248, 250

Mohenjo-daro, 76, 174, 256, 258, 260

monsoon rains, 10, 105, 106, 128, 195

Montréal, 50, 261

Morrow, Karen, 197n13

mud, -lime mixture, 126, 131

Mughals, 142, 148

Mughal, old capital, 160; rule, 78

Mukti Bahini, 160

Multan, 40

multidimensional, 13, 16, 19, 27, 82, 118

Multiconflictual, 18, 19

Mumtaz, Kamil Khan, 159, 162n14

Munro, Vanessa E., 197n13

Mural, 88, 89, 168

Muslim, culture, 15, 27, 74, 173; nations, 161

Muslims, 92, 154, 156

N

Naeem, Anila, 19, 173–182, 175n1, 176n2, 177n4, 178n5, 247, 248, 251

Naimul, Karim, 216n4

Naseeruddin Khan House, 31, 255

nation-building, 14; -state, 18, 155, 158

National College of Arts, 159, 259

Nature, 12, 12n3, 18, 166, 167, 169, 180, 185, 194, 196, 198n20, 202, 213, 215, 216, 217, 240

Naval Housing, 37, 38, 44, 45, 142, 255

Nepal, 85

Necropolis, 16, 64, 65, 73, 82, 92, 109, 113, 150, 256

Nehru, Jawaharlal, 34

Nelson, Margaret K., 241n25

neoliberal, 19, 183–192, 194

neoliberalization, 184
Nixon, Rob, 236n10
Nokia, 99
Neutra, Richard, 35
Ngũgĩ wa Thiong'o, 73
Nizam, Mariyam, 66, 247
No-Objection Certificates NOCs, 178, 180, 187
Nur Jahan, 145
Nurturing, 209n16, 210, 213

O
Oman, 85
Otero, Marina, 232n10
Otherwise, 154, 189, 237, 244
Opportunity, 15, 44, 59, 60, 145, 157, 161, 201, 214, 219, 234, 240
Oxford Brookes University, 33, 159, 174, 176n2, 255, 262
Oxford School of Architecture, 33, 141, 159, 174, 255

P
Pajouhesh, Pani, 193n1, 194n5, 197n14
panorama elevators, 56
Pakistan, Chulah, 17, 95, 112, 121, 130, 131, 132, 150, 167, 168, 210, 211, 221, 223, 224, 225, 229, 231; Council of Architects and Town Planners PCATP, 13, 94, 162, 167, 171, 171n19, 174, 258; East, 160, 161; National Bank of, 181; Navy, 38, 44; People's Party, 15, 37, 38, 142, 161; Railways, 187; State Oil, 15, 55, 222, 247; Transparency International, 95, 259; Tehrik-i-Taliban militants, 101; West, 161
Pakistani, Army, 60, 101; nationalism, 155
Pasqui, Gabriele, 232n9
Paris, 169, 172n21, 211
Parnell, Susan, 190n15
Partition, 27, 34, 94, 154, 156, 158, 159
Patriarchal, 13, 16, 205, 236
Pawaro mountains, 198
peace, spiritual, 20, 214
pedestrian, street, 115; walkways, 43; zone, 86, 115
pedestrians, 150, 157, 177
Penner, Barbara, 207n7
Pentland, Alex, 234n3
People's Housing Programme, 15, 37, 162
Peshawar, 80, 144, 172, 256, 260
Piketty, Thomas, 84
planet, wounded, 237, 240, 241, 242, 243; wounding the 236, 239, 240, 241, 243
Planet Earth, 237, 241
planetary, care, 18, 21, 234–244; destruction,
212; healing, 244; wounds, 236, 243
plaster, 41, 65, 74, 126, 131, 133, 169, 213, 223
platform, cookstove, 224; elevated, 29, 125, 128, 131, 214n1;
Ponti, Gio, 162
Politecnico di Milano, 20, 95, 226, 227, 230, 233, 247, 249, 250, 257
policy; policies, 16, 20, 80, 88–95, 147, 162, 170, 173, 182, 175n1, 190, 194, 200, 204, 205, 208, 220n1, 236, 241; development, 222; public, 73, 189, 202, 203
politics, 22, 89, 157n9, 160n13, 185, 185n3, 186, 186n8, 190n14, 194, 194n4, 194n7, 242n26
pollution, 21, 106, 131, 210, 222, 240
poor, poorest, 14, 43, 121, 124, 130, 142, 144, 162, 170, 189, 190, 194, 195, 214, 220, 222, 231, 236n10
Porter, Bill, 170
Portoghesi, Paolo, 170n10
positionality, 200
postcolonial, nation-states, 158
post-Partition, 19, 34, 156
poverty, 105, 141, 149, 185, 186, 190, 222, 224, 240, 241, 241n24
Povinelli, Elizabeth A., 235, 235n6, 239, 240n21
power, 15, 16, 86, 160, 161, 184, 185, 186, 188, 191, 185n3, 186n8, 191n16, 194, 197, 209, 235, 238, 239
prefabrication, 16, 122, 257
President House Murree, 38
primary school, 100, 108
Prince of Wales, 110
Princess Salimah, 171
Prins Claus Fund, 82, 175
private realm, 207
privatization, 19, 188; outsourcing and partnering as a form of, 189
public, buildings, 54, 235; education, 73, 78, 86; non-commodified good, 211; goods, 192, 211; health, 187, 192; imaginaries, 234; infrastructures, 232n10; park, 56; practice, work, 243n29; improvement projects, 184, 189; platforms, 54; policies, 203, 204, 205; -private partnerships, 19, 181, 182, 184, 187, 188, 194n2; realm, 49, 208; sector, 49, 177n4, 181, 182, 185; space, 49, 86, 89, 115, 118, 119, 141, 143, 184, 187, 190, 208, 211
production, 39, 167, 201, 202, 206, 207, 231; of care, 11; of reproduction, 207; social, 199; of time, 11
protection, 18, 80, 84, 89, 126, 173, 174, 175, 176, 203, 216
pugree, 178, 179
Punjab, 39, 80, 156, 162, 164, 255; Special Premises Ordinance, 175
purdah, 47
Putin, Vladimir, 234, 234n2

Q
quality control, 129
Queen Mary's School Lahore, 33, 255
queer, 235, 253
Qureshi, Fauzia, 170n8

R
race, -critical, 235, 239n17
Rachel, Rakes, 243n29
Rahguzar, site, 87, 115, 116, 118, 150; walking street , 87, 118, 119, 257
Rajasthan, 223
Rahim, S. A., 159
Ramzi, Shanaz, 168, 169n4, 209n19
Rashidi, family, 103; Paras, 103
Raworth, Kate, 210, 210n25
rebuilding, 12, 62, 71, 97, 98
reconstruction, 148, 157, 186, 186n6, 208
refuge, 215
refugee, 154, 155, 195, 200, 218, 241
recovery, 97, 98, 102, 204, 249
reforestation, 100
rehabilitation, 175, 180, 182, 188, 214
Rehman, Parveen, 196
relational epistemology, 209, 209n16
religion/regligons, 13, 19, 155, 184, 194, 239
Rendell, Jane, 207n7
repair, 53, 64, 73, 83, 98, 125, 148, 156, 179, 181, 182, 208, 221
reproduction, 196, 206, 207, 208, 228, 229
resistance, 19, 91, 102, 105, 124, 199, 200, 208; resisting, 199
resources, 12, 49, 59, 90, 97, 109, 111, 149, 161, 170, 188
responsibility, 10, 11, 19, 39, 145, 160, 163, 165, 167, 178, 182, 183, 202, 208, 219, 236, 241; civic 183
restoration, 63, 64, 65, 73, 80, 87, 116, 150, 180, 181, 182
Rice, Jennifer, 194n4
rights, human, 19, 20, 89, 121, 144, 150, 170, 203, 207n3, 249, 251, 262; to the city, 204; to housing, 18, 19, 170, 201–205, 239n20
Rights of Admission, 186
Rogers, Ayesha Pamela, 78
Rohingya refugee camp, 218
Rolnik, Raquel, 19, 20, 201–205, 239, 239n20, 248, 251
roti (bread), 15, 37
Roy, Arundhati, 185, 185n3

Royal Institute of British Architects RIBA, 95, 159, 257, 261
Rudofsky, Bernard, 74
Ruination, 12, 16, 18, 21, 241, 242
rural, 18, 19, 60, 62, 102, 109, 150, 167, 185, 188, 189, 193, 194, 195, 196, 197, 198, 200, 202, 204, 210n22, 210n24, 223n3

S

Said, Anwar, 159
Said, Edward, 185, 185n5
safe, architecture, 108, 111, 113; houses, 121, 122, 135, 150; toilets, 17, 121, 133, 150; communal spaces, 125, 197; structures, 98
sanitary, units, 42, 121, 133
São Paulo, 189, 251, 253
Schaflechner, Jürgen, 195n10
Schreiber, John, 50
Second Battle of Swat, 101
Serageldin, Mona, 83
seriality, handmade, 16, 68, 121
Sethi House, 80, 256
settlements, informal, 47, 143, 185, 189; new, 189
Shah Abdul Latif Bhittai, 198
Shah ka takya, 198
Shahalami, Gate, 156; market area of, 156
Shaikh Shahzad Camp, 101
Shalimar Gardens, 39, 92, 142, 171
Shahrah-e-Faisal Boulevard, 51, 70
Sharah-e-Kemal Ataturk, 157
shelter/shelters, 10, 10n1, 15, 16, 17, 37, 67, 68, 71, 101, 102, 103, 107, 122, 126, 150, 151, 170, 214, 229, 230, 231, 232, 241; cyclone, 214, 215, 215n3, 216n3; desperately in need of, 98; emergency, 12, 16, 66, 208; essential, 98; safe, 108, 14; prefabricated, 10, 10n1; zero-carbon, 11, 12, 17, 67, 119
Sher-e-Bangla Nagar, 160
Shikarpur, 177, 178n5
Siddique, Abu, 214n1
Sikh, traders, 156
siltation, 64
Silva, Kapila D., 175n1, 178n5
Sindh, Building Control Authority SBCA, 178; Cultural Heritage Preservation Act SCHPA, 175; Department of Culture, Government of GOS, 180; Flood Rehabilitation, 107; Heritage Advisory Committee, 175, 259; High Density Development Board, 179; Ordinance, 187n11, 264; Province, 10, 64, 74, 80, 84, 105, 107, 108, 109, 125, 126, 132, 135, 175, 287, 222, 246
Sindhi and Baloch tribes, 193
Sir Ciryl Radcliffe, 225
Sir J. J. College of Architecture, 157

Siran Valley, 98, 99, 100, 172, 256
Sitara-e-Imtiaz, 95, 174, 257
Siza Vieira, Álvaro, 95
skills, 10, 33, 63, 109, 111, 169, 206, 209, 224, 229, 238
skyscraper 49, 57, 239, 239n17; skywalk, 49, 53
slum conditions, 46
Smith, Dorothy, 194
social media, 114, 147
South Asia/South Asian, 19, 60, 149, 154, 154n3, 160, 160n13, 185, 189, 195n10, 220, 223, 258
spaces, community, 17, 121, 134
spatial schism, 207, 211
Sponenburgh, Mark, 159
Srinivas, Smita, 190n14, 190n15, 191n17, 198n18
St. Clair Wilkins, Henry, 57
St. Petersburg, 234
starchitect, 206, 222, 222n2
state, ideology, 19
State of Conservation, 178
steel, and glass, 55, 208; construction, 56
Stone, Edward Durrell, 159
stove/stoves, clean cooking, 20, 220; fires, 220; smokeless, 17, 111, 112, 121, 130; wood-burning, 20, 210, 220, 221, 223
stucco work, 144
street-festival, 169, 175
structural engineers, 66
subcontinent, 156
Sub-Saharan Africa, 149
Sufi Hussain Shah Bokhari, 198
system/systems, of support, 177, 237

T

Tabassum, Marina, 232
Taj Mahal Hotel, 174
Taliban, 66, 101
Tando Allahyar, 193, 195
Tange, Kenzo, 95, 162
Taxila, 169
Teaching, 12, 13, 18, 19, 20, 259; teaching methodologies, 18, 20, 226–233
Technological, 11, 74, 184n2, 219
Technologies, 17, 69, 211, 229, 231; construction, 59, 167; traditional, 12, 17, 63, 71, 74
terra-cotta, pavers, 87, 115, 116, 150; tiles, 169
terrace, 142, 144
territorial fragility, 204, 232
Texas A&M University, 159
Thatta, 69, 73, 74, 76, 82, 163

Thaker Lakhmidass Cloth Market, 177
Thayer-Bacon, Barbara, 209, 209n16
The Heritage Cell – Department of Architecture and Planning HC-DAPNED, 175, 176n2, 177, 177n4
the mythical norm, 208
The World Bank, 187, 187n10
Third World solidarity, 161
Thomas, Helen, 19, 166–172, 248, 251
toilets, 110, 149, 150; eco-, 110; Karavan, 134; safe, 17, 121, 133; urgent lack of, 99
Tombesi, Paolo, 232n8
traditional, building skills, 63; technology/technologies, 12, 17, 59, 60, 63, 66, 69, 70, 73, 74, 102, 109, 126, 236, 264; towns, 37, 40, 75, 141; villages, 63, 74
training, construction, 63; for unskilled people, 63
Transferable Development Rights TDR, 179
Trauger, Amy, 194n4, 200n25
Tronto, Joan, 212, 212n33, 241, 241n25, 242, 242n26, 242n27
Tronto-Fisher framework of care, 241, 242
Truijen, Katia, 232n10
Tsing, Anna, 12n3, 239, 239n18, 240n22
Turner, John, 37

U

uncertainty, radical, 232
UNESCO, 65, 73, 78, 83, 84, 85, 92, 167, 171, 172n21, 174, 175, 198n20, 247, 259, 261; delegations, 84; National Advisor, 79; Office in Islamabad, 80, 78, 84, 92, 144, 171; Representative in Pakistan, 84; World Heritage, 16, 78, 79, 82, 256, 259
United Nations UN, 92, 167, 198n20, 208n13, 261; Development Program, 63; Expanded Programme of Technical Assistance, 158; Habitat Award, 17, 95, 130, 257; Conference on Human Settlements, 89, 170, 170n14; Habitat Conference, 89, 170, 260; Rapporteur on adequate housing, 201–205
UNICEF, 167, 257
United States Agency for International Development USAID, 159
United States of America, 158, 189, 249, 259, 260, 261, 262
University of Engineering & Technology Karachi NED, 124, 175, 251, 258, 259
University of Liverpool, 159
University of Oregon, 159
universities, 12, 13, 20, 66, 109, 227, 232
urban, heritage, 76, 77, 175, 177, 179, 180; society, 15, 49; space, 55;
Urdu, 39, 115
urbanism, 22n22, 184n2, 190, 210n21, 212n33, 237n12, 240n22

urbanization, neoliberal, 18
use, 63, 64, 65, 66, 70, 146, 148, 172, 197, 207, 210, 214, 221, 228, 229, 231, 235

V
Valente, Ilaria, 227, 228n1, 229n4
value, cultural, 73, 173
Vandal, Pervaiz, 156, 159n8
Venice Architecture Biennale, 170
Vecsei, Eva, 51, 144
ventilation, cross-, 74; technology, 70; naturally ventilated, 52;
veranda, 28, 32, 42
Vergès, Françoise, 13n5
vernacular, traditions, 73, 122
village/villages, 75, 85, 87, 98, 99, 100, 103, 108, 109, 113, 116, 125, 127, 150, 167, 169, 185, 193, 195, 196, 197, 198, 199, 199n23, 200, 211, 214, 221
violence, slow, 236, 236n10
volunteer, volunteers, 86, 97, 98, 100, 118, 149, 169, 182
vulnerable, country, 148; masses, 22;
vulnerability, 194, 194n7, 240, 241, 244

W
Wade, Steph, 206n1, 209n15, 209n20, 210n23
wadera, 103
Wainright, Oliver, 106n2
Wallace-Wells, David, 235n5
Walled City of Lahore Authority WCLA, 181
walled city/cities, 40, 156, 157, 158, 162, 181
Warner, Jeroen, 194n7
waste, 64, 131, 149, 223, 231; solid, 183, 187; zero, 16, 105, 110, 210
water, clean, 17, 121, 128, 150; drinking, 128; transport the, 128
Water and Sewerage Board, 181
Watson, Vanessa, 190n14, 190n15, 191, 192n18
wealth, 141, 147, 184, 185, 186, 190, 192, 197, 203, 207, 209
Weijs, Bart, 194n7
Weintrobe, Sally, 207, 207n4
Weisman, Leslie, 207n7, 208n10
West, the, 30, 85, 141, 145, 151, 158, 185
Western, industrialized countries, 188; white institutions, 224
wind, -catchers, 28, 69, 70, 74, 76; cooling systems, 69; towers, 54, 69, 70
wood carving, 143
woman, 13, 27, 32, 38, 62, 95, 97, 134, 135, 162, 172, 174, 199
women, are incredible leaders of housing struggles, 205; Black and Brown, 224, 225; communication between, 167; crafts-, 85, 87, 116, 223; designed by, 131; farm workers, 196; Hindu Bagri, 193; Khaskheli, 196; Muslim Baloch, 193; needs of, 14, 15, 17, 37, 59, 99, 149, 211; rural, 19, 193, 194, 195, 196, 200; sheltered places for, 108; space for, 135;
Women Democratic Front, 199
Women's Budget Group, 211, 212n32
work, care, 20, 206, 207, 208, 210; farm, 19, 195, 196, 199;
workers, unskilled, 127
workshop, zero-carbon, 232
World Habitat Award, 17, 95, 130, 257
World Heritage, Convention, 92; Site, 16, 64, 73, 78, 84, 85, 89, 92, 109, 116, 146, 150, 172, 174, 256
worry, 237, 240, 243
wound; wounding, 234–244

Y
Yale University, 159
Yashar, Deborah J., 192n19

Z
Zakaria, Rafia, 20, 220–225, 248, 252
Zaman, Fahim, 197n16
zanakhana, 80
Zaretsky, Elizero, 207n6
zero-carbon, activism, 63; advocates, 235; approach, 227, 229; architecture, 20, 30, 70, 105, 108, 109, 111, 114, 115, 123, 145, 149, 150, 232; principles, 149; shelter program, 11, 67; system, 108, 119
Zero Carbon, Channel, 114, 134, 167, 228, 228n2, 232; Cultural Centre, 109, 110, 111, 112, 113, 115, 116, 127, 169
Zia-ul-Haq, Muhammad, 162
Zindani, 63
Zumtobel Group, 215, 215n3

Imprint

Co-published by Architekturzentrum Wien and the MIT Press
© 2023 Architekturzentrum Wien. All texts © the authors.

All rights reserved. No part of this publication may be reproduced, stored in a retrieval system or transmitted in any form or by any means, electronic, mechanical, photocopying or otherwise, without the written permission of the publisher.

Library of Congress Control Number: 2022941331
ISBN 978-0-262-54609-6

Editors: Angelika Fitz, Elke Krasny, Marvi Mazhar, and Architekturzentrum Wien
Project Coordination: Agnes Wyskitensky
Graphic Design: Alexander Ach Schuh
Proofreading: Brian Dorsey, Kimi Lum
Translations: Brian Dorsey (German-English, 27–35, 49–57, 89–95, 105–119, 121–136, 246–248)
Transcription Interviews: Anna Livia Pugholm Vorsel

Cover: Mural of Yasmeen Lari in the Defence Underpass, Karachi. Video still: Imran Gill, 2022
Paper: Salzer Design White 1.5 100g
Printed and bound by: Gerin Druck GmbH, Austria

This book was published on the occasion of the exhibition
Yasmeen Lari: Architecture for the Future (March 9, 2023–August 16, 2023), Architekturzentrum Wien.

Director Architekturzentrum Wien: Angelika Fitz
Executive Director Architekturzentrum Wien: Karin Lux

Curators of the Exhibition: Angelika Fitz, Elke Krasny, Marvi Mazhar
Project Coordination: Agnes Wyskitensky
Exhibition Design: Alexandra Maringer
Exhibition Graphic Design: Alexander Ach Schuh
Production: Andreas Kurz

Architekturzentrum Wien, Museumsplatz 1, 1070 Vienna, www.azw.at
The MIT Press, One Broadway, Cambridge, MA 02142, www.mitpress.mit.edu

Public funding for Architekturzentrum Wien (Az W)

Stadt Wien

Bundesministerium Kunst, Kultur, öffentlicher Dienst und Sport

Az W is supported by

ARCHITECTURE LOUNGE
Architekturzentrum Wien

A good part of the Architekturzentrum Wien's comprehensive program is supported by the contributions from its membership program, particularly the contributions from its Architecture Lounge partners. This platform for highly committed companies and associations attributes top priority to knowledge exchanges and networking. Learning, networking, and hospitality are the terms that best describe this field of communication at the nexus of architecture, business, and politics.

Architecture Lounge Members:
ARWAG Holding AG
BDN Fleissner & Partner
Bundesimmobiliengesellschaft m.b.H.
Buwog Group
EGW Heimstätte Gesellschaft m.b.H.
Eternit Österreich GmbH
Gesiba, Gemeinn. Siedlungs- & Bau AG
Gewog – Neue Heimat
Grohe Ges.m.b.H.
iC Projektentwicklung
Immobilien Privatstiftung
Kallco Development GmbH
Kallinger Projekte GmbH
Mischek Bauträger Service GmbH
Neues Leben Gemeinn. Bau-, Wohn- und Siedlungsgen.
Österreichisches Siedlungswerk AG
Österreichisches Volkswohnungswerk
Sozialbau AG
Strabag Real Estate GmbH
Vasko+Partner Ingenieure
WBV – GPA Wohnbauv. f. Privatangestellte
WKÖ – Fachverband Steine-Keramik
Wien 3420 Aspern Development AG
Wienerberger Österreich GmbH
wohnfonds_wien
WSE Wiener Standortentwicklung GmbH